Jerry Krause
and His Chicago Bulls

OTHER McFARLAND TITLES
BY ŁUKASZ MUNIOWSKI

*Turnpike Team: A History
of the New Jersey Nets, 1977–2012* (2023)

*The Sixth Man: A History
of the NBA's Best Off the Bench* (2022)

Sex, Death and Resurrection in Altered Carbon*:
Essays on the Netflix Series* (2020)

Three-Pointer!: A 40-Year NBA History (2020)

Jerry Krause and His Chicago Bulls

The Scout Who Built the Dynasty of the 1990s

Łukasz Muniowski

McFarland & Company, Inc., Publishers
Jefferson, North Carolina

All photographs are from Steve Lipofsky, Lipofskyphoto.com.

ISBN (print) 978-1-4766-9265-4
ISBN (ebook) 978-1-4766-5345-7

LIBRARY OF CONGRESS AND BRITISH LIBRARY
CATALOGUING DATA ARE AVAILABLE

Library of Congress Control Number 2024021217

© 2024 Łukasz Muniowski. All rights reserved

No part of this book may be reproduced or transmitted in any form or by any means, electronic or mechanical, including photocopying or recording, or by any information storage and retrieval system, without permission in writing from the publisher.

Front cover: (inset) Chicago Bulls general manager Jerry Krause; (center) Bulls players Scottie Pippen (33), Michael Jordan (23) and Horace Grant (with glasses) celebrate with teammates during a timeout in a 1991 game at the Boston Garden (Steve Lipofsky/Lipofskyphoto.com)

Printed in the United States of America

*McFarland & Company, Inc., Publishers
Box 611, Jefferson, North Carolina 28640
www.mcfarlandpub.com*

Acknowledgments

I am enormously indebted to everyone who was willing to talk about the late Jerry Krause. Melissa Isaacson and Sam Smith clarified certain things. Ian Thomsen found time in his busy schedule to talk basketball. Clint Johnson taught me about the importance of Clarence "Big House" Gaines for basketball, as well as for American society. Patrick Reardon described what it was like to live in Chicago during the time of the Bulls' success, while Bill Savage educated me about the complicated history of the city. Wojciech Michałowicz told me stories of covering the Bulls as a foreign correspondent. I could listen to Rick Telander talk about sports, politics, art and life in general for hours. Lee Lowenfish enlightened me about the nature of scouting and shared the notes from his interview with Jerry Krause. Shawn Fury is the biggest basketball historian and fan I know.

I have to single out three people who were close to the hero of this book and who provided a unique perspective: Al Vermeil, Karen Stack Umlauf and Thelma Krause. Coach Vermeil offered stories about the training methods, the players and Krause himself. Karen was very generous with her time, patiently answering all my questions and all my emails. I want to especially thank Mrs. Krause for her kindness and generosity. I hope that with this book I did her husband justice.

I also want to thank all the authors, beat writers and journalists whose articles and works I cite in this book. I have nothing but admiration for their devotion to the craft and would not have been able to write this book without all of them.

I owe many thanks to my editor, who did an awesome job spotting all the mistakes, big and small. And as usual, I want to thank Gary Mitchem and the good people at McFarland, who published this book.

When Jerry went to the cemetery to visit his father's grave, he saw a gravestone nearby that read: "Here lies the heart and soul of a newsreel cameraman." He said he wanted his to read: "Here lies the heart and soul of a scout." He was cremated, but I had a plaque made.
—Thelma Krause

Table of Contents

Acknowledgments v
Preface 1
Introduction: Public Hanging 3

1. The Scout and the City 11
2. Traveling Man 29
3. Addition by Subtraction 47
4. Top Sellers 72
5. A Big Bill 90
6. You Always Remember Your First 108
7. Suffering from Success 121
8. Good, Not Great 135
9. Tough Guys Don't Dance 150
10. Footwork and Chemistry 163
11. Baby Bulls 179
12. Hall of Fame 192

Chapter Notes 195
Bibliography 211
Index 215

Preface

The story has been told again and again. Michael Jordan, the individual genius in a team sport, the greatest basketball player—maybe even the greatest athlete—of all time, came to Chicago in 1984 and altered the world. As the cliché goes, his influence went beyond sports, reaching such aspects of the everyday as branding, celebrity, economics, politics, and race.

In the background was a cast of captivating characters: the master manipulator Phil Jackson, the ultimate running mate Scottie Pippen, the hard-working Horace Grant, the flamboyant Dennis Rodman, and the diplomatic Steve Kerr.

On the other side were equally engaging foes, like Larry Bird, Isaiah Thomas, Magic Johnson, Charles Barkley, and Karl Malone. In most narratives, the architect of the six-time NBA champion Bulls, Jerry Krause, is often grouped with them. At times vilified, hated, reviled, and ridiculed, Krause revamped and revived the roster around Jordan, adding bits and pieces that worked together and continued to do so season after season, despite constant tension and constant disrespect from his employees and the people who loved his creation but despised the creator.

Krause was born and raised in Chicago. He loved the city and wanted to make it proud by using his gift for identifying talent, on and off the court, to construct an organization that the city could cheer for and identify with. Yet he was widely disliked. This book tries to answer one simple question: why?

I have written this book to be a fair portrait of a famously secretive man and the circumstances that created and shaped him and his image. I refrain from editorializing throughout and even minimize commentary about the numerous quotations in the text, hoping to provide the reader with an unfiltered view of what happened.

This book can serve as a stand-alone account of the Bulls dynasty, but it omits most on-court events, as well as things Jerry Krause did not participate in directly. For those, the reader should reach for works by Sam Smith, Roland Lazenby, Melissa Isaacson, and David Halberstam. If the reader considers this book worthy to be put on the shelf next to those works, I will consider my job done.

Introduction: Public Hanging

On October 31, 2003, the Chicago Bulls were playing the Atlanta Hawks in Chicago's United Center. At halftime the Bulls were holding a six-point lead. They were the team of the future, with three former lottery picks in the starting lineup: Jamal Crawford, Tyson Chandler, and Eddy Curry. At just 23, Crawford was the eldest of the three, and their imminent coming of age was supposed to lead to another period of success for the franchise, which had undoubtedly been the most recognizable and successful basketball team of the 1990s. In fact, an argument could be made that the Chicago Bulls were the best sports team of that decade.

All three were drafted by the man who was now being celebrated for his achievements, as well as his devotion to the Bulls organization, Chicago sports, and the city of Chicago in general. Here was a man who embodied the blue-collar ethic of the Rust Belt. During a conversation for this book, Chicago historian and journalist Patrick Reardon said, "Chicago likes to think of itself as a muscular place, comfortable with grittiness. It considers itself a brawny, gutsy place, as opposed to, say, New York, which is fancier, or Boston, which is proper, or Los Angeles, where everybody is off the beach."[1]

The man in the middle of the court was in no way muscular. Nobody would mistake him for a factory worker, a farmer, or anybody making a living with their hands. Nobody would think of him as an athlete either. He was short and had a gut, yet from that gut came the feelings that made him so good at his job.

This man was not seen as a hero, and he was not in need of being humanized. If anything, it was the other way around. Surrounded by heroes who were physically gifted, naturally handsome, and charismatic, he stood out for all the wrong reasons.

He was constantly mocked, ridiculed, and belittled by the people he brought into the organization and who worked for him. In any other business he could just fire them with no scrutiny or criticism. It would be expected of him to do so, as otherwise he would simply look weak.

But his trade was professional sports, where mythologizing is as obligatory as it is marketable. The father of basketball himself, James Naismith, always intended for the sport to allow mass participation, not spectatorship,[2] yet the game did not exactly develop in that direction. While playing the game was easy, playing it at the top level was possible only for the chosen few. Jerry Krause was one of the best at identifying whether somebody had the potential to join that elite group.

He recognized heroes before they would become heroes. He should be appreciated for that, yet the only hero present on one of the most important nights of his life, the celebration of his extraordinary gifts, was there because he had to be. There were no guest speakers, no former NBA players towering over the man sitting next to his wife, Thelma, and his family. This was his night, and yet none of his former associates decided to show up for that occasion.

Scottie Pippen returned to the Bulls after leaving the team in 1998 following a well-publicized contract dispute, which largely contributed to the end of the Bulls' championship dynasty. To say Pippen loathed Krause would be an understatement. After he finally made back some of that "lost" money with the Rockets and then with the Blazers, after being underpaid with the Bulls, Pippen returned to Chicago to mentor younger players. There was no purer representation of mentorship than what he did that night.

Despite his feud with Krause, Pippen shook his and his wife's hands after the ceremony was over. While he remained distrustful of the former general manager and even considered him somebody who made the Bulls a dysfunctional organization,[3] at this particular moment he rose above his animosity toward Krause.

Before, sitting in the middle of the court, Krause had been met with a mix of boos and what the *Northwest Herald*'s Nick Hut referred to as "polite applause."[4] Bulls chairman Jerry Reinsdorf, who hired Krause as vice president of basketball operations and kept him at that position for 18 seasons, was watching from the booth, at a safe distance from the man with whom he had formed the (in)famous duo of the "Two Jerrys," responsible for turning the franchise into a basketball powerhouse.

Both men were too often guilty by association. Less than a decade earlier, during Michael Jordan's jersey retirement ceremony on November 1, 1994—two hours long and televised by TNT—they were heavily booed, to the point that Jordan felt the need to stand up for them and say, "C'mon, now, both Jerrys are good guys."

Only in professional sports can it be necessary for an employee to stand up for the employer. Booing Krause became a sort of annual tradition during championship celebrations, as well as many other public occasions. And yet, Reinsdorf stood by him. Legendary Chicago sports journalist Rick Telander explained that "Jerry Reinsdorf is notorious for hiring people and never firing them. He is very loyal. He was loyal to Krause."

The fans may have hated Krause, but they liked the team he was able to assemble. By all accounts, Krause had a great basketball mind. From recognizing the proficiency of Tex Winter's triangle offense, to finding the right people to execute it, he possessed a true passion for the game itself. That was what Bill Cartwright, whom Krause brought onto the team in exchange for the beloved enforcer Charles Oakley in 1988 and offered the position of head coach in 2001, enjoyed the most about Krause.

When talking to journalist Melissa Isaacson, Cartwright said: "It's so nice talking about basketball to someone who's so excited about it. That's a real basketball person, who can watch just for the pleasure of it. That's Jerry."[5]

Cartwright was still the coach of the Bulls when Krause was commemorated by the franchise. He would be fired 14 games into the season, after a disappointing start.

Johnny Kerr, the Bulls' first ever head coach and longtime color commentator, listed Krause's achievements in less than two minutes, including listing the most notable players that he drafted for the Bulls: Scottie Pippen, Charles Oakley, Horace Grant, Will Perdue, B.J. Armstrong, Toni Kukoč, Elton Brand, Ron Artest, Marcus Fizer, Jamal Crawford, Eddy Curry, and Tyson Chandler, as well as the players he traded for.

Kerr's monotone delivery deeply hurt Thelma Krause, who said: "He used to be a friend, but by that time was not a friend and he should not have been the one to MC. I think he was going through the motions, his voice had no emotion or genuine warmth."

General managers do not often get nicknames, as front office workers have rarely been so highly regarded by the fans as to earn them. There was "Trader Jack" McCloskey, who built the Detroit Pistons around the exceptionally talented point guard Isaiah Thomas. Jerry West of the Lakers or Pat Riley of the Heat, once Laker teammates, had their nicknames transferred from their playing days, the Logo and Riles, respectively.

And then there was Krause, by all accounts one of the best general managers of all time, who was known even among the members of his own organization as "The Sleuth." The secretive Krause hid information about players from everyone else, even the members of his own franchise. He understood it was all he had "in his battle against the outside forces that conspire[d] to grind him into oblivion,"[6] as Rick Telander put it in Krause's 1993 *Sports Illustrated* profile.

Krause conducted 37 trades to win the first championship for the Bulls yet never got the respect he deserved. The ability to part with people is equally as important as the ability to hire them. He did not help his case by alienating arguably the best basketball player of all time, Michael Jordan, and one of the most beloved teammates in basketball history, Scottie Pippen.

Jordan was born in Brooklyn and raised in Wilmington, North Carolina. Pippen was born and raised in Arkansas. Both towered over the people cheering for them from the stands, while their toned, chiseled physiques further separated them from the regular-looking fans, who sought escape from the everyday by watching these godlike characters play. Krause was a Chicago local. What was more, as explained to me by Patrick Reardon, "of everyone around the Bulls, you have the team, you have the coaches, you have the owner who was a rich guy and then you have Krause, who was dumpy, ugly ... and he looked more like a Chicagoan than anybody else."

From March 26, 1985, until April 4, 2003, Krause was responsible for shaping the Bulls' roster. He made the decisions, he called the shots, and yet, even after six championships, he could never shake the status of the underdog.

After a short introduction by Kerr, he stood up, dressed in a black suit, with a microphone in hand, and said in a half-serious manner, with a couple of boos still distinguishable: "Back in 1985, when Jerry Reinsdorf hired me, a close friend of mine told me that if we didn't win, they were going to hang me from the rafters. And tonight, 18 years later, I'm getting hung ... but I'm getting hung with six championship banners."

The crowd cheered. Kind of. If there was ever a chance for Krause to win them over and solidify his place in their hearts—his place in history was well secured—that was it. And so he started to speak about the people he was joining at the top of the United Center and how their legacies intertwined with his.

After briefly mentioning Bob Love, Krause told how Jerry Sloan, an Illinois native, who at the time was beginning his 15th season as the head coach of the Utah Jazz, was his first ever draft choice as a full-time

Introduction: Public Hanging 7

basketball scout. The statement was wrong—not because it was inaccurate factually but because Krause always stressed the importance of the organization over the individual. With his background in baseball scouting, his approach was largely influenced by the way baseball franchises used to operate. As explained to me by Lee Lowenfish: "The strong baseball organizations in the old days made it a point that you don't take individual credit. You give that credit to the organization as a whole." And yet there was Krause, not so much taking credit but blatantly giving it to himself.

Then he talked of Phil Jackson as being "a joy to hire," skipping past the disagreements between the two, which came to overshadow the early vote of confidence that Krause gave the inexperienced coach. Initially Jackson was willing to listen to Krause's suggestions. He not only took to following Tex Winter's advice on playing basketball and picked his mind but also wore one of the championship rings he had earned as a player on the New York Knicks to inspire the young roster.[7] As head coach Jackson instilled an us-against-them mentality, which helped him win over the players but alienated the front office. During interviews, he still spoke about how "Jerry Krause was like the only person that really stayed in touch with [him] from the NBA world,"[8] but he continued to undermine the general manager's efforts to build relationships with the players.

Just as they did with Jordan, the fans sided with Jackson, so in order to be on their good side, Krause became the voice of the organization, saying that Jackson "won us a lot of championships."

Speaking of Jordan, he named him along with Jerry Sloan as the "two greatest competitors ... to ever be here." Putting Jordan next to Sloan might have been a slight to the former, but not for Krause, who had said years earlier, "there is no higher compliment than that. I thought Jerry Sloan was the toughest practice player I'd ever seen 'till I saw [Jordan]."[9] For Krause, Sloan was the gold standard, a player held in such high regard that when the Sloan-coached Jazz met the Bulls in the 1997 NBA finals, he said that the team reflected the coach: "they're tough, they're nasty, they're competitive."[10]

And Krause never let anyone forget that he was the one who scouted and picked Sloan.

The same could not be said of Jordan, whom Krause inherited from the previous regime. Even though Krause knew who he had in Jordan, he could never say that he discovered him, like he did with Sloan, Earl Monroe, Scottie Pippen, or Horace Grant.

Krause built the roster around Jordan, repeating some variation of "Michael's the only one I want to keep, the rest of them can go now"[11] through the years. In three years, he got rid of dysfunctional players surrounding Jordan and turned the Bulls into a championship contender, or so the narrative went. He was one of the people responsible for the turnaround—along with the players, the coaching staff, and every other member of the organization who did their jobs—yet in his quest for credit, which was stubbornly taken away from him, he remained even more stubborn in his fight to reclaim it.

With one hand in the pocket of his jacket and the other holding the microphone, Krause now thanked Reinsdorf, whom he called "the greatest owner in sports." Reinsdorf watched from his booth as Krause thanked him for giving him the opportunity to run the franchise.

Then Krause thanked the Bulls' longtime conditioning coach Al Vermeil and his "left arm" Karen Stack Umlauf, who worked for him as an assistant essentially from the second week he took on the position of vice president of basketball operations.

Why left and not right?

"Did he say left and not right?" asked Umlauf, and a smile instantly appeared on her face. She was speaking from her Northwestern University office, where she works as the director of women's basketball operations. "I guess it's because he used his right hand and the left not so much, so I was maybe filling in for some of the things he was not able to do on his own; it was that sort of analogy."

Then I asked her about the serious expressions she and Vermeil had on their faces. Umlauf does not remember clearly why that was, although it might have to do with "the disappointment that he was not getting the credit that he should have in that moment."

After thanking front office employees, players, and coaches, Krause moved on to his family: his stepson David, his stepdaughter Stacy, his son-in-law, and his granddaughter, whom he called "Grampy's girl." When Krause mentioned his wife, Thelma, in the most affectionate and emotional moment of the ceremony, he invited her over, hugged her, and placed a somewhat awkward kiss on her forehead.

Thelma Krause was smiling, but during our conversation she admitted that "she had [her] game face on." Inside she was fuming at the disrespect. Still, she got the biggest applause of the night. After all, here was this secretive executive letting his guard down for a moment and giving people a glimpse into his private life—something he almost never did ... right?

Thelma Krause said that that was not the case; people just were not interested. "Oh, he would tell you about his personal life. He was not going to tell you who he brought in to interview or who he was going to see, but if you asked about his family, he would tell you."

After admitting to forgetting to thank the Bulls' longtime equipment manager John Ligmanowski, Krause, with his voice cracking, went on to mention "the most important group of people," the Chicago fans. With pride, he spoke about being born and raised in the Windy City, "the greatest city in the world," before turning to the Bulls players standing behind him. He asked the fans to "stick with these young people, they're special"—after all, he had drafted and traded for them—before thanking everybody one last time. With his hands outstretched, he was hugged by the young players.

With the theme from *Jurassic Park* playing in the background and a banner with the words "GENERAL MANAGER JERRY KRAUSE 6 NBA TITLES" being unveiled, the teary-eyed executive had finally made it. He was one of the guys, which was described by numerous Bulls employees as "an unrealistic urge."[12] In an article published after Krause's resignation as general manager, Sam Smith described him as "seldom one of the guys, but one of a kind,"[13] and stressed how Krause really wanted to belong, yet was never accepted, just tolerated. At best.

Well, not anymore. The underdog proved his doubters wrong yet again and the banner solidified his well-deserved place in sports history, while the players surrounding the man almost three times their age provided his basketball career with a welcome, warm closure.

Krause's story was unlike any other in professional basketball and it contained no easy victories, just as it lacked decisive defeats. He reportedly turned down a potential $1 million book deal because it came with the condition that he was supposed to write a tell-all memoir. This book does not reveal the whole story but tries to tell its larger part, simply because it deserves to be told. It is about a persistent underdog who worked his way up to the top yet never got the respect he deserved. Here, Krause's infamous, supposedly dynasty-ending statement that organizations win championships makes sense. I would argue that it always made sense, because basketball culture is something that cannot be overlooked.

Krause's fate was closely tied to his surroundings, the people he employed, and the ones he ignored for certain positions. This book is not a typical biography, a complete life story of the (in)famously secretive man, but an attempt at understanding him as a basketball scout and as an executive.

Still, a backstory is crucial in understanding the motivations of every hero. The same can be said about every villain. In order for both to be captivating, their pasts need to fuel their present; the perception of the acts must be more important than pure facts.

Jerome Richard Krause was neither a hero nor a villain. Too flawed and insecure to root for, and too easy of a target to demonize, it is incredible that somebody so successful at finding certain qualities in people and seeing how they could work together was so bad at making others respect him, let alone like him.

When he first got the job with the Bulls, in 1976, the *Chicago Tribune*'s Robert Markus described him as "that nice guy who finished up the track."[14] Forty years later, posthumously, that guy was inducted into the Hall of Fame. By all accounts he was a winner, yet few people outside the front office considered him nice. And those who did were never really heard.

When *The Last Dance* documentary series aired, the image of Krause as a villain once again came to the forefront. "Blame" was the word thrown around most often next to Krause's name. It was easy to forget that Jackson and Jordan both left Chicago behind, while Krause stayed and still lived there. What tends to be overlooked, as was pointed out in a farewell column by Al Hamnik following Krause's departure from the Bulls, was that "Jordan loathed Krause and wanted greedy Phil Jackson to have more power. When Krause refused to bow at MJ's feet, Jackson left and Jordan followed in a hissy fit. So don't hate Krause. Hate Jackson and Jordan for tripping over their egos."[15]

The intention of this book is not to redirect hate, cast blame, or clear anybody's name but to show the other side of the well-known story of the Bulls dynasty, one with a sharp focus on roster construction and the interactions between the team, the staff, and the front office.

It is about making hard decisions and learning how to live with them.

It is about the basketball life of Jerry Krause.

1

The Scout and the City

When talking about the importance of the NBA's coming to Chicago in 1961, Northwestern professor Bill Savage stresses that "Chicago did not need to prove anything with the NBA. The NBA would want to be in Chicago because of its market, which was the second-biggest and is now the third-biggest media market in the country." It was not so much that Chicago needed the NBA to validate its position on the American landscape but the other way around. Basketball needed a big market.

When the NBA came to town, Chicago already had founding franchises in baseball's National and American Leagues, the National Football League, and National Hockey League. That did not mean that there were no basketball fans in the city or that the history of basketball in Chicago started with the Chicago Packers and 1961's first overall draft pick, Walt Bellamy.

Bellamy was a 6'11" center, a future Hall of Famer whose trade from the Knicks a few years later would help New York win two NBA championships. The tough, team-oriented play of the Knicks would inspire an up-and-coming New York businessman, Jerry Reinsdorf, to one day own a basketball team, as well as develop the philosophy that he would want that team to follow. Bellamy was a great player, but trading him turned the Knicks from a good to a great team. And Reinsdorf himself witnessed the magic of "addition by subtraction," which was the approach taken by Krause in the initial stages of organizing the Bulls roster around a talented youngster named Michael Jordan.[1]

The coach of that Knicks team, Red Holzman, would also influence two people crucial to the Bulls' outlook, its coach and its general manager. Reinsdorf and Krause bonded over their admiration of how these Knicks played, how tough and devoid of ego they were as a group.

Phil Jackson was a reserve on those Knicks championship teams, a big man who could play center, but was also comfortable as a forward, as long as he was helping his teammates. He internalized one of the lessons preached by Holzman: "On a good team there are no superstars. There are great players who show they are great players by being able to play with others as a team."[2]

Back when he was a scout for the Baltimore Bullets, Krause earned great praise from Holzman when he stumbled upon the Knicks' coach at an airport in St. Louis. Holzman appreciated Krause's work ethic and advised him about spending time on the road by watching tapes of earlier games instead of sitting in front of the television in the hotel room.[3] Each man appreciated the other's eye for talent.

Another man who often accompanied Krause on the road was Earl Lloyd, the first African American to play in the NBA, who also worked as a scout for the Pistons after his basketball career concluded. Krause recounted how during a tournament they got a chance to see Earl Monroe, a sophomore from Winston-Salem State University, a historically black public university in North Carolina. When seeing him play, both men decided to stay for the whole game, even though it was the eighth contest of the day they had attended, and it was after midnight.

Monroe started to play basketball at 14. He was not recruited to college and played pickup ball in Philadelphia recreational centers while working in a factory. Clarence Gaines, the head coach of Winston-Salem State Rams basketball team, took notice of Monroe's natural abilities. The racism of big-scale universities benefited Gaines, because otherwise Winston-Salem would not be able to recruit Black teenagers from the North, such as Monroe.

As explained to me by Clint Johnson, the author of Gaines's biography *They Call Me Big House*, the coach thought that Black northern teenagers were better skilled because during harsh winters they went to the gym and played basketball instead of football or any other outside activities during much lighter Southern winters.

The fact that both scouts got to see Monroe that night was a combination of factors, yet it would not have been possible if Krause and Lloyd did not do their jobs to the best of their abilities. Both men agreed to not share their secret with anybody, and during subsequent scouting trips they saw Monroe become one of the best players in the country, Lloyd could not pick him first overall in 1967, as the Pistons' head coach decided on Providence's Jimmy Walker instead.

Krause, on the other hand, was able to convince the Bullets to select Monroe, partially due to his experience scouting for the team since 1962, as well as the simple fact that he just would not shut up, going on and on about the abilities of the players that he liked. Yes, he was stubborn, but he could back up the information that he acquired with hotel receipts and luggage tags.

He joked that his autobiography should be titled *One Million National Anthems* because of the number of games he attended, both baseball and basketball. He scouted both sports for 12 years simultaneously. "In those days you could physically scout both sports, because … the basketball draft used to be the third week of March, the Monday after the NCAA Finals, which were on Saturday, and the baseball draft was in the first week of June, so you had plenty of time to get from one to the other if you wanted to which I did and nobody else could or did."[4]

Few scouts spent as much time on the road as Krause, and that was how he managed to earn the respect of fellow lifers. Everybody else just had to accept his devotion to the job.

"I knew what I was getting into," said Thelma Krause about how she handled her husband being away so often.

Krause was also a willing listener, picking up bits and pieces from the legends of the game. One of such men was Eddie Gottlieb, the Jewish Ukrainian coach and executive, who brought Wilt Chamberlain to the league back in 1959 thanks to the NBA territorial draft. Working as an executive during a time when centers were the cornerstones of team success, Gottlieb taught Krause that "when you have good big people, and you have the chance to get another big man, get him."[5]

When asked in a 1989 poll conducted by the *Philadelphia Daily News* to pick three top centers in NBA history, Krause settled on Bill Russell, Kareem Abdul-Jabbar, and Wilt Chamberlain.

In his profile for *Sports Illustrated*, Rick Telander describes Krause as follows:

> Krause is a scout of epic proportions, flaming obsession, monumental quirks, the only man ever to be an executive in both major league baseball and the NBA, with all of his clout having arisen from the simple premise that he can ascertain better than almost anyone else who can throw, hit, run, catch and shoot well enough to play in the big leagues.[6]

That sort of devoted, unrelenting work ethic is a source of pride for Chicagoans. Thelma Krause explained that "he wanted the city to be proud of him, just as he was proud of the city."

Krause attributed his work ethic to his parents, Paul and Gertrude. The families of Mr. and Mrs. Karbofsky, as they were originally called, fled Russia, where they were risking death from anti–Jewish violence known as pogroms, which continued to reappear at times of crisis. The continuous outpourings of violence against the Russian Jewry had their roots in the 18th century, when they entered the Russian class society consisting of "the nobility, the clergy, the peasantry, and of merchants and townspeople. In 1780, all Jews were ordered to register in one of the two latter estates, with full enjoyment of all corresponding rights, privileges, and responsibilities."[7] They were looked down upon by the predominantly Christian society, and even those trying to enter the social fabric suffered abuse. In the late 19th and early 20th centuries, three waves of pogroms swept the country.

The Karbofskys changed their name to Krause, because Jerry's father, Paul, wanted to pursue a career in amateur boxing and did not want his parents to find out he was fighting for a living. The Karbofskys were a family of bakers, they were poor, and Paul wanted to earn some extra money in the ring. As Krause reminisced when talking to Telander: "He fought Barney Ross three times and got knocked out three times. He didn't have a high school diploma, but he was honest and worked hard."[8]

Both of his parents worked full-time, and young Jerry had to fend for himself. Thelma Krause told me that "his parents were a solid unit and he felt that they neglected him. He did not have the social skills one would expect that he should have. But that's how he was raised, they worked together, and he was alone most of the time."

The Krauses settled in Albany Park on the Northwest Side of Chicago. Originally a farming community, Albany Park experienced a building boom in the early 20th century. With it came an influx of residents, initially German and Swedish immigrants and later European Jews, and it became a predominantly Jewish neighborhood until the 1950s.[9] Jews from Russia and territories under Russian dominion, such as present-day Poland, Ukraine, Belarus, and the Baltic countries, started migrating to Chicago in the 1870s and settled around Maxwell Street. By 1930 Jews from these territories made up around 80 percent of the city's Jewish population. Jews from Germany settled on the north side of the city, along with other Germans, so these neighborhoods were not seen as Jewish, whereas Maxwell Street was a typically Jewish area, with most people speaking Yiddish.

During our talk, Bill Savage dispelled the common misperception of inner-city migration in Chicago as monolithic. In the first generation of Jewish migrants who came to Maxwell Street, when a family prospered, they moved to Lawndale, to the West Side of the city. Savage told me that at the time "Lawnsdale was around 95 percent Jewish." Maxwell Street became part of the Black South Side, following the expansion of African American neighborhoods. However, some Jewish shopkeepers stayed behind and there were some relationships formed and bonds established. These could either be positive or exploitative.

Therefore, Savage concluded, "it is hard to generalize about Black and Jewish relations."

Jerome Richard Krause was born on April 6, 1939, the same year the inaugural World Professional Basketball Tournament took place in the city of Chicago, organized as the first competition to crown the world champions of the sport. The New York Renaissance Big Five took the title that year. In 1924 a team from the historically Black South Side won the Colored Basketball World's Championship. After some name changes and trials and tribulations, winning over local fans by playing up-tempo basketball and arguing over money, the 1924 champions in four years became the Harlem Globetrotters, eventually taken over by Abe Saperstein, who came up with the name while still working as a promoter.

As explained by hoops historian Thomas Aiello, the name had nothing to do with New York's Harlem; its function was to "code the team as Black for potential white audiences who might be surprised or offended by the race of the players."[10] The team was not from New York, but it soon acquired that showboat, eye-pleasing style associated with the city, as the grittiness of Chicago simply would not sell outside the region.

Pat Reardon said that the placement of Chicago is crucial in understanding what it stands for, as there is nothing of its size in the Midwest to rival its status as the center of the region: "Part of what makes Chicago different is that it's at the crossroads of a lot of transportation and economy. The reason it grew in the 1800s was that it linked the mining and the farming of the west with the money of the east."

This was the environment and culture in which young Jerry got to grow up, spending time with the local kids. They would sometimes get into trouble, "but nothing criminal or illegal," as Thelma Krause was wont to point out with a smile.

Jerry Krause was an only child, but he would say that he had two brothers who were dead, as one was a stillborn and the other a miscarriage. Even though they never took their first breaths, his willingness to include them among the living showed how deeply affected he was by their missing presence.

As a typical only child, young Jerry would sometimes set his parents against each other in order to get the response he wanted, until his father put an end to it.[11] He grew up enamored with his father's work ethic and referred to him as a "bulldog," which was the highest praise one could get from Krause. Paul Krause taught him early on to evaluate people not on the basis of race or skin color, but by how hard they worked. He also taught Krause to battle criticism with humor and wit.

Following his dad's advice, Krause used to always carry two pennies in his pocket, so that when somebody would say: "You ain't worth 2 cents [Krause could] show him the two pennies."[12]

When reminiscing about him, Krause said: "He used to have a motto: 'Patience plus Perseverance equals Success.' I've got that written down on everything, at home, in my office. There's a lot to it."[13] During our talk Thelma Krause, unprompted, brought up "PPS" as the family motto when talking about his courtship of her, which she characterized as "persistent. Very persistent." Krause even named his Arizona fishing boat *PPS*.

As recounted by Telander:

> Paul Krause worked for the Cook County assessor's office for a time, then ran a neighborhood delicatessen and finally opened a shoe store in Norwood Park, a northwest-side area that was heavily Polish-German and Catholic. "It was very anti–Semitic," says Jerry. "They burned out Jews. When I went to Taft High School, you know what the number of Jewish students was? One." Every day Krause felt the contempt others had for him: "They'd yell, 'You kike!' 'You sheenie!' 'You Jew bastard!' I had to fight, and I learned about prejudice."[14]

This claim was disputed by several people, including two of his former schoolmates.[15] Thelma Krause told me a story about a bigger boy, whose last name was Peterson, who served as Jerry's bodyguard in high school. The boy presumably died young. Mrs. Krause added: "I have to believe it's true, even if it's not true, because that's how he felt."

The differences between the experiences of the Jewish immigrants and their children and African Americans were clear, as best evidenced by their relationship with the police. *Boss*, Mike Royko's biography of Chicago longtime mayor Richard J. Daley, describes how "the immigrant family looked to [the district captain] as more than a link with a new and strange government: he was the government…. When a downtown office didn't provide service, he was a direct link to government, somebody to cut through the bureaucracy." However, the relationship was based on the social and financial standing of a given family, since "in poor parts of the city, he has added role of a threat. Don't vote, and you might lose your public housing apartment. Don't vote and you might be cut off welfare. Don't vote, and you might have building inspectors poking around the house"[16]

Reminiscing about his time growing up, Krause said: "All I talked about when I was younger was sports. If I couldn't play professionally, I figured I'd write."[17] As a kid and a teenager, Krause played baseball as much as he could. In high school, at 15 years old, he became a copy boy for the *Chicago Herald-American*, while running semipro baseball teams and evaluating baseball and basketball talent. Bill Gleason, who was working there at the time, said that Krause "talked and talked and talked. He worked and worked and worked."[18] Gleason developed genuine sympathy and appreciation for Krause and would be one of the few journalists to personally congratulate him whenever the Bulls won championships, as well as defending him in the press numerous times.

He was nicknamed "J.G. Taylor Krause," after J.G. Taylor Spink, at the time a highly regarded sportswriter, who would eventually lose his status due to his racist views, particularly being a strong opponent of integration in baseball. Among his heroes, Krause named sportswriters James Enright, Warren Brown, and Wendell Smith. Later he expanded that group to include Ira Berkow of the *New York Times*, Bob Ryan of the *Boston Globe*, and Chick Hearn, the Lakers broadcaster.[19]

When criticizing journalists writing about his team, particularly when they revealed information that Krause would prefer to keep secret, he brought up these names, saying that as opposed to most writers producing pieces about the Bulls, his heroes stood for journalistic integrity. Even Gleason, who was on Krause's side and genuinely liked him, wrote: "The thing that disappoints me the most is that this guy comes out of the newspaper business and doesn't understand how to deal with the press. He worked in the same office and hero-worshiped two of the more caustic writers in Chicago history in Warren Brown and Harry McNamara and yet he can't handle criticism from the press."[20] It is unknown if his previous experiences in the press influenced his obsessive secrecy, but Krause was probably the least cooperative executive in sports history when it came to talking to the press.

As relayed to me by journalist Ian Thomsen: "He was always playing defense with reporters instead of taking the initiative with information. When you spoke with him everything was off the record, but it just wasn't useful information anyway."

Krause's approach to sharing information was no secret. When he was asked in 1988 which NCAA (National Collegiate Athletic Association) conference was the best, he replied: "You don't want to ask me any questions. I'm a lousy interview. I don't talk about college players before they're drafted and I don't compare conferences."[21]

At age 21 Krause gave up on his journalistic career: "I didn't have the creative ability to put words together. I wanted to excel at something. I got into scouting and knew I could be a success at that."[22]

At William Howard Taft High School, Krause became a warm-up pitcher for the Eagles under coach Jim Smilgoff, who, just like Krause, was a Chicagoan and a Jew. Smilgoff was so highly regarded in the city that he conducted summer training for the Cubs, and in 1958 he was promoted to vice principal at Taft. Apart from his work at the school, he was a football statistician during prep-school playoffs, wrote books about baseball, and was a scout. Annually he organized his Midwest Baseball camp. Krause held Smilgoff in such high regard that he rode "his bike eight miles each way each day so he could continue at Taft."[23]

"Taft was on the other side of the city and it was not easy to get there. I don't know how he got there, but he did," said Thelma Krause with admiration.

He was not athletic, nor he did not possess the potential to become an athlete, but Krause had an undeniable eye for talent. Through his connections Smilgoff was able to put him in touch with Yankees scout Fred Hasselman, whom Krause described as "a fat old man, this wide, maybe five-six."[24] Krause found himself enjoying being on the road, fetching sandwiches and coffee for the older, experienced talent evaluator.

According to Lowenfish, Hasselman "saw that this kid, who was a teenager, really loved the game and was willing to do what he could to find players. Scouts back then were obsessed; being a scout was their lifetime commitment." Years later Krause gave his thoughts on scouting to Adrian Wojnarowski: "Scouting is a zest. It is fun for me, I enjoy it. It's something I was born, I think, to do, I was born to evaluate. God gave me some things. He had to give them to me. And I had to educate them and get a little better at those skills, but it's God-given in a lot of respects."[25]

Lee Lowenfish explained to me what made Krause such a good baseball scout:

> He came of age right after World War II and baseball was still the national pastime, played all over the country, and the level was very erratic. You can't judge a player when he's getting big stats against opponents who are not very good. And the hardest thing in scouting is to project. You see a kid, 19 years old or younger, who is dominating everybody, but how is he going to go against better competition?

Krause said that the key to making such evaluations and projections was gathering as much data as possible. During his time it was less about numbers and more about the eye-test, seeing with his own eyes whether a player was worth drafting. That was why it was so important for him to attend games and see in person what a player was capable of. Sometimes it was just a small interaction that convinced Krause to give a particular player a closer look. One time he said, "I can shake a guy's hand and tell whether he's got good hands."[26]

1. The Scout and the City

When he first got the Bulls job in 1976, as player personnel director, he was already mocked for his supposedly exaggerated knowledge of basketball players, with his critics joking that "he even knew some that didn't exist."[27] Other people appreciated his work ethic, especially those who chose the same professions. As Krause said to Lee Lowenfish, who was interviewing him for his book on baseball scouting: "Scouts are attracted to other scouts and scouts hire other scouts." Lowenfish was quick to add: "They're hunters, it's a calling and they're looking for people who have the same sense of calling, because you're not going to have a normal life if you aspire to the top."

During his conversation with Wojnarowski, Krause gave the example of an outfielder, who might never catch or throw a ball during a game: "you have got to really be careful, you have to understand what you are doing and you have got to be a bulldog, because you have got to go back and find out. You have to get that guy in batting practice. You have got to get that guy to throw for you."[28] When watching baseball, Krause learned to focus on the details, which expanded his understanding of how physical attributes could translate to on-court or on-field performance. According to Telander, Krause was more than a sport expert: "To go from baseball to basketball meant that you were a scout of talent, not just a sport scout."

This was what happened when Krause took over the Bulls in 1985 and invited Karen Stack, then 23 years old, to join his staff. "I was already working at the ticket department and it became a joke with our ticket manager that Jerry stole me from him. Jerry was like: 'oh, you can type, you know basketball, you're with me,'" she reminisced, impersonating Krause's low voice.

It is hard to say for sure which baseball players Krause was responsible for scouting and drafting, because the credit never went to a single person, but to the whole organization. The credit given to the whole franchise, the need to recognize the contributions of everybody employed by it, will return much later in this story as one of the reasons behind the flawed relationship between Krause and Michael Jordan. The price for sharing success was an almost complete lack of recognition and respect.

Telander told me about a team photo from Krause's time managing the Taft Eagles, in which he is captioned as "unidentified boy."

After graduating from Taft, Krause attended Bradley University in Peoria, Illinois, majoring in English and physical education. He was roommates with Barney Cable, who would go on to become a professional basketball player, enjoying a nine-year career in the NBA and the NBL. The connection would allow Krause to get his first taste of working for a basketball franchise a couple of years later.

While studying he continued to write for *Peoria Journal Star* and work for the WLS radio station, and then was a staff writer for the Chicago bureau of United Press International. Prior to the United Press job, he worked in the Chicago Cubs business office. During his conversation with Lowenfish, Krause referred to the job as being "a flunky," earning $65 a week. After working as a gofer and doing some scouting for local basketball franchise, the Chicago Zephyrs, he moved to Baltimore with the franchise.

In 1963, when Cable was playing for the Zephyrs, Krause was noticed by head coach Bobby "Slick" Leonard, as he was always hanging around the team. Leonard eventually offered him a job as a scout. When reminiscing about the job offer, Krause claimed that he got it because he proposed innovative methods of scouting. Leonard said that Krause was just persistent and would not stop hounding him. The two struck up a friendship that lasted for the rest of their lives.[29]

At age 24 Krause became the team's publicity director, statistician, and scorer's table publicist (among other things), while still remaining responsible for scouting basketball players. During baseball season he scouted baseball players. As pointed out by longtime Chicago sports journalist Sam Smith, in those days "nobody scouted games, they read scout magazines and did the draft off things like that.... Jerry was trying to carve out a career."[30]

He was so occupied with work that he neglected basic, everyday things. For a month, following the franchise's relocation from Chicago to Baltimore, he lived with Leonard and his family. The Hall of Fame coach reminisced that Krause "had a problem with dandruff and he didn't keep his shoes shined, so I got him some Head and Shoulders and a can of shoe polish and made him clean up. It was like having inspection every day."[31]

Thelma Krause reminisced that she put in a lot of work for her husband to dress properly, investing in tailor-made clothes.

There is a common misperception about Krause, one regarding his unwillingness to talk to the press. Umlauf suggests that things were not that simple, that he was not reluctant to speak but rather to share information that might be used against him and his team. During our talk she said that while Krause "just wanted to do the work, I think he did like the press conferences and talking, and he always had good answers for things. He was just not going to give you what you wanted."

"Nowhere does it say that the general manager's job is to talk to the press. You are supposed to run a basketball team. And that's it," said Al Vermeil.

Krause's favorite topics were baseball and basketball, and during his early scouting visits for the Baltimore Bullets he established two important relationships that would influence his outlook on professional basketball.

Morice Fredrick Winter was 17 years older than Krause, who was so enamored with him that throughout his life Winter remained the only person he ever referred to as "coach."[32] On his first day of work as an executive, Krause called Winter at 7:00 a.m. and offered him a job on the coaching staff of the Bulls.

The future basketball genius was born in Texas, which earned him the nickname "Tex" when his family moved to California. A pole vaulter with Olympic aspirations that were put to rest by the outbreak of World War II, Winter was for two years, 1940 to 1942, the best player on the Compton Tartars Junior College basketball team. In 1942 the high-scoring guard's team made it to the final of the state Jaycee tournament. After a year at Oregon State, Winter entered the navy, where he served as a fighter pilot until the end of the war.

Winter played out the final year of his NCAA career at USC, under coach Sam Barry, where he learned the triangle offense: a team-oriented style of play, which required the players to form triangles on the court, pass the ball, and set screens. Barry's system was developed on different basketball courts and under different basketball rules. The three-second violation was already in place, which forced the dominant big men to move away from the basket and remain in motion, but only in 1944 did the NCAA rulebook introduce defensive goal-tending, which limited the centers' defensive impact.

Winter adapted Barry's invention to the broadened lane and the three-point line, but the essentials remained the same: "the triangle works when it's played unselfishly, when each player on the floor has the ball about 20 percent of the time and when each realizes his role and also realizes that everyone has a role in the offense."[33] The same rules applied to Winter's basketball philosophy: "Executing basic fundamentals of the game while moving at a fast pace. Being fundamentally sound, but yet quick."[34]

That way of thinking about basketball was born during Winter's sole year at USC, but it was shaped at Kansas State, where Winter became assistant coach under Jack Gardner in 1947. He worked there for four seasons before returning to take over the team in 1953, following two years at Marquette as head coach.

Despite Winter's successes as college head coach, being the assistant coach was the role he truly excelled at, because he could focus on developing and implementing his basketball strategy. Two years prior to taking the assistant position on the Bulls, he publicly acknowledged his limitations, as well as the changing landscape of college basketball: "I enjoy going out and meeting the kids and families, but I don't like getting down in the gutter and kicking in doors. I think the coaching profession is above that, but that's what it's becoming more and more about."[35] But that was later, after eight league titles won during his 15 years at Kansas State. Roland Lazenby writes:

> In fact, it was Winter's Kansas State team that defeated Wilt Chamberlain's team in the Big Eight conference in 1958, leaving the gifted giant so frustrated that he decided to leave Kansas early to play with the Harlem Globetrotters. For Winter, it was the ultimate victory of team basketball over the brilliance of an individual player.[36]

The other head coach with whom Krause forged a relationship early in his career was Clarence Gaines, whose legacy concerns primarily what he did off the court. Working at HBCU Winston-Salem State, he exhibited a strict yet nurturing and caring attitude toward his players. Because he was entrusted with young Black athletes by their parents, Gaines considered it his responsibility to raise them. Some of the players in fact referred to him as "daddy."[37]

Gaines was nicknamed "Big House" because when he entered Morgan State in Baltimore as a football prospect at 6'5" and weighing 265 pounds, a college worker said: "The only thing I've seen as big as you is a house."[38] He demanded respect with his physique alone. In 1945 Gaines graduated from Morgan State with a degree in chemistry and became assistant coach at Winston-Salem State, hoping to return to school in a year or two and become a dentist. He took over the team a year later and remained at the head coaching position for 47 years.

In 1945 Winston-Salem State Teachers College was a women's college, with just a small number of boys. During our talk Johnson recounted that when Gaines started out, "he had no money and no recruiting budget, so he asked graduate students, as they spread across the country, to recruit for him. He said, 'Let me know if you see any Black teenagers who can play basketball.' He did not see many of his recruits in person until they arrived to Winston-Salem."

Such was the case with Earl Monroe, whom Coach Gaines was reluctant to take in at first because of the fact that he started playing basketball relatively late and was not an exceptional high school player. When Gaines entered the train on which Monroe arrived, the future Hall of Famer described Big House as "a big, looming, bear-like figure standing in the doorway."

The CCNY point-shaving scandal of 1950-51, which involved seven schools, made the success of the Winston-Salem State Rams basketball teams possible. Thirty-three college players were involved in fixing games. The Northern schools responded to gamblers giving money to Black teenagers by cutting down the number of Black recruits. The unwritten rule of recruiting was that a college brought in one African American player on a basketball scholarship and another one to be his roommate. If more were brought on, the university would risk upsetting other students.

While racism in the south was more explicit, that didn't mean that it didn't exist elsewhere. Once, out of the blue, during a talk with Johnson, Gaines said:

> You know what's the most racist place I've ever been to? New York City. Down South there are signs that say "Colored Drinking Fountain" or "Colored Waiting Room." I would know where I could and could not go in the South and I could live with that. In New York I would cross a line and I did not know it before it was too late. And it was so dishonest.

For 20 years Gaines had access to some of the best basketball players in the country, until the 1966 NCAA Championship game, in which an all-Black Texas Western Miners team would beat an all-white Kentucky team, ushering in a revolution in African American player recruitment. Eventually little schools, like Winston-Salem State, simply did not have the resources to compete against bigger programs. Gaines continued to coach and educate young Black men. He even struck up a relationship with the local police, who would inform Gaines whenever his players did something bad.

One year prior to the Miners' landmark win, at age 25, Jerry Krause made the first pick of his NBA career. Well, sort of. In the third round of the 1964 draft, with the 21st pick, the Bullets selected Jerry Sloan. Krause especially appreciated Sloan's toughness: "he was phenomenal, he'd mean 20–25 points to his team *without* scoring."[39] Sloan was tough, relentless, and stubborn, and while that made him a great basketball player, the same characteristics allowed him to confidently refuse to come to Baltimore and return to college for an extra season.

A year later, with his education complete, the Bullets once again selected Sloan, who this time was no longer a best kept secret. The ultimate decision was made by Bullets general manager Harold "Buddy" Jeannette, who had coached the team the season prior, but was replaced by Paul Seymour, a former basketball player and coach, who ventured into the liquor business before returning to coaching. Jeanette admitted: "Truthfully, I've never seen Jerry play but my scouts are very high on him."[40] The 6'5" Sloan was seen as a versatile defender, capable of guarding multiple positions. He also took great pride in his defense: "When I look at the box score, I look to see how many points my man scored, not how many I scored."[41]

Sloan was the youngest of 10 children and his father died when he was just four years old. Early on he learned the value of hard work by helping his mother on the farm whenever possible, while attending college and working heavy construction jobs in the summers. Sloan was proud to be from McLeansboro, Illinois, situated 300 miles south of Chicago. He enjoyed working on his farm even after becoming an NBA player and then coach.

He was also a great basketball player. In 1965, after a three-year career playing for Evansville College, he was "widely regarded the greatest player in 45 years of Aces' basketball."[42] Nicknamed the "Fabulous Fox," Sloan brought college scouts to McLeansboro as a high school senior and did the same for Evansville. Coach Alex Hannum of the San Francisco Warriors scouted him as a potential first or second overall pick in the 1965 draft, but holding both, he decided to go instead with Fred Hetzel from Davidson and Rick Barry from Miami. Barry would become one of the best scorers in league history, instrumental in bringing the first championship to the Bay Area franchise. Davidson would produce its second draft lottery pick 44 years later, and once again it would be the Warriors who made the selection. The player in question was Steph Curry.

Sloan was promised a bonus for signing with the Bullets, but he did not show up for the team's press conference. He informed the team about his unwillingness to sign the deal just six hours prior to the event. Following Sloan's no-show, fans began prank-calling the Bullets' offices, pretending to be Sloan and apologizing for the absence. Executive vice president Herb Heft complained that his franchise became "the laughingstock of Baltimore."[43] The Bullets offered Sloan $14,000 per season; he wanted $15,000 plus a $7,000 signing bonus. The disgruntled Sloan eventually signed the deal and played one season in Baltimore, where he came off the bench.

In 1966 Sloan was picked up by the Chicago Bulls in the expansion draft and became the first player whose number was retired by the franchise. A couple seasons into Sloan's stellar career, Krause said: "Everybody laughed at me, they said there was no way he could play in the NBA. But he had done so many things as a senior, intangible things, that I simply fell in love with him."[44]

The Bulls were Chicago's second attempt at an NBA franchise. Well, third, to be exact.

The Chicago Packers employed Harry Hannin as their general manager. Hannin worked for 12 years under fellow Chicagoan Abe

1. The Scout and the City

Saperstein, whose newest endeavor following the Globetrotters was the American Basketball League. Chicago had a franchise in the ABL, the Chicago Majors, also owned by Saperstein. The ABL was supposed to launch the same year as the Packers entered the NBA, 1961. The league folded after one and a half seasons, and it is mostly remembered as being the first to introduce the three-point shot on a permanent basis. The Packers were coached by Jim Pollard, a five-time NBA champion with the Minneapolis Lakers. Journalist Bob Frisk characterized Pollard as "likeable" and "classy" in the article introducing him to Chicago fans,[45] but these characteristics did not translate to on-court success, as the team ended the season with 18 wins and 62 losses.

After the season owner David Trager renamed the team to Chicago Zephyrs. Thirty-two-year-old Jack McMahon was the new head coach and Frank Lane the new general manager. The year prior McMahon had led the Kansas City Steelers to an ABL-best record, 58–28. The Zephyrs would fire McMahon 38 games and 12 wins into his two-year contract.

After another disappointing season, which saw the Chicago franchise win 25 games, it relocated to Baltimore. Initially going by Zephyrs, it was renamed before the start of the season to the Baltimore Bullets, as the defunct Maryland franchise was called in the ABL/BAA/NBA from 1944 to 1954. The name was supposed to create a feeling of continuity, making professional basketball feel at home in the city. As for Chicago, it had to wait its turn. Fortunately, it didn't have to wait long, as in two years NBA basketball was revived in the Windy City.

Dick Klein, the founder of the Chicago Bulls franchise, initially failed to buy the Zephyrs and keep them in Chicago. He reportedly had an oral agreement with David Trager to buy the team for $600,000, but after vacationing in Phoenix he learned that the franchise was moving to Baltimore. Klein was an exceptional basketball player at Northwestern University and later played professionally for the Chicago American Gears of the National Basketball League. That team folded in 1948.

In 1963 Klein formed Chicago Basketball Corp. and started organizing investors from Illinois and neighboring Indiana in order to get the money necessary to establish an NBA franchise.[46] One of his associates was Jerry Colangelo, who was brought along by Klein and whom Klein convinced to get into basketball. Klein ran the franchise along with Colangelo and five other people.

The expansion costs eventually amounted to $1,600,000.

Klein's unrelenting optimism made the return of NBA basketball to the Windy City possible. He always overestimated the players and the team, which he was referring to as his "Baby Bulls," because of the core of the roster consisting of inexperienced players: Keith Erickson,

McCoy McLemore, Jerry Sloan, and Jim Washington. The first star of the team was 31-year-old Guy Rodgers, who the Bulls acquired prior to their first season for two players and cash. Rodgers averaged 18 points and 11.2 assists, which at the time was the league record.

The team played their home games at the International Amphitheater, with occasional excursions to Evansville, Indiana. It was the location which inspired the name, as the Amphitheater was located adjacent to the Union Stock Yards and there was a sense of strength associated with the short, newspaper-friendly name.[47] After two years, in 1968, the Bulls moved to Chicago Stadium.

During their first season there the price of tickets ranged from $2 to $5, which was relatively low and, as pointed out by Sean Dinces, "affordable even for workers without a college education, especially the nearly one-third of the city's workforce employed in union-dense manufacturing industries."[48] This was a rare instance of egalitarianism in a deeply divided city, which Bill Savage characterizes as "racially segregated, politically run by what was known as the Machine, which put Irish white people in front of everybody else."

Richard J. Daley, the city mayor from 1955 to 1976, ran the Machine. Daley was the chairman of the Democratic Party. Control of its treasury allowed him, through local spending, to ensure voter support from all neighborhoods, rich and poor. He gave out positions to labor union leaders and offered governmental work only to trusted contractors. Republican businessmen had to support the Machine to keep their businesses afloat, simultaneously limiting their party's chances at winning the elections. Mike Royko writes that "unlike New York, Los Angeles, and other major cities, Chicago has no independent parties or candidates jumping in to threaten, or at least pull votes away from the leaders. It is no accident. Illinois election laws are stacked against an independent's ever getting his name on a voting machine."[49]

With the city consequently losing manufacturing jobs, due to labor being more and more outsourced, either to Southern states or foreign countries, Daley's idea of saving the city's economy was by investing in the Loop, the main section of downtown Chicago. In order to revitalize the Loop, Daley "oversaw several massive developments during the 1950s and 1960s that forced thousands of Blacks out from the area," as he feared that the presence of African Americans around and in the downtown area would scare off potential investors.[50]

The Bulls initially did not draw. At Roberts Stadium in Evansville, more than 11,000 people watched the Bulls take on the Philadelphia Sixers and win 129–122, limiting the dominant Wilt Chamberlain to 20 points. The team finished the season 33–48 and made the playoffs in their rookie campaign.

Their coach, Johnny Kerr, was named NBA Coach of the Year and turned down the offer to coach at his alma mater, University of Illinois Urbana–Champaign, despite the college game being much larger in the state than professional basketball, as was the case around the country. In fact, the NCAA was so big at the time that the head coach of another college from Illinois, De Paul's Ray Meyer, rejected a job offer from the Bulls, which opened the door for Kerr. Even though they were swept by the St. Louis Hawks, there was still a lot of optimism surrounding the franchise, as no expansion team entered the NBA so decisively. The Bulls finished the season with $50,000 in financial losses, which was far less than the projected $250,000, reviving the sport in the Midwestern city that was known as "the graveyard of professional basketball."[51]

Seven hundred miles away, as his hometown team was spending the summer trying to capitalize on its first successful season in the NBA, Jerry Krause was in Baltimore, with the Bullets holding the second pick. He was still involved in scouting baseball players for the Cleveland Indians, while continuing to push for Monroe's selection in the draft along with fellow Bullets scout Bob Ferry. Apart from scouting college players, Krause was also attending exhibition games to pick up on things professional players were doing during games, like how they were dribbling the ball or setting up for rebounds. He also befriended James "Jim" Enright, a basketball referee and sportswriter, who in 1979 would be inducted into the Basketball Hall of Fame for his 30-year refereeing career.

Most importantly for his personal life, he got married in 1976, to a woman named Sharon. They had a big, fancy wedding in Baltimore, but almost everybody who knew him thought he was making a mistake. His father even said to him: "You can escape, I'll cover you." They divorced after two years.

Professionally, though, things were looking up. Krause wanted Monroe, who led Winston-Salem to its first Division II championship, the first time an all-Black school had won the title. Monroe did not consider professional basketball a valid career option, as not many Black Division II players made it into the NBA. There was also another issue with the 6'3" Monroe that could be considered a problem. He was not a systemic player, but a natural, who was given free rein by coach Gaines.

Clint Johnson reminisced how Gaines thought out loud about the outcome of a potential confrontation between his all-Black team and the 1966 Texas Western Miners: "they were playing like white guys, but my Black players were playing like Black guys." Miners coach Don

Haskins initiated a team-oriented system, which was not particularly flashy, while Winston-Salem relied more on fastbreak basketball, a lot of running and quick passes. It was unclear how Monroe would handle the transition to the NBA, which relied on predominantly white audiences coming to games and buying tickets. Gaines was not particularly interested in attracting scouts, as he was more concerned with keeping his players out of trouble and giving them a foundation to succeed later on in life. As he said to his players: "You came to college to become a man." He demanded respect, honesty and integrity, and gave the same back to his players. Krause said of him years later: "Bighouse [sic] has done more for race relations in North Carolina than anyone else. He's more than a basketball coach."[52]

It seemed that Monroe was going to quit the Bullets and professional basketball as a whole, discouraged by playing for a losing franchise. The player complained to sportswriters that "if pro basketball didn't pay so well he'd just as soon take off the uniform and do something else for a living," despite said sportswriters encouraging him to just play his game, as he had the potential to be "one of professional basketball's next super stars," predicting that he would win Rookie of the Year.[53] This was exactly what happened, as Monroe became the most dominant NBA freshman in the country.

Years later Jerry Krause said that "when Earl Monroe came to Baltimore, he saved the franchise. The Bullets would have been in Houston without him."[54] After the season Krause was once again promoted, although this time the job opportunity came from a different franchise. "The Sleuth" was about to get a chance at scouting for his hometown team.

2

Traveling Man

On August 4, 1968, Martin Luther King, Jr., was assassinated in Memphis and over 140 American cities were swept by waves of violence. In his book on the significance of year 1968 in American sports, James C. Nicholson summarizes by saying that "once the nation's major urban areas calmed, dozens had been killed, 2,500 had been injured, and hundreds of buildings had been burned, causing millions of dollars in property damage. Police had made 20,000 arrests, and 65,000 National Guardsmen had seen riot duty in the worst American domestic disturbance since the Civil War."[1] Among the cities to suffer most devastation was Chicago, including the surroundings of the Chicago Stadium.

Richard J. Daley pledged during his 1967 inaugural mayoral election speech that "As long as I am mayor, law and order will prevail." This would be put to test a year later, during the riots, with Daley issuing instructions to 10,500 police officers "to shoot arsonists and looters— arsonists to kill and looters to main and detain." When asked about children committing crimes, the mayor replied, "You wouldn't want to shoot them, but with mace you could detain youngsters."

The reasons for the destruction of the West Side specifically, with most of the predominantly Black South Side being left unscathed by the riots, were purely historical. The South Side was inhabited by African Americans who had arrived in the city up until the 1930s, whereas the West Side was populated by Blacks who moved there after World War II. In the South Side the community elected Black politicians, whereas the West Side had "plantation wards," which, as Bill Savage explained, were run by white aldermen despite the population within these wards being up to 90 percent African American. The Black voters in the neighborhood usually did not have a Black candidate to vote for, since the white Machine determined who would run for office. Therefore "Blacks on the West Side had no political power, with no sense of connection to the neighborhood."

The riots over King's murder erupted on August 5, 1968, and lasted until August 7. Over 2,000 people were arrested, and 210 buildings damaged. On the day of King's funeral, August 9, the *Chicago Tribune* ran an editorial which described the murder as "a crime and the sin of an individual," while adding that "moral values [were] at the lowest level since the decadence of Rome," the proof of which was "mixed company, with no supervision" being allowed at university dormitories, people dressing immodestly and using "four-letter words." The rioters were described as indulged by the whites unwilling to take the hard line against crime, most notably criticizing the shootings as "police brutality."[2]

Two of the greatest rivals in professional basketball history, Bill Russell and Wilt Chamberlain, were supposed to face off once again in the Eastern Division playoff series between the Celtics and the Sixers the day after King's assassination. As retraced by James C. Nicholson, "after a sleepless night, Russell, along with Chamberlain, was inclined to postpone the game. But the men also worried that a late cancellation would precipitate a violent reaction from angry fans."[3] Game One of the series took place as planned; Game Two was postponed due to the national day of mourning. Both Russell and Chamberlain were present at King's funeral in Atlanta. The city itself was one of the most crime-infested in the country, yet the funeral took place without serious outbursts of violence.

Apart from racial tensions within the United States, another issue faced by the basketball teams (as well as any other businesses) was the spike in violent crime, which grew by 135 percent between the years 1960 and 1975.[4] The violence simultaneously led and was fueled by "residential segregation, urban decay, white flight, and the concentration of poverty in ghetto neighborhoods."[5]

The circumstances for joining the Bulls were not ideal for Krause, who at age 30 was named senior talent scout, while he continued to look for talented baseball players in the summer, this time for the Baltimore Orioles. Franchise owner Dick Klein second-guessed his employees, Johnny Kerr and Al Bianchi, in the press, did not listen to trade and scouting advice, and was more concerned with turning out a profit than building a good basketball team. Bianchi left for Seattle after the first season; Kerr quit to join the expansion Phoenix Suns after the second.

Klein decided to employ Dick Motta, a three-time Big Sky champion with the Weber State Wildcats, because he wanted a tough, hard-nosed coach, one who would reflect the attitude of Chicago and its inhabitants. During Motta's 12 years at Weber, the team went 237–64.

Klein explained his decision as follows: "I wanted a man, who had been a winner at three levels of basketball, who could take less than the best players and compete with the best and who was young enough to take the grind of the NBA schedule. That formula fitted very few men. Motta was one. I found he had a similar philosophy to mine about the way it should be done."[6] After the hire Klein said: "Dick's teams were well-drilled, they knew what they were doing, they worked hard and they played rough. We were delighted to get him."[7]

Motta did not waste any time in confirming his reputation when, during the first day of training camp, after one of the 17 rookies quit, he said: "I'd wish he'd show up for practice tonight. I'd like to have a sacrificial lamb. When he showed up I could order him off the court and that would be a good example for the rest of the guys."[8] The two-hour-long practices were excruciating, filled with drills, one-on-one play, and running. The breaks were devoted to practicing free throws. While he did not look the part—the Madison Square Garden guard famously refused to let him into the arena, not believing that he was an actual coach—Motta was a strict disciplinarian, bordering on authoritarian. During one early season workout he fined a veteran player $500 for not shooting the ball.

When taking over the team, at just 36 years old, with no experience in professional basketball, Motta said: "There is no doubt in my mind I will have total and absolute authority over player personnel and acquisition of players."[9]

He referred to Krause as *his* scout.[10]

Krause developed a system of sorts, using a checklist of 20 physical and 10 mental capabilities that a player should possess. The most important factor Krause was looking for was courage. Guts. That system of evaluation remained unchanged throughout his career as a scout, as well as a basketball executive.

When the Bulls entered the NBA in 1966, they became the 10th team in the league and played in the Western Division. Two years later the NBA expanded to 14 teams and the number of regular-season games grew from 81 to 82. The Bulls remained in the West and finished their first season under Motta with 33 wins, four below the last playoff spot.

Due to tensions between Motta and Klein, the board of directors decided to side with the coach. The man responsible for bringing the investment team together was accused of tearing the basketball team apart, creating friction with his decisions. Klein resigned as general manager, although it was not a secret that the board did not want him running the Bulls anyway. He was replaced by Pat Williams, a 29-year-old former promotion director of the Philadelphia Sixers. Motta was satisfied with the decision, which he influenced, saying: "I was told this summer to sit tight and things would work out for me as coach of the Bulls. They certainly have."[11]

Williams's primary function was marketing the team, while Motta was responsible for constructing the roster. In his first season in Chicago, the Bulls missed the playoffs. Motta blamed the team he inherited for that. "We were in sad shape.... We had no rookies, no new faces. When we started this season we had ourselves a three-year plan to make the playoffs."[12] After just one year the team was back in the postseason.

However, interest in the Bulls grew because of Williams's marketing. Part of it was giveaways to fans sitting in lucky seats, meeting Chicagoans regularly in their places of habitat, organizing grocery nights, and a wrestling show, involving the Bulls' first PR specialist, Ben Bentley, facing off against a "declawed, defanged, muzzled, sedated" bear named Victor,[13] as well as getting great press due to the general manager's willingness to talk to journalists even on the most difficult of topics.

The most controversial issue was the NBA's reliance on Black players, which was supposedly keeping white audiences away from games, especially in the aftermath of the 1968 riots. Asked about the rising influence of African Americans on the outlook of the city and their number on the Bulls roster, Williams responded: "Nothing alarms or concerns me about the current surge of black pride, Afro dress, and so on. On the floor, it's our guys against their guys, regardless of color."[14]

Williams's "master stroke" was Benny the Bull, a mascot who became a local celebrity.[15] Landey Patton, the man wearing the red suit, with hooves, horns, tail, and all, was so popular that he was recognized in public and asked for autographs without the costume on. Two years after winning over children and their parents, the 30-year-old Patton resigned, having gotten a job negotiating office space rental for corporations and businesses. While the team performed better, Patton complained: "It's not the same as in the first season. I can't explain why, but the crowds don't react the way they used to."[16] The crowds attending games did not change, as the Bulls continued to bring in around 10,000 fans per night, 2.5 times more than the 3,500 attending Bulls games when Williams took over.

Following the 1969-70 season, in which the Bulls returned to the playoffs, the team held the 11th pick in the draft. With future Hall of Fame guards Calvin Murphy and Nate "Tiny" Archibald available, the Bulls picked Jimmy Collins instead. Six other teams passed on them before they were picked as the first and second picks of the second round, but that mistake prompted Motta to introduce Krause as the man who talked him out of taking Archibald in the draft. All the teams that passed on Archibald—except for the Cincinnati Royals, who got him in the second round—were proven wrong before the regular season by the 51-point shooting performance by the 5'11" guard during the Aloha Basketball Classic.

Krause valued Collins more than Archibald because of his defensive ability. When approached by the *Albuquerque Journal*'s Ben Moffett at the New Mexico State–Utah State game about Collins, Krause concluded in typical Sleuth fashion: "I'm not going to tell you what it has taken me a season of research to find out. But I will tell you this. If he is drafted high, it means he can play defense. If he doesn't, it means he can't."[17] Collins was also contacted by the NFL's Minnesota Vikings, but he signed with the Bulls on a three-year contract. Krause valued Collins so highly that he put the New Yorker third in that year's rookie ranking, behind only Pete Maravich and Bob Lanier, two future Hall of Famers, whom the Bulls had no chance of landing with the late picks that they held.

Motta was not fond of Collins, who in his rookie season played 8.7 minutes per game and appeared in just 55 contests. The disdain of the coach toward his player was most visible during a late season game played in Las Cruces, New Mexico, in the arena where Collins had played college ball. Fifteen thousand fans came to watch the local idol play in the NBA, as the Bulls were taking on the Cincinnati Royals, yet Collins never got off the bench. After the game he said: "It's nothing new to me to sit on the bench the entire game. In fact, I haven't played in the last 10 games."[18]

The fans booed Motta's decision to not bring in the player, and the coach did little to increase the NBA's marketability in the region. Collins demanded a trade, but he did not get his wish and stayed in Chicago for one more uneventful season before quitting the NBA altogether.

After witnessing the results of the decision to pick Collins, Motta decided to do the scouting himself, overruling Krause. In the second round he infamously picked Howard Porter of Villanova, who was also signed by the ABA's Pittsburgh Condors. The teams were about to go to court over the rights for the player, but they eventually reached an agreement, and the Bulls signed the NCAA Final Four Most Outstanding Player to a five-year deal worth $1.5 million. Porter was ruled ineligible for the honor because he signed with the Condors while still a college player. That controversy impacted Porter's draft stock; up until that point he was considered one of the best players in the country. The consequences of that signature were massive: Villanova, who made it all the way to the final, forfeited all of its wins since Porter signed the deal and returned the money it received for progressing so far in the tournament.

That did not matter for Krause, since he had already moved on to work for Suns general manager Jerry Colangelo. Colangelo was willing to not only pay his salary but also shell out an additional $30,000 per season to cover Krause's travel expenses. During his last season on the Bulls, Krause watched 142 college games in person. Colangelo appreciated that dedication: "I was out scouting one time and went to a gym that had 75 seating capacity. I figured if there was one person in the world I might see there, it would be Krause. Sure enough, there he was."[19] Colangelo, just like Krause, was from Cook County, Illinois, and from 1966 to 1968 worked for the Bulls holding various jobs, from marketing director through scout to assistant to team president.

Krause was so used to life on the road that he did not move out of Chicago to work for the Suns. Approached by journalist Dave Kindred at a game between Louisville and Dayton, Krause described his usual routine while scouting: "I'm going to Chicago now. Gotta drop off this laundry, pick up my other laundry, go to Lafayette, La. Helluva tournament down there. Southwestern Louisiana, Long Beach State, Pan American and Texas-El Paso. You think there won't be some players there? Wow!"[20]

The University of Louisville was a significant place for Krause, because he scouted a local boy from Kentucky, Wes Unseld, whom the Baltimore Bullets selected second overall in the 1968 draft. Overlooked because of his size, at 6'7" Unseld was still able to outscore and out-rebound fellow centers, winning the Rookie of the Year and MVP awards in his first season in the NBA.

Krause preferred Otto Moore and Charley Paulk to Unseld, but Bullets head coach Gene Shue really wanted Unseld.[21] In 2001 the *Washington Post* published a Bullets scouting report from 1968, which ended with an underlined statement in capital letters: "I DO NOT FEEL WE SHOULD GO FOR HIM UNDER ANY CIRCUMSTANCES." Bob Ferry commented on the issue: "The Bullets had two scouts back then—me and Jerry Krause. And I didn't write that report."[22] Asked for comment, Krause said he did not remember whether he wrote the report or not but added that the Bullets needed his approval to make the pick, so he was still involved in the selection.

Moore was picked sixth and Paulk seventh overall, and both were long out of the NBA when Unseld retired from professional basketball in 1981. With his decision to select Unseld, Shue preserved Krause's reputation, which landed him a job with the Suns. This would be a lot harder one year later, following the whole Collins debacle. In 1971-72, his second NBA season, Archibald improved from averages of 16 points and 5.5 assists to 28.2 and 9.2, respectively. Not drafting him turned from a regular-sized mistake to a terrible one.

The 1972 NBA draft was the first on which Krause left his imprint as a head scout for the Suns. Colangelo and Krause were looking for team-first players, who were more concerned with winning than filling stat sheets, labeled in their scouting reports simply as "O.K.P."—Our Kind of People. In the first round the Suns took defensive specialist David "Corky" Calhoun of Penn State, whom Krause had seen play 10 times the previous seasons, passing on Julius Erving (who would join the ABA instead) and Paul Westphal.

In the second round, seven years after he pushed the Bullets to select Jerry Sloan, Krause picked Don Buse, another defensive-minded player out of Evansville. The 6'4" Buse was slightly shorter than Sloan, a lesser scorer and rebounder, but a better ball handler. Colangelo said: "Krause is looking at a Buse and hoping for a Sloan. He seems to think Don has a good chance of making our team, and we're looking forward to seeing him at our rookie camp in June."[23] Buse was also drafted by the ABA's Virginia Squires but signed with the Indiana Pacers from his home state. He would eventually join the Suns after five seasons with the Pacers in a player swap for guard Ricky Sobers.

The two picks did not pan out as planned, but a year later Krause would make his best addition to the Suns by bringing in head coach John MacLeod, whom he met when scouting University of Oklahoma's Clifford Ray as a potential draft pick for the Bulls. The Chicago franchise selected Ray with the fifth pick of the third round of the 1971 NBA draft, one of the last roster recommendations made by Krause. Ray had a bad reputation, but he proved to Krause he was definitely O.K.P. when he wrote on a question sheet provided by the scout: "Mr. Krause, you won't find my name among the top scorers in the country, but you will find it on rebounds and blocked shots. I want to be the next Bill Russell in the NBA."[24] When he was traded to the Warriors in 1974, Ray was welcomed at the airport by team captain Rick Barry, who said that the team could win a championship with Ray playing at center. Ray recounted that story to Krause after the Warriors won the 1975 championship,[25] and Krause continued to retell it with pride.

MacLeod, much like Krause, started off as a baseball player, but unlike Krause was a very good one, who never got to become a pro due to an injury. He also played basketball at Bellarmine College, but by his own admission was "not a very good player. But [he] was fairly good at defense and could pass the ball. [He] started maybe only once or twice in college."[26] The time on the bench allowed MacLeod to develop the ability to watch, which was another characteristic he shared with Krause.

Krause had so much confidence in MacLeod that he put his job with the Suns on the line, stating publicly that if he did not pan out as head coach, Colangelo could fire him as well.

Prior to selecting Pippen, Krause described MacLeod as his greatest scouting find. If that was not enough praise, Krause compared MacLeod to Tex Winter, whom he already held in the highest regard, while characterizing Winter as "too nice a guy to coach in the NBA."[27]

When Colangelo picked the last head coach the season prior, Butch van Breda Kolff, he lasted just seven games before Colangelo stepped in and replaced the excitable and energetic coach with himself. Van Breda Kolff, who took the Lakers to the NBA Finals in 1968 and 1969, was fired after threatening to fine the Suns' star player, Connie Hawkins, for missing practice. This proved to be the final straw for Colangelo, who was not pleased with how the coach was running the team.

Just like the coach, Krause was not particularly liked by the players, as he would exceed his privileges, reportedly asking for massages from team physicians in the middle of practice.

"Jerry hated massages so it's very doubtful he was in the trainers' room getting them," said Thelma Krause.

Furthermore, when players were in practice, Krause criticized them to the trainers, while praising them when he knew they could hear him. One of the Suns players, 6'7" forward Lamar Green, was able to expose him by hiding a tape recorder beneath a Jacuzzi. To get back at Krause, Green appeared dressed as a tribal warrior and began dancing and stirring the water in the Jacuzzi around Krause, as if he were being cooked.[28]

Krause was also not particularly liked by his co-employees, due to his secretive nature. Oftentimes he would not even inform fellow scouts and coaches about where he was going to on a scouting trip, let alone who he was going to watch.

In the 1972-73 season, due to the coaching turmoil and a preseason which seemed wasted, since it contributed to the head coach losing the job, the Suns managed to win just 38 games. The next season, devoid of controversy, with the head coach having the front office's full support, they regressed by eight wins.

The team officially entered rebuild mode after Hawkins was traded to the Lakers, all while Motta's Bulls made the Western Conference Finals. This had been the plan all along, to take a step back and pick the right players—at least according to Krause, who explained his roster-building philosophy as follows: "I think you draft yourself into contention or potential championship, then add the extras through trading. The key to winning in the NBA has been defensive center play and rebounding. It's pretty hard to trade for those type of guys. In most cases they must be drafted."[29]

Since Krause started working as a scout, almost a decade prior to making that observation, the Celtics, the Knicks and the Bucks had all drafted their dominant big men—Bill Russell, Dave Cowens (Celtics), Willis Reed (Knicks), Lew Alcidor (Bucks)—while the Sixers and the Lakers traded for theirs (Wilt Chamberlain).

In 1975-76, after five seasons of missing the postseason, the Suns made it all the way to the finals, and they did that by sticking to Krause's strategy of getting a good big man in the draft. Colangelo was named Executive of the Year and NBA freshman Alvan Adams won the award for the Rookie of the Year. The 6'9" Adams peaked in his first season, making the All-Star team with career-high averages of 19 points, 1.5 steals, 1.5 blocks, and 5.6 assists (good for eighth in the league).

The 1975 fourth overall pick had already caught Coach MacLeod's eye when he was in high school. MacLeod spoke of him with appreciation when he was still working at Oklahoma and Adams became the 1972 Player of the Year in the state: "He can do it all. I don't think there's any doubt that he could start next year in college."[30]

The coach stayed true to his word and started the 21-year-old during his last season with the Oklahoma Sooners. The Suns drafted Adams mostly because of his relationship with the head coach, but the center fit right in alongside forwards Gar Heard and Ricky Sobers and guards Curtis Perry and Paul Westphal. Sobers, just like Adams, was a rookie.

As the 1976 finals were still going on, rumors were circulating whether MacLeod would leave Phoenix after the series, as he was heavily recruited by the Bulls' new director of player personnel.... Jerry Krause.

Krause did not participate in the construction of the Suns roster, as in November 1975 he again left a team which was on the brink of breaking out. He became the head of the Sixers' college scouting program. This was a one-year deal from the start, as the man presiding over the Sixers scouting up until that point, Jack McMahon, was suffering from back problems and was unable to travel.

Krause was hired by his former employer, Pat Williams, who left Chicago to become the general manager of the struggling Atlanta Hawks before taking over the Sixers. The team from Georgia was bad and it was not drawing, so Williams reached for his old bag of tricks. As enumerated by Clayton Trutor:

Williams brought his halftime staples down to Atlanta with him, including Victor the Wrestling Bear and Little Arlene, the era's most famous competitive eater. Interspecies wrestling matches and hotdog eating contests became the midgame norm during the 1973-74 season. On other occasions that winter, the Hawks gave away prizes for the fan with the largest feet in the arena and for fans that weighed in at more than 250 pounds. Williams also added Easter Egg Hunt, Secret Santa, and Trick or Treat nights to the Hawks' promotional slate.[31]

He was gone after just one season.

Scouting for the Sixers brought along a new development in Krause's scouting career, as he found himself attending high school games, looking for the next Darryl Dawkins (fifth overall pick in 1975) or Bill Willoughby (19th overall pick the same year). Williams downplayed the scouting trips, stating: "It's not nearly as serious a thing as last year, but our position is, if there's an Oscar Robertson out there, we'd at least like to know."[32] Krause was happy to participate, as knowledge was the currency he valued the most.

Krause was such a permanent fixture at college and high school games that during the NAIA (National Association of Intercollegiate Athletics) tournament in March 1976, a scoreboard campaign urged him to buy a tournament T-shirt. To the joy of the organizers, Krause did. Working for the Sixers, Krause said that he got to attend more than 300 games that season and predicted in a talk with journalist Fred Stabley, Jr., that Robert Parish was going to be among the top picks.[33]

While the prediction was very much on point, Krause passed on the center when picking for the Bulls in 1976—bringing the 42-year-old Parish to Chicago 20 years later brought little consolation. Parish fell to eight and with their 12th pick the Sixers picked swingman Terry Furlow. When describing the pick to said journalist, Krause said: "I've found Terry to be a very outstanding person. I've seen him four games and met him a number of times, and I'm sure he'll have no trouble getting along with people." Furlow bounced from team to team, facing serious drug issues. He died in a car crash in 1980 while driving under the influence.

Krause scouted for the Sixers, but was drafting for the Bulls, who were picking second in the 1976 draft and went with Scott May, the small forward and NCAA champion under coach Bob Knight at Indiana University. Apart from Parish—who they admittedly were trying to land in a trade—the Bulls also passed on Adrian Dantley, Alex English, and Dennis Johnson, all prominent professional players.

The Bulls made the pick with no head coach in place, now that Motta was gone as both a general manager and a head coach. This was inevitable, as he described the roster that he himself constructed as "the worst team in the league" while, as *Chicago Tribune*'s Bob Logan humorously wrote, blaming "hostile referees, writers, fans, scheduling, or munchkins."[34] Things got to the point that the young players organized a press conference in defense of the criticized coach. Veterans, while mostly present, did not speak up. As a former college coach, Motta was able to influence younger players, and it was even suggested that it was Motta who forced the rookie John Laskowski and others to go to the bat for him.

The defense did not do much to turn the tide, and the Bulls eventually finished the season with a league-worst 24 wins. Motta stopped hiding his bitterness and complained that he was not valued enough by the people in the city, accusing the beat writers of trying to "build a career on [his] dead body," adding: "I never expected to be here this long anyway."[35] He continued to position his players and himself against everybody else, building a sense of community by alienating everybody outside the team. A similar us-against-them mentality, albeit used in a gentler, less authoritarian manner by Phil Jackson, would bear fruit 15 years later.

Motta left the Bulls for the Bullets, where his hard-nosed coaching would result in two finals appearances and one NBA championship. The Bulls got nothing in return and were left with a mess that Krause and general manager Jon Kovler, who doubled as the franchise co-owner along with Lester Crown, were supposed to clean up. Krause came with Jerry Colangelo's recommendation: "I told them Jerry is loyal and a hard worker. He's been around the NBA and he knows basketball. Jerry's made mistakes, like all of us, but that organization needs some loyalty."[36]

The team Krause inherited would lack one loyal Bull on its roster, as Jerry Sloan was forced to retire due to knee problems, but he also indicated that he wanted to stay with the team: "I wouldn't want to be considered for head coach now, and the man they hire must be free to name his own assistant. If the new coach wants me … that might be worked out."[37] Things would be worked out a year later, with Sloan joining the coaching staff.

Krause did not fumble his first important decision by selecting May, because he was overruled by Wirtz and Kovler, who actually made the selection. When the Hawks traded the first overall pick, Wirtz and Kovler backed out of the commitment made to Parish that they were going to pick him, as he supposedly came with a $1.8 million price tag.

Chicago Tribune's Robert Markus referred to May as "the surest bet to be a star.… Krause would be very safe in drafting May. It would be a choice hard to criticize."[38] When the ABA disbanded in 1976, the Bulls

Krause called Jerry Sloan, shown here as the head coach of the Utah Jazz in 1996, the toughest practice player he ever saw ... until he saw Jordan practice.

were also able to add power forward Artis Gilmore to the roster. Originally picked 117th in the 1971 draft by the NBA's Bulls and seventh by the ABA's Kentucky Colonels, Gilmore chose the latter, as they could simply give him more money. With the rival league now gone, the Bulls were free to claim their player. Krause missed Gilmore's introductory press conference, because he was running the fourth-round draft pick Keith Starr through a series of physical tests prior to signing him. That earned Krause significant criticism but was just one more misguided decision in a whole string of mistakes made by the executive.

The biggest mistake occurred when Krause was hiring the new head coach. Krause wanted Ray Meyer, the 62-year-old coach of DePaul Blue Demons, and offered him a three-year deal worth $60,000 per season (at least according to the press).

"As long as I knew him, Jerry always told me he did not offer Meyer the job," clarified Thelma Krause.

At DePaul Meyer would have to work three years to earn his annual NBA salary. DePaul was (and still is) a Jesuit university, its president at the time was the Rev. John R. Cortelyou, and the school enjoyed an impeccable reputation in the Chicago area as an important part of the community, much more important than the struggling NBA franchise. Keeping the winningest NCAA coach at a respected college program was way more important than letting him join one of the worst professional basketball teams.

Granted, the Bulls were the sole professional basketball team in the state, but the dysfunction in the front office, the drug issues within the roster, and the fact that the Bulls simply were not drawing all factored into the program operators vetoing the move. Krause tried to explain that Meyer simply misunderstood him when they were talking on the phone.[39] By putting himself at the center of the negotiations, the director of player personnel acted more like the general manager. Krause demanded to make all the roster decisions, including being the head of team scouting.

On September 1, 1976, three months after he had taken the job, Krause resigned, allegedly because of personal reasons. Allegedly he had applied for a job at the NBA offices. It was no secret, though, that the Bulls made him the scapegoat for the failed negotiations. Had Meyer became the coach, the (supposed) move would be Krause's masterstroke. Years later Krause reminisced, "I walked out with my tail between my legs. It was something I had wanted to do all my life, and suddenly, it was over."[40]

There was no NBA job. Instead, Krause began scouting for the Seattle Mariners. By the end of November, the *Chicago Tribune*'s Bill Jauss wrote a long commentary piece urging the Bulls to rehire Krause, whom he described as a "native Chicago workaholic with a head full of basketball knowledge."[41] Jauss claimed that it was Krause who got Alvan Adams for the Suns, ignoring the connection that the center had with his college coach John MacLeod. Interviewed for what was basically a puff piece, Krause said that he could get along with coach Ed Badger, the assistant coach promoted to head coach after Krause was forced to resign.

The expansion Mariners welcomed Krause's expertise, who found himself once again working for a baseball franchise from the Pacific Northwest. Ten years earlier he had worked as general manager for Portland Beavers of the Pacific Coast League. His first find was Arturo Sanchez, a 17-year-old from Caracas, Venezuela, who was signed by the Mariners' farm team. Sanchez did not necessarily pan out as Krause intended, but the scout soon found another job for himself, working for the Los Angeles Lakers.

In January 1977 he was named chief scout for the Lakers and was marketed to the fans in California as having "a hand in selecting 10 per cent of the players currently in the league,"[42] which was a Hollywood-worthy exaggeration. He was tasked with scouting players based east of the Mississippi, while the Lakers general manager, Bill Sharman, was scouting prospects based west of the river. Krause was mailing in his reports.

He scouted Jack Sikma, the 6'11" center playing not far from Krause's home in Chicago, for the Illinois Wesleyan Titans. Holding the sixth pick, the Lakers passed on Sikma, who was selected eighth overall by the SuperSonics and in two years won an NBA championship with the Seattle team, on the way to a Hall of Fame career. Upon his selection, Sonics coach Bob Hopkins described Sikma as a "pure shooter" and compared him to.... Alvan Adams.[43]

Another player scouted by Krause was Oral Roberts University's Anthony Roberts, whose breaking of the National Invitation Tournament or NIT's single-game scoring record with 65 points Krause witnessed in person. Despite Krause's praise of the player, the Lakers passed on him as well, as did many other teams. The talented scorer was picked 21st overall, by the Denver Nuggets. He did not have much of a professional career, but the player selected after him, as the last pick of the first round, proved to be Krause's masterstroke.

The Lakers held three 1977 first-round picks: sixth, 15th and 22nd. With their first, they went with NC State's forward Kenny Carr, who brought a reputation to the NBA of somebody whose body language was conveying a bad message. He was considered a sulker and a quitter. Carr started playing basketball at 14; earlier he played football. He won the Olympic gold medal with the national basketball team prior to joining the Lakers' training camp.

Brad Davis of Maryland, the second Lakers pick and the player whom Krause had personally convinced to enter the NBA a year earlier, was a playmaker, supposed to battle for the starting position with the last pick of the first round, Norm Nixon. The 6'2" Nixon joined the Lakers from Duquesne, a small program in Pennsylvania, but he acted as if it were him who was the highly-coveted prospect. One Lakers coach said: "The thing about Norm Nixon is, he came into camp as if he had led the league in rebounds, assists, and free throws the past season and for the last five years in a row."[44] However, his lack of hesitancy to shoot differentiated Nixon from Davis, as did his quickness and hard defense. Bill Sharman spoke highly of Davis and his reputation, describing him as "a good passer, a super kid," and praised his attitude, but Nixon was just better equipped for the NBA.[45]

Davis found himself stuck behind Nixon, not able to find playing time. Carr also had issues cracking the rotation, which prompted *The Evening Sun*'s Michael Janofsky to write that "Carr is to Laker forwards what Davis is to the guards, only he gets about 50 percent more floor time. Mostly he sits: watching, learning, clapping and twisting orange towels."[46] The Lakers cut Davis at the beginning of his second season in Los Angeles, and after two years of bouncing around the league, and being cut by the Pistons prior to the start of the 1980-81 season, he was able to get signed by the expansion Dallas Mavericks. He stayed there for 12 years, earning the distinction of being the first player to get his number retired by the franchise.

During the offseason, as Krause was once again off working for the Mariners, looking for the next big thing in baseball, the Lakers announced that they were retaining the scout's services. One of his first scouting assignments was the Purdue–Indiana State University game. While claiming he was looking at Wayne Walls of Purdue and Harry Morgan of ISU (both eventually went undrafted), he added, "naturally while I am here, I will turn in a report on Larry Bird and Joe Barry Carroll. We are always looking to the future, the years ahead."[47] The Lakers were not as forward-thinking as the Celtics, who picked Bird sixth in the draft overall, even though he was still staying in college for one more year. His class graduated in 1978, but he joined ISU a year later. Initially Bird went to Indiana University and quit after a month and reentered college at the much smaller Indiana State University.

Another future prospect scouted by Krause was Mike O'Koren from UNC, a tough Jersey kid who eventually ended up playing for the home state Nets, picked sixth in 1980. The Lakers were holding the 26th pick in the draft and they picked Ron Carter, the first player to be drafted to the NBA from Virginia Military Institute. Carter was waived prior to his second season as pro.

The future-looking Krause announced the All-American starting five of college players to watch in 1978-79: Darnell Valentine, Mike O'Koren, Sidney Moncrief, Larry Bird, and James Bailey. The biggest name missing was the first overall pick in the 1979 draft, a Michigan State sophomore named Earvin Johnson, who made Krause's second team. Joe Barry Carroll headlined Krause's third team.

Krause, criticized for talking too much to the press—imagine that—was particularly appreciative of Bird, whom he described as combining Jerry Sloan's grit and Rick Barry's shooting, all the while being "the biggest forward in the history of the college game to be blessed with precision passing and dribbling skills."[48] He called O'Koren "an outstanding defensive forward and one of the few players who could have stepped off the campus at the end of his freshman year and into an NBA starting job."[49] He characterized Indiana's Mike Woodson as having "the best natural quickness of any of the standout forwards in the country."[50]

Before leaving the Lakers, Krause managed to find one more gem for them, a player instrumental in bringing five NBA championships to L.A. with the quality the scout valued the most—stellar defense. And the pick was made on the urging of Krause, with the promise that the team would select the player if he was still available. Luckily for the franchise, he was. When Krause attended a game between New Mexico and Brigham Young, he did it to see Marvin Johnson, the eventual second-round pick of the Bulls. He left impressed with Michael Cooper, an African American swingman, who played unselfishly on a high-scoring team. The fact that the player did a great job of containing his man, future Celtic Danny Ainge, in a game that took place at Brigham Young, "the toughest place in the country for a Black kid to play," proved to Krause that he had guts.[51] The Church of Jesus Christ of Latter-Day Saints, BYU's sponsor, has long held racist views and Black players coming to play in Utah were oftentimes discriminated against.[52]

In early November 1978, Chicago White Sox president Bill Veeck employed Krause as a scout, calling him the team's "Scout at Large." Krause gave up scouting basketball and focused solely on baseball. He explained his decision as follows: "You have film to study in basketball, there is no film in baseball. A scout has to be at the ballpark. You don't have rainouts in basketball. A baseball scout has to be gone from home a lot more."[53]

2. Traveling Man

One of the tasks Krause undertook was to get through the language barrier separating the English- and Spanish-speaking players. Bridging the communication gap was intended to allow Latino players to have a better chance at succeeding in Chicago. Krause did a lot of scouting in the Mexican League and saw how hard it was for Mexican players to transition into life in the United States.

When he stayed in Mexico, he put his writing skills to the test, penning long letters to his future wife, Thelma. The two had met earlier in the year, on October 11, 1978, at a Jewish singles dance. Thelma went with a friend and Jerry attended only because the event took place during the World Series, with the Yankees playing the Dodgers. Krause was friends with the Yankees' manager, Bob Lemon, and he did not want to watch his team lose the game, so he went to the dance. Just like Jerry, Thelma was divorced. She had two children, Stacy and David, who were almost 10 and almost six.

> I mistakenly gave him the phone number to work, and he kept calling me at work. I had midterms, because I was still studying. And I finally relented when he said that he was going to bring dinner on a Friday night. I was at home, with my children and when he came in they were like: "Who the hell is that?" He had this hat and this plaid jacket, and he brought pizza, which he thought was wonderful. But it really wasn't.

The next night they were supposed to go out for their first official date, but Krause had to go to the hospital. Thelma made other arrangements for the evening and he continued to call her at home, but she was not there. When she came home, he asked her where she was and she tried to put him down, end the relationship before it even started. At that point she did not know how persistent he could be when he wanted something. After their meeting at the dance, he had told one of his friends that he met a woman he was going to marry.

Not willing to take no for an answer, Jerry handwrote her a five-page letter, utilizing his journalistic skills and showing her his more passionate, sentimental side. She decided to give him one more chance. Thelma still has the letters he wrote to her in the late 1970s. Later on they used the telephone to stay in touch.

Initially, he was awkward around her kids, but they eventually saw the same things Thelma saw in him. After a while he transitioned from "Jerry" to "Dad" and that filled him with pride. When David was 10 and Stacy was 14, they adopted a dog. "It was the children's and Jerry's dog," Thelma Krause emphasized with a smile during our talk. The dog was named Tofi, "because she was found behind a Baskin-Robbins store."

Tofi was a rescue and the Krauses immediately fell in love with her when they saw her in the adoption center. When she died, they had a statue of the dog made. It still stands in Thelma Krause's home.

With a wife, children, and later a dog, Krause could enjoy family life during brief moments when he was not on the road. That was until March 26, 1985, when his career, his life, the city of Chicago, the NBA, and professional sports in general would forever change.

3

Addition by Subtraction

In the summer of 1984 Jerry Reinsdorf, the chairman of the Chicago White Sox, was in New York having dinner with George Steinbrenner, the owner of the New York Yankees. The two were friends and would oftentimes talk about the hardships of running a professional sports franchise. The former idolized Harry Truman, the latter George Patton and Vince Lombardi. Reinsdorf avoided the limelight and was loyal almost to a fault; Steinbrenner relished the attention, placed enormous expectations upon people, and openly feuded with them when they were not met. Reinsdorf was a native New Yorker, born in Brooklyn, who left the city and picked Chicago as his habitat in 1957. His move coincided with his favorite baseball team, the Brooklyn Dodgers, leaving for the West Coast. Steinbrenner was from Ohio and moved to New York, where his expensive hirings, costly firings, and very public feuds provided constant fodder for the press.

During that particular dinner Steinbrenner started complaining about his certain possession in Chicago—a 10 percent stake in the Chicago Bulls franchise. He got into the Bulls in 1972, when the franchise was generating excitement and games had an average attendance of 10,000 people. Ten years later, even the Chicago Sting soccer team was outselling the Bulls.

According to Reinsdorf, the problem was that people running the team had no time to actually run it. He added, somewhat casually, that "[the Bulls] wouldn't be losing money if I would be running them."[1] This was not the first time somebody had talked to Steinbrenner or majority owner Arthur Wirtz about saving the Chicago franchise. In 1982 Al McGuire, former head coach at Marquette, had suggested through his agent that if the Bulls would hire him as a consultant, he would improve the relations between the players and the management. Wirtz dismissed that statement, calling it "stupid and absurd."[2]

This was also not the first time Reinsdorf considered branching out and trying his hand at a different sport. In May 1984 he and Eddie Einhorn, who owned the White Sox, were announced as possible buyers of the Chicago Blitz football franchise, which was $2 million in debt. The USFL approached both men about the possibility, and Einhorn decided to bite. The franchise folded the same year.

A week after the conversation between Steinbrenner and Reinsdorf, Lester Crown called Reinsdorf. Crown owned one-third of the Bulls. Twenty-four percent belonged to the Wirtz family, whose patriarch, Arthur, partnered up with Crown in 1972 to buy the controlling stake in the Bulls from Dick Klein.

Arthur Wirtz died in 1983, with his family inheriting the stake in the Bulls; the full ownership of the Chicago Blackhawks hockey team, which the Wirtz family has held since 1966; and the Chicago Stadium, where both franchises played. Wirtz was primarily a businessman, not a sports fan—he owned sports franchises and organized sporting events at the stadium because he wanted to make money. According to one former Blackhawks player, Stan Mikita, during the remodeling of the arena somebody asked Wirtz whether he wanted the seats painted, to which he replied: "I don't want paint on the seats. I want butts."[3]

Reinsdorf's favorite basketball team were the 1970–1973 Knicks, who were incredibly popular in their city. According to the NBA's long-time commissioner, David Stern, who presided over the league's global ascent and who grew up a Knicks fan, those teams "were the earliest indicators that professional basketball players could actually blur the lines between athlete and entertainer, become crossover celebrities and walk alongside America's most popular."[4]

When Reinsdorf officially became the Bulls majority owner on March 1, 1985, he probably did not hope to emulate their success. He publicly declared that he had no plans when it came to the front office or the coaches he wanted to bring in. He bought 58.6 percent of the franchise for $9.2 million and in order to take care of the investment, he declared: "I will be visible, I will be seen, I will be actively involved with this franchise."[5]

This statement alone made Reinsdorf welcome as the new owner. As Telander explained to me, the fans in Chicago "are interesting. They know the players, the personalities and if you try hard, they will like you.... They don't like people who are not good at what they do, but they do appreciate effort."

Other NBA owners and executives were enthusiastic about the purchase as well. Ted Turner, who also owned professional baseball and basketball franchises in Atlanta, said that the move was "terrific." Lakers general manager Jerry West commended the Bulls for improving

3. Addition by Subtraction

during the 1984-85 season, adding that it was "good for the league to get another team up here."[6]

The Lakers themselves contributed to other NBA franchises getting a chance to grow, not only thanks to their savvy marketing and flashy style of play, but also because of their lucrative spending. In 1981 the franchise signed their star point guard Magic Johnson to a 25-year contract for $25 million, coming into effect at the beginning of the 1984-85 season. It was the less-prominent purchases, though, that furthered the talks of putting a salary cap in place, along with a collective bargaining agreement (CBA) that would protect the owners while also taking into account the wellness of the players. Franchise owner Jerry Buss gave raises to all of the players on the Lakers' roster, like when he signed Mitch Kupchak, a role player, to a seven-year, $5.6 million deal in 1981. As pointed out by Joshua Mendelsohn, "fellow owners ... feared his cavalier increases were pushing the league salary scale beyond what other markets could sustain. Buss simply didn't care; he believed that the higher salaries were part of running a sound business."[7]

In order to level the playing field between the teams, a salary cap was put in place. The 23 NBA teams were not to exceed the $3.6 million pay limit. The CBA was introduced because only seven of these franchises were turning a profit, which was a consequence of the lucrative spending within the league due to its involvement in the bidding war with the ABA for the best talent. The NBA emerged victorious, but the success came at a price. David Stern was now looking for a way to save the league from imploding, with the Cleveland Cavaliers, Indiana Pacers, San Diego Clippers, and Utah Jazz on the verge of folding during the early 1980s.

A direct consequence of the new limits was that some teams were somewhat erratically signing players with the intention of exceeding the cap before it was too late. Some players also wanted to protect their interest and sign large contracts while they still could. One of them was the 36-year-old Lakers center, Kareem Abdul-Jabbar. In the summer of 1983, the native New Yorker was a free agent. Three years removed from his sixth (and final) MVP award, he remained dominant, averaging 21.8 points, 7.5 rebounds, and 2.2 blocks per game. He was pursued by his hometown Knicks, the Nets, and the Bulls, with the first two soon backing out of the negotiations because they could not afford his salary. The Bulls were willing to orchestrate a trade in order to get Abdul-Jabbar the two-year, $4 million deal that he wanted. The shape of the Bulls' roster depended on whether they would be able to get Abdul-Jabbar, who, in turn, was skeptical of joining a team so filled with uncertainty. The Bulls general manager, Rod Thorn, said: "a lot depends on what happens with Kareem, and we probably would not be able to go after other free agents if we sign Kareem."[8] They were not able and did not, nor did they sign any notable players. Abdul-Jabbar stayed in Los Angeles.

The Bulls went 27–55 in the 1983-84 season, their first under coach Kevin Loughery, and held the third pick in the 1984 NBA draft. There was dysfunction in the front office, as team owner Bill Wirtz was highly critical of Loughery for not playing the best player on the team, shooting guard Reggie Theus, and of Thorn for trading him mid-season to the Kansas City Kings. The fans sided with Theus and booed the head coach when he was introduced before games. The Bulls lost 14 of their last 15 games and were one loss shy of earning the coin flip for the first overall selection and the chance of landing a center.

Hakeem Olajuwon and Patrick Ewing were seen as the two best college players in the country, both centers and both about to enter the NBA draft. Ewing decided to return to Georgetown for his senior year, which left Olajuwon and Kentucky's Sam Bowie as the top two big men in the draft. Both were off the board when it came the Bulls' time to pick, so they decided on Tar Heel Michael Jordan. Capable of playing as a point guard, shooting guard, and small forward, Jordan was about to become a member of the USA basketball team, which was to participate in the 1984 Los Angeles Olympics.

Prior to the international competition, Jordan was not seen as a standout player. The *Chicago Tribune*'s Bob Logan mentioned Bowie, Charles Barkley, Melvin Turpin, Sam Perkins, and Wayman Tisdale as the players that the Bulls should be targeting, as they could potentially play center.[9] Upon selecting Jordan, Thorn said that he wished the player would be 7'1", adding that there were no good offers for the pick. One of them included Chicago-born power forward Terry Cummings; a different one concerned center Tree Rollins, a defensive specialist, who would end his 17-year NBA career with an average of 2.2 blocks. Both had very good careers, but weren't comparable with Jordan's illustrious time in the NBA.

However, after the Olympics, which the U.S. won and Jordan dominated, the spotlight turned to the 6'6" rookie. After the tournament and the exhibition games, Loughery said: "I don't think any player in a long time came into the league with this kind of hype."[10] Jordan's athletic gifts were accompanied by a superior work ethic, one that made him the first player to arrive to practice and the last one to leave. He needed to dominate every play, every game, and sometimes Coach Loughery would just let everybody go home early, because Jordan was wearing them out.[11]

Loughery was an established coach who had won two ABA

3. Addition by Subtraction

Championships with the New York Nets. The fact that he worked with Julius Erving fueled the comparisons between the promising rookie and Dr. J., who was slowly heading toward retirement. Phil Jackson, who got his start as a coach under Loughery in 1978, appreciated his "maverick style of leadership."[12] Back with the Nets, when Loughery was thrown out of games, Jackson would take over the coaching duties. Just as he knew who he had in the inexperienced coach, Loughery also knew he had hit the jackpot with Jordan.

However, his status as head coach became uncertain on March 25, 1985, when Thorn was dismissed as general manager. His six-year run was tumultuous, with the Bulls making the playoffs only once. He went through six head coaches, including Thorn himself, and only two—Jerry Sloan and Loughery—worked with the team for longer than one season. During the 1983-84 season the Bulls were 21st in attendance out of 23 teams, while during the still ongoing season they jumped up to ninth. This was part of an overall trend in the city of Chicago, a sports synchronicity, which gave the inhabitants a feeling of hope and optimism. As told by Savage:

> The sports scene in Chicago was pretty dismal, in general our sports teams were kind of jokes. This begins to change in the early 80s: in 1983 the White Sox win their division, in 1984 the Cubs win their division, the Bears are in the playoffs and advance to the game before the Super Bowl, in 1984 Jordan joins the Bulls, in 1985 the Bears win the Super Bowl and the city has this buzz around it, that its sports teams are getting better.

That optimism was palpable and made the firing all the more hurtful for Thorn, who said to the press two days after being dismissed: "I am personally sad because now the team is starting to turn things around and there are good days ahead, but I won't be a part of it."[13] The turnaround was made possible thanks to the heroics of one player, known simply as "Mike," who soon would captivate the whole world with his flashy plays and charisma. Other notable names on the roster were small forward Orlando Woolridge, who was Willis Reed's cousin and went to Notre Dame on his recommendation, and center Dave Corzine. The man tasked with turning this roster into a contender was Jerry Krause.

The first thing Reinsdorf noticed about Krause was that he was talking a lot. For three years they had built a relationship while trying to improve the White Sox, discussing drafting and trading baseball players. Krause was present at every meeting and he always had something to say. As noted by Sam Smith, Krause "had an annoying habit of repeating his opinions,"[14] which made it hard to listen to what he actually had to say, but Reinsdorf was willing to overlook the naysayers and the doubters.

Years later, in *The Last Dance* documentary, he reminisced that he asked around the league about Krause and everybody said: "'Don't touch the guy.' He had a way of alienating people. But I wasn't hiring somebody to win a personality contest. I wanted somebody who truly believed in building a team the way I wanted to, and Krause was the guy."[15]

And Krause was persistent, hounding Reinsdorf and talking about the improvements that could make the franchise better. Reinsdorf's vision matched that of Krause, who immediately stated that the change was not going to happen overnight, but would be a matter of years, simply because he wanted to trade away everybody except Michael Jordan.

This was the narrative Krause began pushing later. When interviewed for Lazenby's book on Jackson, he said: "I had nine players I didn't want and three I did. I wanted Dave Corzine, I wanted Rod Higgins, and I wanted Michael. The rest of them I couldn't have cared less about."[16] When talking with Wojnarowski, Krause described the roster as "Michael Jordan and 11 guys I didn't want."[17] After the 1987 NBA draft, with Michael Jordan and Dave Corzine the only two players remaining on the roster, Krause said that he was "cleaning out the garbage before the Cadillacs come in."[18]

As Krause put it: "Reinsdorf ... knew me, and he knew he was getting a scout, and he wanted that."[19] Still, because he was not a basketball expert, Reinsdorf reached out to former Knicks great Bill Bradley for advice. Bradley vouched for Krause.[20]

Krause got the job with a month's worth of basketball still left to play, so that he could evaluate the players that he had on the roster. Not the one to make harsh decisions, the Sleuth went to work and first got into organizing his own team in the front office. His first important hire came just a week into the job.

Krause was big on finding people and giving them chances, putting them in the positions to succeed. He referred to them as "my puppies," which he saw as a term of endearment.[21] Karen Stack Umlauf was the first of such hirings. She was a basketball player at Seton Academy, an all-girls Catholic high school in South Holland, Illinois. As a senior, she attended Oak Forest High School, where her team made it to the state's Final Four and went on to play at Northwestern University. A standout post player, Umlauf wanted to continue playing basketball after college, so she spent a year in France and came back to play for a local professional team, the Chicago Spirit, which folded rather quickly.

She was looking for a job and an acquaintance from the Northwestern's marketing department, David Rosengard, got a job with the Bulls

3. Addition by Subtraction

and asked her to submit her resume there, because the franchise needed immediate help in the ticket department. It was not that they were not selling tickets, but the other way round—Jordan's ascension created such a buzz that the team needed people to handle the ticket requests, because there were so many of them.

Umlauf was responsible for organizing the base of season ticketholders, which increased by over 10,000 after Jordan's rookie year. In 1984 the team sold around 2,000 season tickets. A couple of years later David Rosengard, the Bulls' marketing director, was fired. The belief was that with Jordan, the tickets were selling themselves. Rosengard saw it differently. Talking about Reinsdorf, he said: "When the guy at the top feels like he's uncomfortable with another guy in one of the important chairs in the organization, it's his bat and ball."[22]

Umlauf was looking at different jobs, some of which paid more, but working for the Bulls allowed her to be close to the game that she loved. One thing she knew was that she did not want to teach speech-language pathology, but her degree would come in handy in the opportunity that Krause had for her, just as her experience in organized sports did.

Umlauf herself recounted: "What is attractive to employers is having somebody who played sports, understands discipline and teamwork, is organized about their schedule, and is competitive. Those are good employees to have in your field." Krause predicted that she would outgrow the job anyway, so he decided to speed up her development. The ticket manager joked that Krause "stole" her, but he simply asked: "You can type? You know basketball? You're with me."

Rosengard was not particularly happy because he lost a great worker, a challenge-oriented person, who was willing to do whatever was asked of her. In David Halberstam's *Playing for Keeps* Brian McIntyre recounts that in the 1970s only one person was assigned to the Bulls ticket office.[23] Stack was hired as part of the expansion of that division, but she did not stay there for long.

The 23-year-old would form a lifelong bond with Krause, as he would talk to her about players and ask her for perspective, which made her feel appreciated. Much smaller than her, he would sometimes hug her, joking about the difference in height. More importantly, there was mutual trust there and Krause made it a habit to tell Stack and other members of his office how he appreciated them. When he valued somebody, he would praise that person to others, telling them about what good job they were doing.

Krause was feeling the pressure early on. Reinsdorf's decision to fire Thorn, one of the most respected and liked executives in the NBA, was not popular. Asked about his solution to the state of franchise,

Krause said: "people want to know right away, what's wrong with the Bulls? I tell them it's a lot easier to decide from where they're sitting than it is in the catbird seat, when I put myself on the line."[24]

And Krause made it easy for people outside the organization to hate him. In our interview, Telander noted that to his knowledge Krause never admitted to a mistake, at least in public. This need to be respected and appreciated came from him always being the underdog. As explained poetically by Telander: "Jerry Krause had been forever at the bottom of the drain, the sewer system. Nowhere could he go and be respected for who he was. He was not the life of the party, a jolly little fat man. He was a miserable guy."

To the outside world he was forever bound to remain a fish out of water, a short, pudgy guy who did not fit in, despite numerous efforts. As pointed out by Sam Smith: "Jerry always tried too hard to work his way in."[25]

Krause idolized two Reds, Holzman and Auerbach. Both were also short for NBA standards, both standing at a mere 5'10", yet they commanded respect from much taller and stronger athletes. Krause had a personal relationship with Holzman from his scouting days, which worked in his favor when talking about the job with Reinsdorf, who wanted the Bulls to reflect the same sense of ruggedness and selflessness as the championship Knicks teams. Auerbach was much more intimidating, as he kept everybody on their toes.

Just to fast forward a bit, during the summer of 1985 Auerbach called Krause about a trade. He wanted to give the Bulls his point guard, Sam Vincent, for a second-round pick. Krause had a couple of hours to decide. He asked around about Vincent, who nobody had anything negative to say about, but still backed out of the deal simply because it was brought up by Auerbach. "Auerbach had beaten so many people so badly in trades going back so many years that I was afraid of him. I hoped I got that same respect later on, but certainly he got that respect from me and I would not deal with him."[26]

The most interesting thing about this trade proposal was that Krause really liked Vincent as a player and got him for the Bulls during the 1988 trade deadline.

When Krause took over the team, the locker room culture was not great. Most but not all of it was caused by the former regimes. In 1979 the Bulls lost the coin flip that would land them the first overall pick and point guard Magic Johnson. Picking second, the Bulls took big man David Greenwood. During Jordan's rookie season Greenwood was averaging 6.1 points and 6.4 rebounds, mostly coming off the bench for the Bulls, while Johnson was a two-time NBA champion and the best point

3. Addition by Subtraction

guard in the league. Interestingly, Johnson initially preferred to play for Chicago because it was closer to Michigan, where he grew up and played college basketball. He also wanted to team up with Artis Gilmore, at the time one of the better big men in the league.[27]

"It's a fascinating discussion," said basketball historian Shawn Fury during our conversation. "I'm a Magic homer and I think he would turn the Bulls around, they would've been a fast-breaking team, but he wouldn't have had that L.A. aura, embody the perfect fit between the player, the city, and the organization. I can't say he'd win five titles with the Bulls, simply because the East was so tough, but they could've competed for a title or two."

In 1982 the Bulls selected Quintin Dailey seventh overall, even though they knew the talented player was trouble. In 1981 Dailey had been accused of sexually assaulting a woman in San Francisco. In 1982 he pleaded guilty to a charge of aggravated assault. The Bulls did not care and signed him anyway, which resulted in the franchise becoming the first professional basketball team to be welcomed home and away by pickets of women's rights advocates, protesting against Dailey's presence in the NBA. The player begged for a second chance during interviews, all the while developing drug and alcohol dependence.

Dailey was still on the Bulls when Krause took over. So was Orlando Woolridge, who was developing a drug habit of his own, which he would admit to in 1988 as a member of the New Jersey Nets.

Dailey and Woolridge were the two best players on the team after Jordan. Both were setting a bad example for their teammates, but luckily for Krause, the one that mattered was not interested in escaping reality. If anything, he was shaping it, wearing his signature shoes and appearing in commercials, staging unique performances game after game, increasing the recognizability of the Bulls franchise. As the spotlight shone brighter, the cracks in the organization gained exposure, which negatively affected the NBA as well.

The players' addictions reflected those of the general population, as America was entering a period of deindustrialization with manual labor being outsourced to foreign countries, which offered cheap labor to American companies. Ever since the 1920s managers had been either closing down their companies or investing in new industrial facilities in the suburbs.[28] Numerous programs were established in the 1950s and 1960s to reinvigorate the manufacturing industry within cities, but the capitalist drive for cheap labor and cost-cutting wherever possible was stronger than local bonds, loyalty, and employee welfare.

In 1971 the Chicago Union Stockyards officially closed. The South Works area in South Chicago, centered around a steel mill controlled by U.S. Steel, began to decline due to downsizing. The meat and steel markets were no longer what they used to be, as refrigerated trucks and highways allowed meat companies to operate from smaller, cheaper locations outside the city. In the second part of the 1970s the steel market was in crisis, and while it would eventually heal, the South Works could no longer be salvaged. The result of these changes was rising poverty in the African American community of Chicago.

Bill Savage pointed out that both industries provided a chance to escape poverty for Black teenagers, who could start work at a factory at age 16 and earn a decent living, but when they shut down, "the economic basis of what Black stability and prosperity there was, was obliterated by deindustrialization."

In her personal history of the process taking place in the Windy City, Christine J. Walley recounts: "While Southeast Chicago's steelworkers were used to long periods of layoffs and the mills' erratic ups and downs, the permanent closing of heavy industry—the reason why everyone was there in the first place—was simply unfathomable. The closings, not surprisingly, were met with bewilderment and disbelief, and they set in motion profound shifts within economies, families, and individual psyches."[29] The city had to change its identity, transition from being an industry-oriented metropolis into something new, yet unknown. During the first wave of deindustrialization, from 1979 to 1986, the Chicago metropolitan area lost 358,000 manufacturing jobs, which accounted for 87 percent of all firings and layoffs in the area during that period.[30]

Rising unemployment resulted in spikes in crime, violence, and drug abuse. The use of drugs was not solely restricted to social pariahs. As reported by *Time*'s Michael Demarest, cocaine became the "all–American drug" of the early 1980s, "in part precisely because it is such an emblem of wealth and status, coke is the drug of choice for perhaps millions of solid, conventional and often upwardly mobile citizens."[31] When Bahamian drug runners came up with a way to combine cocaine, water, and soda to create its cheaper offspring, crack, American drug dealers were quickly able to double the profit of a hundred dollars' worth of pure cocaine by selling it in $10 vials to inner-city drug users. Because of its affordability, regular users "might purchase a $10 vial three to four times a day," as recounted by Russell C. Crandall.[32]

In 1983 the NBA, in cooperation with the NBA Players Association, instituted an antidrug program that decreed that any player could be randomly tested for the use of cocaine and heroin. Multiple offenders were banned from the league and could not return for at least two years.

The league's drug issues came to light in 1980, after the *Los Angeles*

3. Addition by Subtraction 57

Times' Chris Cobbs reported that from 40 to 75 percent of NBA players were using cocaine.[33] Eliminating the prevalence of drugs in the league was a long, uphill process. As pointed out by Scott Ostler from the same publication six years later, "in today's NBA, avoiding drug problems is like hitting free throws—it's an unglamorous but important part of a team's overall game."[34] In some cases the easiest way of avoiding a drug problem was getting rid of the player with the problem.

However, Krause was not one of the guys who would turn their backs on troubled players. Both Dailey and Woolridge stayed on the roster. Krause even drove Dailey to the airport when the player was heading to rehab, and visited him in the clinic. Rick Telander said, "As a general manager you are always a bit of a cutthroat ... you get rid of a player and bring in somebody who can help you a little bit more, or you do it because of the salary cap and other financial reasons, and it destroys a guy. It might destroy his whole family. But you have to do that stuff!"

In the summer of 1985, 7'2" reserve center Jawann Oldham wanted to renegotiate his contract, according to which he was about to make $175,000. Oldham wanted a significant raise, of around $300,000, as he was 27 and looking for financial safety for the last years of his career. Krause's stance on not renegotiating contracts would not change through the years and would eventually result in the dismantling of the Bulls' championship dynasty. Oldham did not like the way he handled the contract and later trade negotiations, saying: "Jerry Krause didn't know what he was doing and I couldn't work for that man."[35]

At this point Krause was evaluating potential Bulls coaches, all the while indicating to journalists that Loughery's job was secure. One of the names on Krause's list was Georgetown's John Thompson. Thompson was reluctant to discuss the potential job in the press, stating: "Kevin [Loughery] is the coach here. I would feel very disturbed if somebody discussed my job. I'm not going to discuss a job that isn't open."[36] Having coached at Georgetown for 13 years and being the first African American coach to win the NCAA Division I in 1984, Thompson actually worked himself into exhaustion during the 1984-85 season, but showed no sign of leaving D.C.

Loughery's firing prior to the start of the 1985-86 season, which had been hinted at ever since Reinsdorf took over the Bulls, was supposedly caused by the same "philosophical differences" that got Thorn fired. The Bulls had made the playoffs for the first time in four seasons, but that was not enough for Loughery to salvage his position. Loughery later admitted that his job had been at risk ever since Krause joined the front office: "I know Jerry Krause too well and he doesn't want people working for him that know him. See, you have to have respect for your general manager."[37] The statement was not true, as Krause actually wanted to work with people he had known for years, like Tex Winter, Phil Jackson, or Tim Floyd.

When Krause was asked to confirm that Stan Albeck, who coached the Cavaliers, the Spurs, and the Nets, would get the job after Loughery, he said: "I can't. I have to go my own way. It's not in my best interests to do so. You can speculate all you want, but you have to say I refused to comment."[38] Albeck was soon announced as the next head coach. The hottest name on the market, Albeck was connected with job openings in Philadelphia, Los Angeles (where he had a home), and New Jersey, with the Nets still hoping he would return.

Albeck, John MacLeod, and Jack Ramsay were mentioned by Krause as the three coaches he wanted. He knew both Albeck and MacLeod, the former from their time with the Lakers in 1977 and 1978, with Albeck being the assistant coach there. Ramsay was one of the best and most influential coaches in the league, second in career wins at the time. He had two years left on his contract and was on the way out from Portland, not seeing eye to eye with management, but the coach would leave the Blazers a year later, fired by the franchise after 10 seasons. By the time it came to make the decision, there were only two names in the running, Albeck and Phil Jackson.

Krause first met Jackson when he was scouting for the Baltimore Bullets at the University of North Dakota in the 1960s. Krause, who loved to tell stories, recounted after a quarter century that day he spent with head coach Bill Fitch: "It's in a snowstorm. We're watching film, and Fitch says, 'I want to show you something about this kid you'll never believe.' He introduces me to Phil, and he takes him out in the back of an old two-door Ford behind the gym. And Phil sits in the back seat and opens both doors at once. Fitch says, 'That's how long his arms are.'"[39]

Jackson was selected with the 17th pick of the 1967 draft by the Knicks. The Bullets hoped to pick him up later on, after deciding on Jimmy Jones with the 13th pick instead. While a much better player, Jones joined the Bullets in 1974, after seven successful seasons in the ABA and the team already in Washington. Jackson retired in 1980 after a 12-year career in the NBA, winning two championships with the Knicks, all the while learning the importance of defense. Being sidelined with a back injury during his third season allowed Jackson to watch how basketball was played. From Coach Red Holzman he also learned how it *should* be played.

Through the years Krause kept in touch with Jackson, especially when, following a year-long hiatus from basketball, Jackson got into

3. Addition by Subtraction

coaching, taking over the Albany Patroons, a Continental Basketball Association team parented by the Knicks. The CBA had wanted Jackson to work in the league ever since he was available for the coaching job, because of his status in the NBA. Initially Jackson was to make a return to coaching in the 1983-84 season at Flathead Valley Community College, with the school trying to reinstitute its men's basketball program after 13 years, but chose to remain in the state of New York.[40]

He learned the responsibilities of coaching the hard way, driving the team van, checking the team in and out of hotels, scouting and training. The CBA was a whole different animal than the NBA, and not only organization-wise. As stated by *The Boston Globe*'s Michael Madden, "the delusion of the Continental Basketball Assn. is that these players are but a sliver away from the NBA when, in truth, all but a very few are flawed.... And the reality of professional basketball in America is that there is the NBA but then a drop off a cliff down to the CBA for those players reluctant to give up the dream."[41] It was also a great place for inexperienced coaches driven by the dream of one day working in the NBA, like George Karl, Dave Cowens, and Bill Musselman.

Ultimately, Albeck signed a three-year deal worth $900,000 and Krause recommended Jackson to come work for him as an assistant coach. Jackson arrived for the job interview from Puerto Rico, where he was coaching during the summer. He looked the part of somebody working in the tropics, as he wore his hair long, had a beard and, as recounted by Jackson himself, "an Ecuadorian straw hat with a blue parrot feather sticking out of it."[42] They went to lunch, then to dinner.

The next day Krause asked Albeck about Jackson, but he already knew the answer—this could not work. Instead, Albeck went with Murray Arnold, Mike Thibault, and Tex Winter. Arnold was a complete greenhorn in the world of the NBA, but he had just finished a six-year stint at Chattanooga, coaching a Division I program. Mike Thibault was already on the staff, having joined the Bulls in 1982 following two seasons on the Lakers, the second of which he finished with an NBA championship, making him the only Bulls staff member with a ring. That gave him no authority because Winter was hired to be the chief strategist, teaching the others the intricacies and efficiencies of the triangle offense. Whether they wanted to learn was a different story.

Years later Krause said that he regretted hiring Albeck the moment he signed the contract.[43] It was somewhat confusing that Krause and Reinsdorf decided on Albeck in the first place, as he had a reputation for not being particularly keen to overwork his players. Mike O'Koren, who played for Albeck on the Nets, said that under him the players "came to practice, did [their] thing and left."[44]

After finding somebody who seemed to be a suitable coach, at least prior to signing the contract, it was time for Krause to prove his scouting chops and pick players who could complement Jordan, 1985's Rookie of the Year, who finished the season third overall in points per game with 28.2 while leading the team in rebounds, assists, and steals per game as well. Even before Jordan's rookie year concluded, Larry Bird admitted "without a doubt" that Jordan was "the best guy [he] ever played against."[45] His ability was recognized by basketball fans around the country. Becky Fenwick of United Video, a company responsible for handling the promotions of Chicago WGN, which at the time held the rights to Bulls games, said: "Michael Jordan is almost as popular as the Chicago Cubs."[46] For her, as for many others, the Bulls and Jordan became one and the same.

Organizing a proper team around a generational talent is a difficult task, but not as difficult as finding that generational talent. As pointed out by Telander, "[Krause] did not get Michael Jordan, Michael Jordan was there. He could never get over it. There is no way to get over it. I can get you a few scientists to work with Einstein or Isaac Newton; it is much easier than finding an Einstein or a Newton. You either found him or you didn't. You either drafted him or you didn't."

The second-hardest thing was drafting the players that would complement that unique individual, which was exactly what Krause did, starting with the 1985 draft.

Prior to player selection, he and Reinsdorf made an important acquisition in signing Al Vermeil to be the Bulls' strength and conditioning coach. Vermeil had been working for the White Sox for a few years, and in late May 1985 he met with Krause and the general manager of the White Sox, Roland Hemond. Vermeil reminisced: "We had dinner together with his wife and my wife, and before that, we talked about different things, and he felt that my role was very important because he saw the improvements that the White Sox players had done under my instruction.... I was the second or third person hired at that time." Vermeil was a high school football coach, then worked for the San Francisco 49ers as the strength and conditioning coach for four seasons under legendary head coach Bill Walsh, where in 1981 they won their first Super Bowl in franchise history. Vermeil would become instrumental in the Bulls' success, working on the strength, power, and speed of the players.

He was such a good specialist that in the year 2000 Bulls coach Tim Floyd preferred his backup center Chris Anstey to stay in Chicago in order to work on his game, instead of joining the Australian Olympic national team.[47]

First deal came on draft day morning, when the Bulls traded for the

3. Addition by Subtraction

San Antonio Spurs' forward Gene Banks, to come off the bench for Jordan and Woolridge. That move was made with other Spurs in mind, as the Bulls would also get George Gervin, one of the best scorers of the 1970s and early 1980s, and John Paxson, who was underused and underpaid on the Spurs.

Years later Paxson recounted: "I did not know Jerry from Adam, but he called me every few days and said: 'Just sit tight, we're trying to figure something out.'"[48] He waited patiently and signed with the Bulls in November 1985, just as Jordan broke his foot. That injury would have serious repercussions, as the Bulls' handling of it would strain his relationship with Krause, leading to trust issues which would never be resolved.

After getting Banks, Krause reached an agreement with the Cleveland Cavaliers to exchange the Bulls' 11th pick and point guard Ennis Whatley for the ninth pick and a second-round pick. The Cavaliers drafted power forward Charles Oakley for the Bulls, as by NBA rules the deal was announced only after the first round of the draft concluded.

Oakley played for a small college, Virginia Union University, because of academic issues. He worked incredibly hard, as he initially had little athletic ability, but turned himself into a physically imposing, muscular player.[49]

Oakley capped off his college career with an incredible senior season, averaging 24.3 points and 17.3 rebounds per game and earning the title of NABC Division II Player of the Year. Apart from his undeniable basketball abilities, what Krause appreciated most was his toughness; he said of Oakley: "I like people who don't take prisoners, and this guy doesn't take them."[50]

Chicago fans booed the trade, but Krause knew who he was getting—an enforcer, who came with a recommendation from Coach Clarence Gaines, whose team played against Oakley for four years.[51] Al Vermeil told me that when Krause went to scout Oakley, he asked Gaines whether he would be seen, to which the coach replied that the Bulls executive would be the only white person in an arena filled with African Americans.

The last trade of the day was the exchange of second-rounder Ken Johnson and Ben Coleman for 7'0" center Mike Smrek, a Canadian who studied at Canisius College in Buffalo, New York. Smrek was the 25th overall pick, and his stock rose after the college season, since the school and the player were not on anybody's radar a year earlier. Smrek was described as having "the disposition of a lamb" and the pick was widely criticized, as height seemed to be the only quality he possessed.

The focus on size was nothing out of the norm during that draft, as

John Paxson (5) was the perfect backcourt companion to Jordan—a tough spot-up shooter (1988).

3. Addition by Subtraction

out of the first 32 picks, 10 were seven-footers.[52] In fact, the Bulls passed on Manute Bol in favor of Smrek. Justifying his decision, Krause said: "We had our reasons for not taking Bol. Strength was a very big concern. He had no offensive ability at all and couldn't shoot. We felt Mike Smrek would be a good player for us in the long run."[53] He was not, and left the Bulls after just one season, while Bol was twice the league leader in blocks.

Apart from rookies, Krause added two veterans to the roster: Kyle Macy and George Gervin. Macy, a 28-year-old point guard, had a successful NCAA career at Kentucky after transferring from Purdue following his freshman year. Joe B. Hall, his coach at Kentucky, described him in 1980 as "the best college guard in the country today and unquestionably the finest playmaker and floor general … maybe even in the game. It is not possible to improve on Kyle as a playmaker because he is the best,"[54] which was a bold statement, considering that one Magic Johnson entered the 1979 draft, in which Macy fell to 22nd overall. Still, the Suns were pleased to get him. Macy was seen as an intelligent player, "a coach on the floor," as the man who picked him, Jerry Colangelo, described him.[55] He had a reliable jump shot as well, but was characterized as lacking the speed necessary to make it in the NBA.

Macy was considered highly marketable when he entered the league. Advertising executive Jim Host said of him: "Macy speaks well, he conducts himself well, he is the essence of the all-American boy. He presents an overall image that not many athletes have projected in recent years."[56] While he was a solid presence on the Suns, averaging 10.6 points and four assists in his five seasons in Arizona, he didn't have nearly the impact that his new backcourt partner, Michael Jordan, had on and off the court.

Macy signed with the Bulls as a free agent, and the Suns received two future second-round picks in exchange. Prior to what turned out to be his last season on the Suns, Macy had already been informed by Colangelo that he should look for another employer, as the team wanted to increase its offensive pace. A methodical, slow playmaker was not somebody that Colangelo saw leading this team.

In case contract negotiations with Macy fell through, the Bulls organized a guards-only mini-camp for eight potential playmakers. Following their early offseason trades, the Bulls had no ball handlers on the roster and even intended to start Jordan next to Quintin Dailey if none made it onto the team.[57] Dailey, however, soon entered rehab, which sped up contract negotiations with Macy. The Bulls also considered signing Norm Nixon, whom Krause scouted for the Lakers back in 1977 and who was playing for the Clippers, but he eventually remained in Los Angeles, following a missed offseason and a 13-game holdout. According to Krause, Macy would simply blend better with Jordan, as he felt that the 6'6" guard "needed a point guard that could shoot the basketball."[58]

While signing an established point guard such as Macy was expected, the same could not be said about acquiring Gervin. The 33-year-old had spent 12 years in San Antonio, playing for the Spurs since their ABA days. He led the NBA in scoring four times and was a beloved figure in the city, but he did not see eye to eye with Coach Cotton Fitzsimmons, who wanted Gervin to come off the bench for the first time since his rookie year, back when he played for the Virginia Squires in 1972-73.

Under Albeck, who coached the Spurs in the years 1980–83, Gervin averaged 28.5 points per game, but he was on the decline, and the Spurs had been shopping him for the duration of the previous season. When discussing Gervin's situation on the Spurs, Albeck said: "They're demeaning the guy, embarrassing him and that's the thing that hurts me. That guy has given them every possible thing he could give."[59] Prior to the player swap, which saw big man David Greenwood, the second overall pick of the 1979 NBA draft, move to Texas, the Spurs were talking with the Cavaliers about trading Gervin for World B. Free, also a talented scorer and two years his junior.

The first crack in Krause's relationship with Jordan occurred when the general manager brought in another Spur, Gene Banks, who played for two years for Albeck back in San Antonio. Albeck made him the starter in Banks's second year as a pro, but after the 1984-85 season, in which Banks lost his starting spot on the Spurs, he left to reunite with his first NBA coach in Chicago. Banks's presence complicated things for another Bulls swingman, Rod Higgins, whom Jordan really liked. When interviewed by Roland Lazenby years later, Krause reminisced: "We traded Rod Higgins. Michael was upset about that."[60]

For Jordan, friendship and loyalty were important. After all, he came up under Dean Smith at UNC, where year after year the alumni would return to train with the college team, offering help and mentorship. These bonds were established for life, and Tar Heels looked out for their own.

Krause ignored that Higgins and Jordan were friends, looking past the fact that Jordan even bought a home close to his. If Jordan did not know it by now, with that trade he learned that professional basketball was a business. Because of the move, Jordan also was not particularly keen to learn from Gervin, making it known he was not pleased with the Spurs legend's arrival in Chicago. Jordan later explained that it had more to do with Higgins leaving than Gervin coming in: "When I said I wasn't happy with the trade, it wasn't anything against Gervin, it was that Rod has to get cut to allow some money to be paid for Gervin."[61]

Kevin Lougherty called Higgins "a coaching delight,"[62] and praised the player for being ready whenever called upon, regardless of how much—or how little—playing time he was getting. When Lougherty left, Jordan expressed hope that his friend would get more chances on the court: "He's a player. He deserved a lot more playing time last season."[63] Instead, under Albeck, Higgins appeared in only five games and went on to have a truly nomadic season, which would see him switching teams three times and appearing in just 30 games overall.

Higgins lived in Northbrook; Chicago was his hometown. While still a member of the Bulls, the team that drafted him in 1982, he was preparing for the inevitable: "If Jerry Krause brings another guard in here, maybe Rod Higgins has to go someplace else. Is that so bad? I'm sure there's a place for him to go."[64] That place would turn out to be Oakland, where Higgins would enjoy the best six seasons of his professional career.

Getting rid of Jordan's friend was a crack, something that could be mended, but what transpired during the season had severe consequences for the relationship between the executive and the franchise player. Even though the Bulls were defeated in every contest of their eight-game preseason, they opened the season 3–0, winning at home against the Cavaliers and the Pistons, and then in Oakland over the Warriors in what was the first game of a three-game road trip. The game against the Pistons was particularly heated, as power forward Bill Laimbeer shoved Jordan, and coaches Albeck and Chuck Daly got into a shoving match of their own, both being ejected from the game, suspended for one more, and fined. Krause stood behind the coach and appealed his fine, which the NBA set at $1,250.

In the game against the Warriors, Jordan broke his left foot when jumping for the ball and landing off balance. The injury occurred in the second quarter of the game, the rest of which Jordan needed to sit out. Originally it was thought that the player injured his ankle; it was only after X-rays were taken in Chicago that the doctors noticed the fracture. He would miss at least six weeks. No one was more frustrated with the injury than the player himself, who also said: "Maybe it's time for the Chicago Bulls to win without Michael Jordan."[65]

Krause knew that there was no replacing Jordan, both on the court and from a marketing standpoint, as the vice president predicted that the injury "will affect attendance at home and all around the league."[66]

For Krause, any short-term solutions via trades were off the table: "I'm not going to disturb the nucleus of this team or mortgage the future of this team for a six-week emergency."[67]

After all, he got the job after treating the Bulls as a long-term project. To fill the roster spot, the Bulls returned to the table with Nixon, drafted by Krause and coached by Albeck, who was an assistant on the Lakers back when Nixon played for them. Nixon wanted a four-year deal worth between $700,000 and $800,000 a year. Krause refused to go beyond $650,000 and three years, as Nixon had just turned 30. There was no way to fit Nixon under the salary cap. Eventually the Bulls signed Ron Brewer, a 6'4" shooting guard, who was waived by the New Jersey Nets.

However, the Bulls had a different guard on their roster who would become pivotal for them and help them throughout the first incarnation of their championship dynasty. John Paxson joined the team just prior to Jordan getting injured, after holding out on the Spurs and waiting for Krause to fulfill his promise to him.

The signing was announced on October 30, 1985, and the Spurs had 15 days to match the offer. Despite sitting out the whole preseason, Paxson came to Chicago ready to play. He was picked up at the airport by Karen Umlauf. She took him to a workout, at Krause's urging, and even rebounded for him. Then Paxson was immediately put into action after joining the team on its West Coast tour, playing 14 minutes against the Clippers. After the debut, in which he had two points, two assists, and a steal, Paxson said: "Everybody made me feel real comfortable. The coaches went over some offensive sets with me, but you're always nervous coming into a new situation like this."[68]

When the team was 4–8 and in need of any help possible to salvage the season, Dailey came back from rehab and rejoined the roster. After entering the locker room, the troubled guard was hugged by everyone. Everyone except for Ron Brewer, who simply was not there, since he was released to free a spot for Dailey. Originally expected to spend six weeks in the rehab facility, Dailey came back earlier. His return was seen by some as rushed, with Krause being accused of wanting to bring him back to help the slumping Bulls. The accusations made little sense, since a bad season would mean a good draft pick.

Meanwhile Jordan was becoming restless, looking for a chance to return to action. The best player on the team was not with his teammates and was not watching games, stating that it was too frustrating for him to be unable to play for the first time in nine years. Instead of rehabbing in the team facility, Jordan returned to North Carolina. He did not particularly endear himself to his teammates when he said of

3. Addition by Subtraction

the Bulls, 8–17 at the time: "I took off for my home in North Carolina for a few weeks ago because I could not bear to watch the Bulls lose."[69]

Prior to his return the Bulls had to release Billy McKinney, a 30-year-old point guard born and raised in the state of Illinois, who unretired in 1985 to finally play for his home state NBA franchise. After nine games McKinney re-retired, this time for good, and in 1987 would start off his executive career as assistant vice president of basketball operations for the Bulls.

One player who benefited from Jordan's absence was Gervin, who missed training camp and had to work himself back into shape. Once he got rolling, he was delivering vintage performances, like on November 19, 1985, against the Pacers, when he went 15/18 from the floor.

Rookie Charles Oakley was also struggling in the first part of the season, once even falling out of the rotation for a couple of games. The knock on Oakley was that he was getting into foul trouble early and was not a reliable offensive option. With Jordan out, more players needed to contribute on the offensive end. Krause earned some valid criticism for passing on another power forward, Karl Malone, selected 13th overall by the Utah Jazz in 1985, who would have been very helpful now that the team needed a scoring power forward.

In his rookie season Malone ended up scoring 14.9 points and grabbing 8.9 rebounds per game, which were solid numbers, but nowhere near the heights that he would reach as a scorer and a rebounder. Oakley picked up the pace in the second part of his rookie season, and in the next two seasons, in which he would average 13.6 points and 13 rebounds per game, he became a great complementary player for Jordan, an interior presence and enforcer whose primary concern was collective success.

After the Bulls lost to the Knicks on December 26, 1985, making the team's overall record 11–21, Krause held a staff-only meeting to determine how to dig the team out of the crisis. Reinsdorf decided to step in and attend his first team practice, as well as meet with Albeck in private. Following the meeting he said to the press: "My job is to ask the kinds of questions that will make people think a little more. It will stimulate Jerry and the coaching staff to think about things."[70] With a bit over a third of the season gone, Albeck was already in the hot seat, long-term plans and injury to the franchise player notwithstanding.

Meanwhile Jordan's foot finally healed and in three weeks he was expected to return to the team, following two weeks in a walking cast and one week in a brace. Krause was adamant about not rushing his return in order to salvage the season. Jordan was simply too valuable a commodity to risk. When a beat reporter wrote a story discussing which player could be benched once Jordan came back, Albeck responded by refusing to talk to him altogether.[71] The article predicted optimistically that Jordan would be back in January or early February; however, the date of his return had to be postponed yet again; the chance of Albeck saving his job was basically gone. Albeck was easily manipulated by players, executives, and the chairman, listening to suggestions and backtracking when it was revealed whose suggestions he followed. Furthermore, his rotations were confusing, especially to players themselves, as he did not react to the game, but followed what he referred to as his "usual substitution rotation."[72]

On February 2, 1986, Dailey played his last game for the Bulls. In late January he had missed practice and a team flight, indications that something was wrong. Initially Dailey said that he had family problems, but after Krause launched a team investigation the story did not add up. Dailey was one of the frontrunners for the Sixth Man of the Year Award, despite the apparent issues, but once he lost a spot on the roster, there was no chance for him to win the award. Reinsdorf was also not a big supporter of the troublesome player, whom he witnessed eating pizza and a hot dog during an actual game. The next season Dailey signed with the CBA's Jacksonville Jets and was supposed to earn $500 a week, but was picked up by the Clippers before the CBA season started. The Bulls had the right to match the offer, but they decided not to.

In Dailey's place the Bulls brought in 6'4" Michael Holton from the CBA on a 10-day contract. Holton began the season on the Suns, the team that originally drafted him a year earlier, but was cut after four games. It was thanks to his late-game heroics against the Nets that the Bulls put an end to a seven-game losing streak. With averages of 11.6 points, 2.8 assists, and two steals in his first five games, Holton secured himself a roster spot on the Bulls for the rest of the season. However, following Jordan's return, his minutes would decline, and after the season Holton would head out to Portland.

Dailey was not the only one causing disruption within the team. Orlando Woolridge, the best player on the roster during Jordan's absence, failed to show up for the game against the Celtics on March 4, 1986. Krause immediately fined him $3,660 for that game and the previous contest, which Woolridge had also missed. Before the game Krause found out Woolridge was with his agent in New York, even though the forward was cleared by the team physician to make a return after missing 10 of the last 12 games due to injuries. Woolridge's absence allowed rookie Charles Oakley to earn significant minutes and he responded with averages of 18 points and 14 rebounds during a six-game stretch.

When Woolridge returned for the next game, against the Hawks, he got a cold reception from his teammates. When talking to the press, John Paxson had no reaction, Gene Banks refused to comment, and Sidney Green was not willing to forgive Woolridge's absence when the team needed him. Woolridge apologized for his "immature decision," which was caused by ongoing contract negotiations. Much of the blame for how the situation was handled fell on Krause, with some demanding a fine and a suspension. With Dailey gone and Jordan still at "85–90 percent,"[73] as estimated by Dr. John Hefferon, who was handling his rehabilitation, the Bulls needed as many healthy players as possible, especially if they were as talented as Woolridge.

Part of the criticism came from the fact that when issuing the suspension Krause was not with the team either—he was in Los Angeles, scouting Loyola Marymount's Keith Smith. Looking for a point guard who could keep up with Jordan, Krause wanted to take a look at Smith, the 6'4", 185-pound, score-first playmaker, who became the focal point of Paul Westhead's run-and-gun system. Westhead said of Smith: "in our fast break system, it means he handles the ball on every situation. It's up to him to deal to his teammates or shoot. If that chemistry breaks down, we're in trouble."[74]

Earning comparisons to Nate Archibald and being regarded as one of the best playmakers in the draft, Smith was not picked by the Bulls. In fact, not many teams were impressed with his 21-points-per-game average. He was selected by the Milwaukee Bucks with the 45th overall pick, after the Bucks had already selected one rookie point guard, Scott Skiles. After the season concluded neither remained on the roster, and Smith was out of the NBA altogether.

Pairing a former shooting guard with Jordan could actually work, as the two could share playmaking duties, and the future would show that a typical point guard could not mesh with Jordan's ball-dominant style. However, it was the handling of Jordan's injury that already had some journalists in the country calling for Krause's head in his first full season on the job. Krause organized two of the best orthopedic specialists in the country, Dr. Stanley James of Eugene, Oregon, and Dr. John Bergfeld of Cleveland, Ohio—through the years of retelling the story their number grew to five—so that Hefferon could consult them on the results of Jordan's CAT scans. The doctors instructed Jordan to be extra careful about his foot and not put too much pressure on it. Instead, he ignored their directives and played pickup basketball while in North Carolina, where he had gone under the pretense of working on his degree.

Reinsdorf said that it was like Jordan forcing the team's hand, indicating that he was going to greenlight his return, because "if we let him play, at least we have some control over how much he plays. If we knew Michael was going to be good, that's one thing. If he is going to be naughty, I think we're better off letting him play here so at least we can watch over him."[75] A player directly opposing the franchise should be disciplined, especially since the franchise did not want to put his health at risk.

By allowing Jordan to play, against his better judgment, Krause would look weak as an executive. He got a second shot at the job of his dreams, working for his hometown franchise. If Jordan were to reinjure his foot, Krause would definitely be fired, as well as go down in history as the man who finished the career of one of the most promising athletes in history. Hefferon, on the other hand, saw Jordan's passion to return to play and reclaim his identity as a basketball player as worth the risk, saying to Krause that if the Bulls did not allow Jordan to play, "he would probably never forgive them."[76]

Krause recounted that when confronted about playing pickup games, Jordan said that he could play, to which Krause responded: "Michael, you work for this team, I work for this team. We are employees of this team. He did not like that. Michael got mad when I said that."[77] This may imply that for Krause basketball was a business, whereas for Jordan it was much more. That is far from the truth, as Krause's devotion to basketball was, if anything, at least very similar to Jordan's. When I asked Rick Telander about the parallel between the two, he said:

> They were both exceptional people. The case for Jordan is obvious, not so much for Krause, because as an executive you don't personally win or lose, you draft, it depends if somebody is available, you do things based on how much money you got, it is more financial stuff, not as clean-cut as being a great athlete. But he was in that narrow, narrow sphere as exceptional as Michael Jordan. Clearly not in a way Jordan would respect and I would not put the things Jordan did on par with what Krause did.

Jordan overruling the Bulls is part of his legacy. A player putting himself above the organization that drafted and developed him now serves as proof of how special Jordan was. Instead of giving them credit, Jordan ridiculed the executive and the owner. They never played the game; they did not know his body like he did.

After a two-hour meeting, Jordan was cleared to play with a time restriction. Krause wanted to be on the record that it was he who instructed Albeck to not play Jordan for more than 14 minutes per game, to protect the navicular bone in his superstar's left foot. By making it clear that it was his decision, he was trying to retain job security in case something happened to Jordan. Because nothing did, and the Bulls

3. Addition by Subtraction

made the playoffs, their postseason push ignited by Jordan's return (and Albeck not sticking to the minute restriction), Krause became a villain, blamed for pulling the reins on the best player of all time. Jordan proved Krause was mistake-prone, not trustworthy, maybe not knowledgeable enough to be a general manager in the NBA. Luckily for Krause, Jerry Reinsdorf was in his corner, and he was willing to support him and his vision.

4.

Top Sellers

The Bulls made the 1986 playoffs, even though they shouldn't have with a 30–52 record. Michael Jordan's 63-point performance against the Celtics happened even though he was not supposed to be on the court, especially not for 53 minutes of a playoff game against the Celtics in the Garden. One of the greatest performances in basketball history was a triumph of the individual versus the organization. Jordan openly made statements like "Jerry Krause and I basketball-wise just don't get along,"[1] solely on the basis of Krause's careful approach to his injury.

Order needed to be restored.

Reinsdorf and Krause could not punish Jordan for his insubordination because he was so popular and beloved that there was no chance of winning a public argument with him. But somebody needed to go. Coach Albeck was forced to cut short his two-week vacation to San Antonio in order to meet with Reinsdorf and Krause. They talked for three and a half hours; no decisions were made, but rumors were circulating that the Bulls were considering former NBA player Doug Collins as his replacement.

According to Will Robinson, Collins's college coach, Krause decided to employ the inexperienced coach because of vanity. Robinson recalled that he said to Krause: "'You take say a Dick Motta and you won't get credit for picking a coach. Dick Motta already is a good coach. But if you take Doug Collins and he succeeds, and I'm telling you he will succeed, you will get all the credit for that.' That seemed to impress him. And that's why he gave Doug the job."[2]

Collins was 34 years old at the time. He was born and raised in the state of Illinois and played college ball for Illinois State, a true native son if there ever was one. Prior to making himself eligible for the 1973 draft, the 6'6" Collins left as the leading scorer in his university's history. He was the first overall pick as a consensus first team All-American. His selection was delayed twice due to communication problems. The franchise that picked him, the Philadelphia 76ers, got into an argument with the league, as they wanted the fourth overall pick of that draft as well. The pick belonged to the Seattle SuperSonics, who signed ABA's John Brisker, whose NBA rights belonged to the Sixers. Landing two lottery picks would have been great, but Collins was as good a prize as any, as he supposedly possessed "the quickest hands and feet in college."[3]

After an eight-year career with the Sixers, the highlights of which were his four All-Star Game appearances, he turned to coaching, starting off as an assistant at Penn and Arizona State. At the moment he was working as a television analyst for CBS. He also worked for Krause for 10 days and prepared reports on some players around the end of the 1985-86 regular season.[4] Even though Albeck had one more year guaranteed on his contract and would get $250,000 from the franchise anyway, Krause admitted that he had talked to Collins and called him "a very bright young man."[5] However, Krause said that they were not talking about Collins taking over the Bulls, just having a regular dinner.

The decision to fire Albeck was not a popular one. He was an experienced coach, especially in comparison to Collins, who was rumored to take his place. The fact that Reinsdorf trusted Krause so much was also met with displeasure. Krause stepped in for Rod Thorn, another well-liked and respected figure, and the team actually declined under his rule. Albeck would be the second coach fired by Krause, and he had not even been the vice president for two full seasons.

The *Chicago Tribune*'s Skip Myslenski and Linda Kay interviewed an unnamed franchise investor, who described Krause as "a bad person in a very bad job," and complained that "Jerry Reinsdorf [was] very defensive about him."[6] Reinsdorf was particularly unhappy with how the Bulls performed without Jordan under Albeck. He wanted Red Holzman's Knicks 2.0. He wanted a team, not a superstar and his supporting cast. Reinsdorf explained that he wanted "no isolation, no one-on-one, very little dribbling and a tenacious defense."[7]

When Albeck said, following his firing, that he was sorry for the fans of Chicago, the statement was directed at the chairman and the vice president. Local press reacted to the unexpected sacking by calling Krause a "Reinsdorf bootlicker."[8] Albeck unloaded on Krause following the firing, describing him as devoid of self-consciousness, disruptive, and "an object of ridicule."[9] According to Albeck, Krause "deliberately drove a wedge between Reinsdorf and [him]," while "Tex Winter's only function was to be Krause's spy in the locker room."[10] He took special issue with Krause entering the locker room, something that had been problematic in the past and would remain problematic in the future. As observed by Karen Umlauf, "Jerry always wanted to rub elbows with the athletes and he would never accomplish that because he lacked the physical attributes."

For their part, Krause and Reinsdorf released a joint statement, in which they described Albeck as "a competent NBA coach who has shown class and character through a difficult season."[11] Albeck took a head coaching job at Bradley University and Krause said he was happy for him not only because he did not have to pay out his whole salary, but because he simply had "no bad feelings toward Stan."[12] Albeck recognized that the Bulls' only chance to be successful was to rely on Jordan. Collins compared Jordan to his teammate on the Sixers, Julius Erving, who was great, but unlike Jordan "played within a team concept."[13] During the season Krause would say with pride: "Doug tells me Jordan is playing much like Erving did when they were teammates."[14] Erving was still an active player, although 1986-87 would be the last season of his stellar career.

Jordan was entering his third season in the NBA, and the boost of confidence that came following his return from injury, capped off with the 63-point performance against the Celtics, would become only more problematic for the Bulls as time went on. Local journalists started siding with Jordan. The *Chicago Tribune*'s Bernie Lincicome wrote prior to the 1986 NBA draft that Krause's primary focus should be on accommodating Jordan and every day he should ask himself: "Have I done something nice for Michael Jordan today?"[15]

The Bulls held the eighth pick in that draft, which was considered so weak that the Sixers traded their first overall pick to Cleveland for forward Roy Hinson. The Cavs picked Jordan's fellow Tar Heel, Brad Daugherty. The Bulls would not pick that high, as Krause could not land a top-three pick despite his attempts to increase his chances of landing one of three centers: Memphis State's William Bedford, North Carolina State's Chris Washburn, and Daugherty. When that failed, Jordan had his eyes on a different player from North Carolina that he wanted Krause to select.

Johnny Dawkins was a point guard from Duke, who had just led the Blue Devils to their first NCAA Final Four in eight years. The rivalry between Duke and the Tar Heels was just becoming serious, with Duke soon to emerge as one of the best programs in college basketball history. The 6'2" guard was mentored by his father, Johnny Dawkins, Sr., who made sure that his son worked on his game from a young age. The future Dukie played with men twice or thrice his age and was adjusting to a physical style of play, so that in the future he would not be intimidated by bigger and stronger players. Dawkins could jump out of the gym, was flashy, quick, and efficient, as he finished the season with 20.2 points per game. When Walter Berry of St. John's collected one of his numerous—seven to be exact—awards for 1986 college player of the year, he said that it should go to Dawkins.[16]

Jordan wanted Dawkins because of his skills but also because of their personal connection—they had the same agent, David Falk. Doug Collins wanted Dawkins as well, as proven by his straightforward statement on draft night: "I'm a tremendous Johnny Dawkins fan, I love Johnny Dawkins."[17]

The night before the draft he even told Duke's Mike Krzyzewski that the Bulls would pick Dawkins. However, Krause, the most important decision maker on the Bulls, considered Dawkins "too slim," lacking "the body to take the sustained punishment of the NBA."[18] Maybe he did not know where Dawkins came from and how used to physical play he was, or maybe he simply was so impressed by the player that he picked that he was not willing to listen to Collins, Jordan, or the fans, who were also hoping for the Dawkins-Jordan pairing.

Prior to the draft it seemed that Krause would go with Dawkins as well, who he described as having "very good quickness and very good speed," and possessing "the potential to be good on defense in our league."[19]

Was that a smoke screen, or did Krause change his mind at the last moment? Whatever actually happened, the player who was selected instead of Dawkins, Brad Sellers of Ohio State, was put in a tough spot. Over 3,000 season ticketholders, who had gathered in the Grand Ballroom of the Chicago Hilton on draft night, immediately started booing when his selection was announced.

When I asked Rick Telander about whether Krause would admit to a mistake—according to Telander he never did—I mentioned drafting Brad Sellers as one of his most critical ones. Upon hearing the name, Telander said energetically: "Oh, I'll tell you a Brad Sellers story! [Krause] told me: 'Nobody's better at throwing the ball inbounds.' What? 'When it's late in the game, you gotta get the ball in, they're pressing, he's 7'0" and he can see the court.'"

Fast forward to May 7, 1989. The Bulls are playing the Cavs in Cleveland. It is Game Five of the first round of the playoffs. There are three seconds on the game clock. Michael Jordan is guarded by Larry Nance and Craig Ehlo, yet he is able to break free, catch the inbound pass, jump, hang majestically in the air, release the shot, beat the buzzer, make the score 101–100, and send the Bulls to the Eastern Conference Semifinals.

The man inbounding the ball? Number 2, Brad Sellers.

That one successful pass did not validate the decision to pass over

Dawkins, nor did it make up for Krause's decision to bypass Jordan in making the selection and alienating him even more in the process. Krause did not do himself any favors by hyping up Sellers to anybody who would bother to listen.[20] To make the case for Sellers, Krause even referred to the 1986 draft as the "best small forward draft ever."[21] The fans might have been more understanding if Krause had gone with another point guard, Scott Skiles, but the executive was scared of his reputation: "Skiles is a tough kid, and I like tough kids. Whether I like him enough to draft him at No. 9 is another question. We'll always have the specter of Quintin Dailey staring us in the face, and sometimes that's not a real good specter around here."[22]

Skiles had been arrested for possession of marijuana and driving under the influence. Considering that a number of players selected in that draft would suffer from substance abuse issues, and the second overall pick, Len Bias, would actually lose his life to cocaine, the fear was somewhat justified, but not regarding Skiles, who would become a serviceable NBA point guard and in 1998 even emerge as one of the candidates for the position of head coach for the Bulls.

Sellers would be traded after three seasons, never becoming the revolutionary wing player Krause envisioned him becoming. He had the size of a Kevin Durant or a Dirk Nowitzki, and Krause was particularly impressed with the shooting touch that the big man possessed, but it was not on the same level as the other two, nor was it a time when such players could flourish. Even though Collins was cognizant of Sellers's ability to play "like he's 6'7","[23] he was not the player that he wanted.

"I loved watching Brad Sellers in college and was excited about what he'd do in the pros. He was taller than Pippen, had the length, in theory should do a lot of different things on the court and I thought he was going to be the total package," said Fury. "When he got to the pros, for whatever reason, there was none of that."

Gambling on a fresh-faced coach and an out-of-the-box rookie were not the only moves made by Krause during that summer. The team had a shooting guard in Jordan and a power forward in Oakley, but the rest of the positions were up for grabs. Sidney Green, the man Oakley was supposed to be the backup to, became expandable after Oakley earned the starting spot. Green was traded to the Detroit Pistons for big man Earl Cureton and the 1987 second-round pick.

The 6'9" Cureton entered the NBA in 1980 and had not yet become a starter in the league. Krause explained the trade as follows: "I saw a tape of one game against the Celtics where he played power forward against Kevin McHale, center against Robert Parish and small forward opposite Larry Bird. And he defended well against all three of them."[24]

In an era of positionless basketball, Cureton would be a great addition. In 1986-87 he ended up playing as a starting center for the Bulls until he was traded to the Clippers halfway through the season.

Green was not particularly happy with being moved. While he complimented Oakley, calling him "a quality player," he immediately added that Oakley "was drafted by Jerry Krause, so I'm sure that had a lot to do with it. I though the only thing we lacked was a center."[25]

Instead of strengthening the middle, Krause weakened it by trading Jawann Oldham to the Knicks for their 1987 first-round pick, which the Knicks got from the Nuggets in exchange for guard Darrell Walker. Krause would turn that pick into the crown jewel of his scouting career, a skinny kid from Arkansas named Scottie Pippen, who would become the quintessential small forward of the 1990s.

For one season, though, Sellers was targeted to be *that* player. Sellers was supposed to take the three spot—although not immediately, as he was involved in lengthy contract negotiations, which did not win him any new fans in Chicago—while Macy and Dave Corzine were nothing more than spot-fillers, as the GM was looking for better players.

Krause wanted to trade for SuperSonics center Jack Sikma, 1979 NBA champion and seven-time All-Star. Because the Sonics were rebuilding, Sikma asked to be traded from the only professional team he had ever played for. He was not sentimental when making the demand: "I don't care about the past. I'm 30 now, and I'll be 34 at the end of my contract. My goal is to be prepared (to retire) at that point."[26]

The Bulls were potential suitors, and 30-year-old Sikma named the Bulls as one of the teams he wanted to play for. With four years left on his $1.5 million a year contract, Krause considered the asking price too steep and passed on Sikma, citing his injury history.[27] The Sonics' Lenny Wilkens complained to the press that dealing with Krause was frustrating, because he was constantly changing his mind.[28] Sikma was eventually traded to the Bucks (along with a second-round pick) for center Alton Lister and two first-round picks, in 1987 and 1989. He enjoyed five solid seasons in Milwaukee, playing at least 80 games in the first three.

Krause would select two championship cornerstones, Horace Grant with the 1987 pick and B.J. Armstrong with the 1989 pick, that he would have had to part with in order to get Sikma.

As for the point guard position, Krause understood better than anyone that he did not need both Kyle Macy and John Paxson. Macy was more experienced and established, but he had a bigger contract. And Krause really liked Paxson. If he could take the guard who barely cracked the Spurs rotation and turn him into a starter on a winning team, his credentials as a scout would be etched in stone, as his ability to spot talent would no longer be limited to the draft.

Jordan also preferred Paxson to Macy, primarily because he remembered when the two were on a college all-star team in Yugoslavia and Paxson, then of Notre Dame, had hit a big, game-winning shot.[29] So Krause worked out a trade for a modest return, as it was no secret around the league that either Macy or Paxson had to go. The Sleuth did his best not to lose his position in negotiations by saying: "Several teams have expressed an interest in Kyle Macy and Indiana is one of them. We're talking to several teams about several players."[30] However, other executives were wising up to Krause's non-statements, and the Bulls got only two second-round picks in return for their starting point guard.

Jordan's opinion of Macy was not that great. Jordan's friend, Buzz Peterson, grew up idolizing Macy and when Jordan made the Bulls, Peterson asked him what Macy was like in real life. He replied: "Get another idol."[31]

The Bulls' starting point guard for the season arrived on draft day via trade for Larry Krystkowiak, whom Krause picked in the second round, and two future second-round picks. He was a pass-first, selfless playmaker, so exactly the opposite of what the team should have been looking for. When talking to Paxson about joining the Bulls, Krause sold him on the idea of creating a team of shooters, who would share the ball and, by using the triangle offense, allow everybody to get their touches and chances to shoot.

And then he reached for Steve Colter.

John Paxson's older brother, Jim, who played with Colter on the Blazers, described him as follows: "I lockered next to him for two years, and he is probably the nicest guy I've ever known."[32] Born in Phoenix and playing college ball for New Mexico State, Colter built himself up gradually, from 10.6 minutes per game in his freshman year to playing every minute of the 28 games he participated in as a senior. He was picked 33rd overall in the 1984 draft by the Blazers and for two seasons earned a reputation as a model citizen and a good point guard, who was once again patiently building up his position up on the rotation and starting 51 games in his second NBA season. His field goal percentage was 45.6 and his three-point shooting percentage was 32.5, while the 27 three-pointers he made was the highest number on the team, but his 8.7 points per game average was good for only eighth on the Blazers.

During his first conference as a Bull, Colter hoped for more opportunities to score, saying that in Portland he only shot the ball "if it was a last resort." He then asked rhetorically: "Is it fun being a last resort? Well, if you're not used to it, no."[33] In Chicago he was expected to score more. The 1992 second-round choice from the Bulls was used in a trade package that landed the Blazers Danny Ainge from Sacramento.

Orlando Woolridge, the second-best player on the Bulls the previous season, was a free agent in the summer. He was wanted by the New Jersey Nets, who had been in search of relevance for so long that they had no problem with paying more than $1 million a year to a player with substance abuse and attitude issues. Some of the Bulls players were against bringing Woolridge back after he missed two games for unspecified personal reasons. Signing him to a five-year contract for over $5 million would only further alienate Jordan. The Bulls were close to trading Woolridge on draft day, but the inner turmoil in the Nets organization prevented that from happening.

The Nets still wanted Woolridge, but the initial, generous offer of two first-round picks for him was no longer on the table. Krause proclaimed that the Bulls would match any offer sheet signed by Woolridge, as he was eager to get something, anything, in return. Larry Fleisher, Woolridge's agent, and Krause did not communicate for three months. Fleisher was the head of the NBA Players' Association and one of the men responsible for introducing the salary cap. Being on his bad side negatively impacted negotiations with basically every NBA player.

Reinsdorf handled the negotiations from that point on. The Bulls got the Nets' 1987 first-round pick and second-round picks in 1988 and 1990.

Jordan could not wait for the new season to start, saying: "I feel like this is my rookie year. I'm hungry and I want everyone on this team to be hungry. I don't go for any of this rebuilding stuff."[34] The best player on the team wanted it to be good right away, and it was Krause's job to surround him with the best talent possible *now*, instead of building through the draft. The difference in philosophies made the already fragile relationship almost irreparable.

Jordan entered an already great team at North Carolina, and it continued to be great and competitive for the three years he was there. With his charisma and magnetism, Dean Smith made it look so easy. Chicago was the third market in the country; Reinsdorf and, by extension, Krause had the money to make the team great. Jordan was schooled by Smith, so he thought he knew how it was done—by bringing in guys like Dawkins, not Colter or Sellers.

With the training camp almost over, Krause was still trying to get Joe Barry Carroll from the Warriors and Eddie Johnson from the Kings. Carroll, the first overall pick of the 1980 NBA draft, was ready to move on from the Warriors, who had already selected Chris Washburn with the third pick in 1986 to be his replacement. The 7'0" Carroll's NBA career was seen primarily through the prism of the trade that landed him in Golden State. The Boston Celtics held the first pick, but Red Auerbach orchestrated the move in which the pick went to the Warriors, while the Celtics got their starting center, Robert Parish, and the third pick in the 1980 draft, which they used for power forward Kevin McHale. While Carroll was able to put up solid numbers—and not contribute much of anything else—Parish and McHale won three NBA championships with the Celtics, made the All-Star team numerous times, and would eventually enter the Basketball Hall of Fame. Eddie Johnson was a score-first small forward and one of the first modern sixth men, who despite coming off the bench would play 30 minutes per game and ignite the offense as a leader of the second unit.

The prospect of bringing in Carroll or Johnson was particularly intriguing to Jordan, who said: "No way we should pass up getting players of that caliber if they're available."[35] Krause's inability to land even one did not help their relationship.

Krause's trades infuriated Jordan, as more than half the roster that had begun the previous season was now gone. Frustrated, he said: "I just wish they would settle on who is going to be here and then get on with it."[36]

Krause continued to meddle with the roster and treat players as instruments, as he did with Alfredick Hughes, the 14th pick of the 1985 draft, who was cut by the Spurs after their training camp concluded. Bulls picked him up soon after that. Krause told the press that he brought him in because the Bulls needed people in practice, adding bluntly, "We told him he'll be with us for practice and if we make another move, he could be out of here quickly."[37] Hughes was cut before the start of the regular season.

Because he could not take out his frustrations on Krause, as he was his *de facto* boss, according to Sam Smith's *The Jordan Rules* Jordan targeted the two men he brought onto the roster instead of Dawkins—Colter and Sellers. Colter reacted by giving his version of events: "I never had a problem playing with Michael. With any guy who's extremely successful like Michael, people are going to want to shoot him down.... I'm not calling him an angel. But who is?"[38]

Steve Colter was not a bad player. He had a signature move, "the Crooked Leg," which involved dribbling the ball behind his back with his right hand and bringing it back with the same hand from left to right, switching direction, and leaving the defender hesitant for a split second, which was enough for Colter to rush past him, toward the basket.

As for Sellers, the player who supported him, at least publicly, during the early days of his NBA career was none other than Jordan, who said, "He has played pretty well.... He adapted well to NBA play.... I think he's going to help the team, and he's going to improve. He'll get more physical as time goes on."[39]

When Colter was traded mid-season and Paxson entered the starting lineup, Jordan became the primary ball handler of the team. Sellers, who was up and down throughout the season, as most rookies tend to be, was one of his primary targets thanks to his shooting touch. In *The Jordan Rules*, Phil Jackson explained that Sellers was drafted precisely because of his shooting ability—so that Jordan could not be doubled, as the small forward could score from almost any place on the court.[40]

Prior to the start of the season, Krause was happy with the roster he assembled, saying: "I know this team will play better than it did last year. We're better coached. We're better defensively. We're quicker, faster. Better chemistry."[41] What he was really or at least equally as happy about were the three first-round picks in the upcoming draft and the $1.5 million of cap space.

This team was not about that one season, but about the future.

That was why he was protective of Coach Collins, reportedly going through his mail at team offices to weed out the most offensive letters. And he surrounded him with an experienced staff. Johnny Bach, Gene Littles, and Tex Winter all had way more experience than Collins, who was supposed to learn from them, just as he did as a player from the Sixers' Gene Shue. He was a tough player and wanted his players to be tough as well. For him, hard work and effort trumped pure talent.

"We aren't going to outtalent any team in the league. Nobody. But we can outwork other teams," said Collins, adding that the Bulls were a long-term project, and his goal was to win 40 games.[42]

If Jordan wanted to win now, he had to do most of the heavy lifting himself. In the opening-night 103 victory over the Knicks, Jordan scored 50 points. Afterward he complained about his teammates' lack of skill and/or effort, saying: "I don't think it's my role to score 75 points a night."[43] He also referred to himself as an underdog.

However, after the Bulls were 3–0 and Collins remained the only unbeaten coach in the NBA, Jordan praised his teammates for pulling for one another, being supportive and not egotistical.[44] For the first two wins Krause wore a blue sports coat and a yellow tie, so when he forgot his attire for the third game, Thelma Krause had to bring him his lucky coat and tie to the arena.

The clothes would stop working as a lucky charm soon after that third win, as on November 7, 1986, the Bulls lost to the Pistons, but they still managed to amass a 7–3 record in the first 10 games. After the first

20 games of the season, they were 10–10, an almost perfect foreshadowing of their final 40–42 record.

South Bend Tribune's Bill Gleason, in a column published on November 13, expressed justified optimism that the Bulls could actually win 40 games. The columnist described "the general manager who looks like a basketball with a mouth" as somebody capable of surrounding Jordan with reliable, competent players, adding that "Jordan might make Krause a genius."[45]

Sellers was initially looking like a good pick as well. On November 14, when the Bulls played the Celtics, he guarded Larry Bird and limited him to just two points in the fourth quarter. The Bulls lost, but still, Sellers was showing signs of being a capable NBA defender. By the end of the year he earned his first suspension for disciplinary reasons, and lost around $6,000 due to fines. Sellers earned the suspension after going home to Cleveland following the Christmas Day loss to the Knicks. Originally the players were allowed to go home, but after the loss Collins demanded that all players return to Chicago. Sellers had already bought his plane ticket and refused to fly with the team.[46]

Colter shot just 26 percent in the preseason and continued to struggle with his shot, making 31 percent of his field goal attempts. Asked whether he should bench him instead of Paxson, who was way more reliable, Collins argued that his team needed Paxson's 10.8 points per game when Jordan was resting, adding that he could not take Colter out, as that would strip him of his confidence.[47] Al Vermeil emailed me a week after our second interview, asking whether we talked about John Paxson. We had not, so he wrote back in an hour or so:

> Every team needs a John Paxson. A player who is consistent, holds things together and can make the big plays when you need them. If you evaluate the first three championships we won. John played an integral part in all three. In the 91 championship, John played great defense and hit the big shots in Game Five to seal the championship. In the 92 championship, John played outstanding defense against Portland. In the 93 championship series against Phoenix, John hit the big shot in Game Six to seal the last championship. What I'm saying, John Paxson rose to the occasion whenever needed. He was a very underrated player.

Collins soon saw what he had in Paxson and agreed to move Colter. On the last day of 1986 Colter was traded to the Sixers for Sedale Threatt, who in 1983 was a sixth-round pick, and who Krause had originally wanted to get in the summer, but Philadelphia declined his offer of a future first-round selection. Krause rarely included first-round picks in trades during that time, which showed just how serious he was about the point guard.

Sixers coach Matt Goukas was particularly reluctant to see Threatt go, saying: "I feel close to Sedale, because I coached him in the summer league. It's unusual enough that a sixth-round pick makes a team, much less had an impact. But he worked hard, was always available, had a terrific attitude. It's a unique story."[48]

Threatt became the sixth man for the Bulls, while Paxson was permanently moved into the starting lineup. The Bulls defied expectations: they won 10 more games than the previous season, with a rookie head coach and a slew of draft picks. Jordan led the league in scoring with 37.1 points per game, 3,041 in total, and steals with 3.2 per game and 259 in total. He made the All-NBA first team for the first time in his career.

Oakley led the league in rebounds with 13 per game and 1,066 in total. He and Jordan were the difference-makers on the Bulls team, which apart from the two draft picks consisted of various castoffs, for whom playing in Chicago served as a last chance to keep their NBA dream alive.

When Jordan was asked about which positions the Bulls should target for improvement, he refused to answer. In private he would push for the team to draft Joe Wolf, but publicly it was just easier for him to complain and criticize, instead of being on record with a solution that would not pan out.

The Bulls were once again swept by the Celtics in the first round. In Game Three Jordan made nine of his 30 shot attempts, after suffering from stomach flu the day before. Before the game the Cavaliers' rookie Ron Harper visited the Bulls locker room, as he was friends with Oakley and Sellers, with whom he played basketball in the summer. Players joked that they should find an extra uniform for Harper, while Collins threw in: "We could use you." In 1994 Harper would really join the Bulls, long after Oakley and Sellers were gone from that locker room.

The mood on the team was way better than it had been the previous season, and Krause also played his part in upholding it, like when he canceled $250 fines that he issued to four of the Bulls players in March. All the while he continued to search for new talent, even making a personal appearance at the Portsmouth Invitational Tournament.

He was looking for the next Charles Oakley or Mike Smrek, both of whom he saw in person during the 1985 PIT and eventually drafted. In 1987 the Bulls were supposed to pick 8th, 10th, 29th, and 33rd. Krause could use all those picks on players he saw at PIT, if he was particularly impressed. Much to his chagrin, the player he wanted was also there. And he was already making waves around the league.

By that time, Pippen was no longer a secret. Prior to his appearance at PIT, he was projected to be picked in the later rounds of the draft,[49] but his stock was rising faster than any other prospect's from his class. When NBA's director of scouting, Marty Blake, saw him for the first time back in December 1986, he was impressed that the skinny 6'7"—Pippen would eventually grow to 6'8"—kid from Central Arkansas could play all five positions. When he graduated from high school, he was just 6'1" and was primarily a point guard.

Pippen retained his ball-handling abilities, while his size and athleticism allowed him to become a versatile player, the proto-forward that Krause thought he was getting in Sellers. His coach at Central Arkansas, Don Dyer, said prior to the draft that "[Pippen] was a point guard most of his life and still has those skills.... I could see him as a tall point guard."[50] Bulls scout Billy McKinney was the only one who bothered to go see a NAIA game and he said Pippen had the longest arms he had ever seen. When Krause asked him whether Pippen was a good basketball player, McKinney answered: "I don't know, competition is terrible.... I don't know if he can play."[51]

The National Association of Intercollegiate Athletics (NAIA) is the inferior cousin of the NCAA, but it still has been able to supply the NBA with talented players like Willis Reed, Elgin Baylor, Jack Sikma, and Dennis Rodman. Pippen was invited to PIT by Blake and made such an impression that he was invited to another tournament, which took place in Hawaii. Pippen performed great, partially due to his close-knit play with 5'3" point guard Tyrone "Muggsy" Bogues.

Bogues reminisces in his autobiography about the pairing: "No one saw us coming. We went undefeated over the entire weekend. Coaches and players kept looking at us, wondering who the heck we were and why we were kicking their more highly-ranked butts."[52]

Both men were selected to the tournament's first team, but Krause was not going to pick Bogues anyway, because of his "one rule" of roster building: "I don't want anyone on the team smaller than me."[53]

With the Bulls season over, Krause was already thinking about the next one. He invited 60 rookies for a four-day pre-draft camp. In the meantime, Krause considered his chances of getting the Rockets' 7'4" center, Ralph Sampson. Three-time college national player of the year, Sampson entered the NBA with extraordinary expectations, and while he did lead the Rockets to the finals in 1986 as part of the Twin Towers duo along with fellow center Hakeem Olajuwon, he unfairly earned the reputation of a soft player because of injuries, which limited him to just 43 games in 1986-87. Sampson played out of position, as a power forward, and as such he shied away from physical play, and was booed by his own fans because of that. It is uncertain how advanced the trade talks with the Bulls were, but when other teams inquired about Sampson, he was reportedly not for sale, especially after signing a six-year, $14.4 million contract in 1986. The Rockets traded him a year into his new deal, in December 1987, to the Warriors, after head coach Bill Fitch gave up on the oft-injured big man.

Other big men the Bulls were interested in were the Suns' Larry Nance and the SuperSonics' Tom Chambers, and both would eventually move in 1988, just not to Chicago. Both trades were supposed to involve Oakley. While the Suns proposed a direct exchange for Nance, the Sonics, apart from parting with Chambers, also wanted to swap picks, their fifth for the Bulls' eighth. Krause did not want to part with Oakley, but he knew he needed to do something, as the Suns, who already held the second overall pick, were also trying to get the sixth overall pick from the Kings in order to draft Pippen. He did not strike them as worthy of being selected second overall behind the surefire number one pick, David Robinson. Power forward Armen Gilliam was a much safer choice, as he was a proven NCAA talent.

The Sacramento Kings, who picked sixth, were reportedly torn between Pippen and UNC's point guard Kenny Smith. Krause pestered them a few times about their pick, offering in exchange the Bulls' eighth or 10th pick and either Gene Banks or Sedale Threatt. The Kings also made Eddie Johnson available, whom the Bulls had wanted a year ago, but Krause had already found his small forward in Pippen. Johnson was a great offensive player and Collins wanted the team to primarily improve on offense, but Johnson's inability or unwillingness to play defense made him less desirable than Pippen. Yes, he was raw, but Pippen's pure athleticism and physical attributes were impossible to ignore.

When Krause, in typical sleuth fashion, saw the Kings' executive Joe Axelson talking to Pippen in the back of the stands during one of the training camps, he knew he needed to act. On the outside he remained secretive, saying "We could trade up, we could trade down, we could do nothing,"[54] but inside he was panicking. One day prior to the draft the *Chicago Tribune* ran a story about Krause pursuing Pippen, which, according to the executive, jeopardized his chances of drafting the forward.

Krause also showed great interest in rookie point guard Kevin Johnson, but it is uncertain whether the Bulls actually wanted him or whether it was just a smoke screen. Until the day before the draft the Kings were rumored to want Scottie Pippen and Horace Grant, but after trading Eddie Johnson to the Suns for power forward Ed Pinckney, Axelson said they were no longer interested in Grant, while Pippen's stock had dropped in his eyes.[55]

If in fact the Kings' interest in Pippen waned, Krause would only have to get in front of the Cavs, who held the seventh pick, in order to get his man. However, Axelson was notorious for giving false statements in public, and the Detroit Pistons' general manager Jack McCloskey delivered a pre-draft statement of his own that could also spoil Krause's chances of landing Pippen: "We tried desperately to move up to get him. He is the most interesting and exciting player in the draft. If he doesn't go in the top 10, something's wrong. I think he is going to be a superstar."[56]

The Spurs, picking first, went with Navy's Robinson. The Suns, picking second, went with Gilliam, and the Nets picked guard Dennis Hopson. The Clippers, who were rumored to like small forward Derrick McKey, went with Georgetown's Reggie Williams instead. Then came the Sonics' turn. They selected Pippen.

The small forward entered the stage wearing a Sonics cap. He was smiling but seemed a bit confused. Earlier in his hotel room he had received a call from Krause, informing him that the trade to bring him to Chicago was in place, he just needed to play along and keep the move a secret. And yet, Pippen seemed somewhat uneasy when talking to reporters, until one of them told the rookie that he might be wearing the wrong cap, as he was part of a trade to the Bulls. Pippen went to Chicago, while the Bulls' eighth pick, 6'11" center Olden Polynice, a 1988 or 1989 second-round pick, and a first-round pick swap in 1988 or 1989 went to Seattle.

This intricate move was made possible thanks to ... the Clippers. The condition for the trade was that Gilliam and Reggie Williams would be no longer available for the Sonics to pick. If either was still draftable, the deal would be off and the Sonics would go with the more established college player. By not picking McKey, as was initially predicted, the Clippers allowed the Bulls to get their player.

The negotiations with the Sonics went on until 2:00 a.m., but they were worth it. Coach Collins was complimentary to Krause during the post-draft press conference: "I think Jerry should be really commended. He could've given up, but he kept whacking away. ... He is just relentless."[57]

Krause himself explained that he had to be stubborn during the negotiations, because he *really* wanted Pippen: "The way I have to do business, sometimes I have to be a bit rough. I'm not concerned about protecting my image. I just hope people respect my judgment, my evaluation of talent and my ability to build an organization."[58]

The professed team of shooters really came together when Krause got Horace Grant from Clemson. The 6'10" power forward led the Atlantic Coast Conference in scoring, rebounding, and field goal percentage.

4. Top Sellers

Grant grew up in Mitchell, a small town in Georgia, and played in Sparta. He was recruited by Clemson along with his twin brother, Harvey, and got a full four-year scholarship. Harvey transferred a year later to Independence Community College, and eventually to Oklahoma. Horace stayed at Clemson for the duration of the scholarship.

Grant was expected to be brought along slowly, as the Bulls already had Oakley, and prior to the draft Krause also got 38-year-old Artis Gilmore from the Spurs in exchange for the 1988 second-round pick. Once Grant came to an agreement with the Bulls—as his contract negotiations lasted a couple of weeks into training camp—Gilmore would take Grant under his wing and teach him about being a professional in the NBA, with Grant doing typical rookie chores, like taking Gilmore to lunch and dinner, and paying for both meals.[59]

On draft night, after the Bulls selected Grant, Reinsdorf ordered four bottles of champagne. During the post-draft press conference, Krause apologized to the reporters: "If our faces are a little red, it's because we stopped off for a sip of champagne to celebrate."[60]

Drinking was not his forte, but he loved to eat, especially during the draft, when he would spend long hours in the office, talking to the employees, as well as taking and making calls. Umlauf reminisced: "When we would be working longer, he would be all about: 'What're we ordering for dinner?' It was how he celebrated." And after the 1987 draft Krause had every reason to celebrate.

Initially Krause was torn between Grant and Joe Wolf out of UNC. Both made the All-ACC team, but Grant received 245 out of 246 possible votes, while Wolf got 184, placing third behind fellow Tar Heel Kenny Smith. Bill Cary of Wisconsin's *The Reporter* referred to Wolf as "perhaps the most publicized high-school athlete ever to grace the athletic facilities of this state."[61] Krause said he initially was a "Joe Wolf guy," and prior to the selection he did not know whether he should take Wolf or Grant, who looked better when brought in by the Bulls for a workout.

Minutes before making the selection he was still uncertain about who he was going to pick. He even referred to Wolf as "a 6'10" version of Jerry Sloan."[62] According to Krause, Reinsdorf then put his arm around him and said: "Go with your gut. Your gut's good."[63] Krause picked Grant. In Roland Lazenby's *Blood on the Horns*, he reminisced how almost immediately after making the selection,

> Dean Smith called me and ripped my rear end, literally. "How could you do that, you dumbell?" Literally. And Michael said, "What the hell? You took that dummy!?!" And for years that's what he called Horace, dummy. To his face. Dummy. Right to his face. Unbelievable.[64]

The best summer pickup would turn out to be assistant coach Phil Jackson. Krause's protégé showed up for the job interview shaved and properly dressed this time. The player who had impressed Krause at North Dakota by opening car doors while sitting in the backseat was brought on to learn the principles of the triangle offense from Winter, which Collins was reluctant to use during games.

Enamored with Jordan, Collins was as much of a fan as he was a coach of basketball, and he allowed his star player to be himself, instead of teaching him how to function in the team-first system that was the triangle. With Jordan playing the point guard position, the ball would not move around as much as Krause had wanted.

The triangle made the typical playmaker position expendable. To illustrate how hard it was for pass-first ball-dominant point guards to adapt to the triangle, Shawn Fury referred to the 2003-04 Los Angeles Lakers, who signed future Hall of Famer Gary Payton to play at the one position: "For 12–13 years he had the ball in his hands and when you put him in the triangle, where he's no longer going to control the game, it becomes obvious that he's going to struggle in that system."

Krause believed that the triangle was the best offense for a player like Jordan, and Collins's unwillingness to instill it made parting ways inevitable. Krause liked Collins as a person. He even offered to borrow some clothes for Collins early in the 1987-88 season, when the coach lost his luggage at the airport. The 6'6" Collins was over a foot taller than Krause.

However, Krause became skeptical of Collins's coaching style. Instead of the natural, free-flowing offense, the Bulls' players had to memorize 40–50 plays, which were called by Collins on the spot, as he was reacting to the on-court events.

Pippen and Grant immediately grew close to one another, and both really enjoyed Chicago. During his first press conference Pippen said: "Mr. Krause and Coach Collins said they will help me learn to cope with the big city."[65]

From a sports perspective Chicago was a city in transition, mostly thanks to the NFL's Chicago Bears. In fact, Jordan and the Bears' quarterback, Jim McMahon, played golf together. The Bears were always the personification of the city's attitude, how its inhabitants viewed themselves. Pat Reardon explained why: "part of it is that you play a lot of the games outdoors in Chicago, which means that you have got to be really tough, but also there's been an emphasis on defense rather than on offense, that's why the Bears are considered gritty ... when you watch Michael Jordan play, you don't think gritty."

Finesse overshadowed the work ethic and the hours put into

perfecting his game. And Jordan expected the same from everybody joining the team. So when Krause was putting in the 16–18 hour workdays, as far as Jordan was concerned, he was just doing his job. When asked about his relationship with the executive, Jordan said, "[Krause] and I, we keep our distance."[66]

5

A Big Bill

Jordan was about to enter the fourth year of his seven-year rookie contract. He was already the main attraction of the NBA, not just the Chicago Bulls. Making less than a million a year, now Jordan was reportedly looking for a seven-year, $30-million deal, which would mean an over 400 percent raise. The way he drew crowds even during the preseason, with the Bulls averaging close to 13,000 fans per contest in the eight games, definitely made him worth it, but Reinsdorf was already earning a reputation as somebody not willing to overspend and renegotiate contracts, just on principle.

Umlauf said that "Jerry Reinsdorf was one of the best owners to have for an executive, because he hired people and allowed them to do their job, but he was also smart. When he saw something was not working, he would say: 'This isn't working, explain to me why we're doing this.' But I don't think he ever was like 'Jerry, you need to sign this guy.'" She also added that he was a shrewd businessman—while unwilling to give out the largest contract in the NBA at the time to its best player, he still made an exception for Jordan and renegotiated his rookie deal, settling on an eight-year, $25.7-million deal.

Jordan admitted that he was going to play out the contract anyway—which Reinsdorf knew, as Jordan was worried about his reputation—while adding that "if you are a concerned owner and an owner that looks after the best interests of his players, then you would [offer the extension] on your own ... if you consider that individual to be in the top elite class."[1]

At that time Jordan's friend, Knicks center Patrick Ewing, was the highest-paid NBA player ($2.75 million). Even his former teammate, Orlando Woolridge, was making $1.2 million, which was almost twice than the $830,000 Jordan was about to earn. In fact, he was not the highest-paid player on his own team, earning less than the 38-year-old center Artis Gilmore. Jordan was 16 years younger and had a bright future in the league, but his present was at times unbearable.

5. A Big Bill

Jerry Krause spoke with compassion about Jordan being always under surveillance from the fans and the media. "Michael's a cult figure which is a sad thing in some ways because it's not easy being Michael Jordan."[2] Collins struck a similar tone, talking about the "lonely life" that Jordan was forced to live because of his fame. He could not go to a restaurant or a cinema without being approached by fans. Oftentimes he had to leave the arena through a different exit and enter the team bus at a place and moment when he would not be bothered.[3] It is remarkable how Jordan was able to focus on basketball despite the frenzy surrounding him. And it is equally as remarkable that Krause was able to keep the rest of the roster intact.

Gene Banks, who was the sixth man on the team for two seasons, ruptured his Achilles tendon in a Baker League game while he was in Philadelphia for the summer. Krause withheld the remaining $100,000 of his salary and banned him from team facilities. With Pippen and Sellers as the two small forwards, Banks would be third in the rotation anyway. Banks complained that he was treated "like some kind of criminal or like I'm on drugs. It's almost like I was a murderer or that I killed somebody's mother."[4] He still expressed hope to return to the team in March.

The rehab did not go as planned, and instead of rejoining the Bulls, Banks moved to Italy to play for Arimo Bologna. In the summer of 1988, he tried out for the expansion Charlotte Hornets, but did not make the roster primarily due to concerns about him reinjuring the Achilles tendon. Banks would play out the rest of his career in Europe, after a short stint in the Continental Basketball Association.

The way he was treated exposed the double standard in the Bulls, as nobody punished Jordan for his participation in pickup games back in North Carolina. It was pure luck that Jordan did not aggravate his old injury. Because he could not punish Jordan, and also for PR reasons, Krause decided to inflict the punishment on a less-prominent player. He also did it for financial reasons, as by not keeping Banks on the roster, he could save up to $246,000 in cap space.

In the middle of December, with the Bulls 14–6, Krause was looking at Sacramento centers LaSalle Thompson and Joe Kleine, and was willing to part with Brad Sellers to get either one of them. Sellers was the starter, while Pippen was coming off the bench. It was clear that Pippen was a work in progress, as his outside shot was not up to par with his incredible athleticism, yet he showed enough promise to part with Sellers.

The search for a center was caused by Artis Gilmore's slow start to the season. With the Bulls team brimming with youth and energy, the

38-year-old big man found it hard to not only keep up with his teammates, but also adapt to the "showtime" style of basketball that Collins wanted the Bulls to play. In the 24 games (23 starts) he would end up playing for the Bulls, Gilmore averaged 4.2 points and 2.6 rebounds, well below his career averages of 18.8 points and 12.3 rebounds.

The Bulls would also have to pay Gilmore the full amount of money he was owed in his contract if he remained on the roster after January 1, 1988. On December 24, 1987, Gilmore was waived and could then be picked up by any other team or just retire, as he was reportedly contemplating retirement and needed time to think about it.

At least that was Krause's version of events. It was later revealed that if Gilmore agreed to leave, the Bulls promised to organize a night in his honor and retire his number. He refused, so the team let him go unceremoniously. *The Times*' Gene Seymour called Krause's version of events "B.S." and criticized Krause for passing on Johnny Dawkins and Karl Malone, as well as not trading for Ralph Sampson.[5] Asked about whether he wanted to be released, Gilmore replied simply: "I did not say that."[6] He signed with the Celtics on January 8, 1988.

Meanwhile, there were talks of another big man being on the Bulls radar, a member of a less successful center duo than the Olajuwon and Sampson. When the Knicks picked Patrick Ewing first overall in the 1985 NBA draft, their starting oft-injured center Bill Cartwright became expandable. The Knicks tried playing the two together, but the experiment amounted to a mere 24-win season and was soon abandoned. In 1987-88 Cartwright was coming off the bench behind Ewing, and the Bulls were offering the Knicks Brad Sellers and some extras.

Cartwright had entered the NBA as the third pick in the 1979 draft. He was forced to move from his native California to New York to play on one of basketball's biggest stages. Cartwright had no chance at becoming NBA Rookie of the Year that year, not with Larry Bird and Magic Johnson fighting for the crown of the best newcomer in the league. But with averages of 21.7 points and 8.9 rebounds while playing for the Knicks, who were getting substantial media attention at the time, Cartwright would have been a contender in almost any other year. His coach, Red Holzman, mostly appreciated his rookie's work ethic, adding that "Bill Cartwright has the mental and physical ability to be a great basketball player."[7]

Statistically he never went beyond that rookie season, though he remained serviceable until injuries derailed his career, but at age 30, as polite, respectable, and easy to get along with as Cartwright was, it was evident that his time on the Knicks was over. The New York fans were done with him as well; they called him "Medical Bill" because of the number of injuries he had suffered.

Krause's plan to keep his interest in the big man a secret was spoiled by somebody spotting the executive at a Knicks game. The move would come to fruition after the season, during which the Bulls were playing Dave Corzine as the starter as they figured things out, evaluating in what direction to go. So when the team slumped, there was no haste to improve the roster at all costs. While Krause was criticized for how he parted ways with Gilmore and the gaping hole the Bulls still had in the middle, the overall mood about this particular roster was optimistic. However, Krause's best player was in the minority and demanded a private meeting before the January 14 game against the Cavaliers. The meeting must have worked, as the public criticism of Krause subsided on Jordan's part.

The team's turn coincided with Chicago becoming the most important city in the NBA for the first weekend of February 1988, with the fifth All-Star weekend taking place in Chicago Stadium. Making use of the opportunity, team representatives of the National Basketball Players Association, as well as most All-Star players, met in Chicago's Hyatt Regency on February 5 to talk about the recently expired collective bargaining agreement. Frustrated with the owners' reluctance to acknowledge that the NBA was changing, the players agreed to act in unison and enforce their agenda. Part of the reason why the CBA was not agreed upon was because players wanted teams to no longer be able to always match offers for the free agents.

The new agreement, signed in April 1988 for six years, would allow unrestricted free agency, putting an end to general managers' shrewd maneuvers, like when Krause was able to get the pick that he turned into Scottie Pippen from the Knicks in 1986 for Jawann Oldham. According to the new agreement, Oldham would just leave with no compensation for his team, just like Oakley was rumored to do after the season.[8] In April the Bulls signed the powr forward Oakley to a six-year, $6 million contract.

The Eastern Conference All-Stars featured three native Chicagoans in their lineup—Maurice Cheeks, Doc Rivers, and Isaiah Thomas—but none came close to receiving as loud of an ovation during their introductions as Jordan did. In Thomas's case the boos outweighed the applause, which must have been disappointing for the man raised in Chicago's K-Town area. He masked his true reaction behind his signature smile.

Thomas was raised by a single mother, along with six brothers and two sisters. His mother worked three jobs at once and did her best to keep her children out of trouble, not afraid to confront gang members who came to her home to recruit her children.[9] Thomas continued to support charities in his hometown, like the Rev. Jesse Jackson's Operation PUSH or the Ben Wilson Scholarship Fund, established in memory of a Chicago basketball player killed by two gang members. Yet his own city booed him during the most important showcase of the season.

The same fans would boo the Bulls' Dave Corzine, and later Brad Sellers, demanding them to play tougher, more physically. Corzine's minutes in home games were limited so that he would not lose his confidence. Al Vermeil recounted that Corzine was a great character guy, who helped Bill Cartwright immensely when he came to Chicago: "Dave has worked with me for the past three seasons. He was a very hard worker and believed in what we were doing. When Bill had a conversation with Dave, Dave told him that it would be to his benefit to work with me. Dave was never part of the championship team, but in terms of my career at the Bulls, he played a significant role in assisting it in a positive way. I will always be thankful to Dave Corzine."

As for Sellers, he was playing out of position, as both Krause and Collins saw him as a small forward, not the stretch-four he would function as today. Sellers was not particularly happy, but he understood his role on the team, saying, "It's a catch-22. We're winning ballgames, so why mess with a good thing?"[10]

Jordan, on the other hand, could do no wrong. That February weekend upheld his status as the most exciting athlete in the city, as he ended up winning the Slam Dunk Contest and All-Star Game MVP after a 40-point performance. The game solidified Jordan's case for the regular season MVP trophy as well. Jordan may not have seen eye to eye with Krause, but the executive substantially improved his chances of winning the individual achievement by trading Sedale Threatt to the Sonics for Sam Vincent. With guards John Paxson and reserve Rory Sparrow dealing with injuries, Vincent could immediately step in as the starting point guard and keep the Bulls' progress on the right path. He did just that, averaging 13 points and 8.4 assists in the 29 games he appeared in.

The season prior Jordan got just 10 first-place votes despite averaging 37.1 points, 2.9 steals, and 1.5 blocks per game, losing to Magic Johnson, whose Lakers went 65–17 in the regular season. Now, even though Jordan's stats were worse, he was playing on a better team. It presumably could have been even better, but Krause turned down offers for the Suns' Larry Nance and James Edwards. The latter would be traded to Detroit instead, win two championship titles with the Pistons, and eventually play for the Bulls at age 40, retiring in 1996 as an NBA champion. The Bulls could have gotten Edwards for center Mike Brown and a second-round pick. Brown was well liked, a culture guy, but he was not on the same level as Edwards, who as a starter on the 1990 Pistons championship team averaged 14.5 points.

Threatt was complimentary to the Bulls and the player he was traded for, saying, "One thing about Chicago, they've got good people here ... I think [Sam Vincent] is a Chicago kind of a player."[11]

According to Krause, the fans also saw that there was something special about this roster: "there was a curiosity about seeing Michael Jordan after the Olympics but then people started to come out because [the Bulls] were a competitive team."[12] The Bulls were one of the league's biggest attractions, second in attendance as an away team, only behind the Celtics. At home the average attendance was over 18,000 per game, three times more than four years prior, before Jordan entered the NBA.

The Bulls finished the season with 50 wins and 32 losses, good for the third spot, and they were playing the Cleveland Cavaliers in the playoffs. The teams went 3–3 during the regular season, and the Bulls similarly split their six games with the Celtics. The Bulls were no longer the underdogs, although it was clear that they needed a big man if they wanted to become serious contenders.

The Bulls beat the Cavaliers in five and the biggest winners of that series were the rookies, Grant and Pippen. Grant was averaging 8.8 points and 8.4 rebounds throughout the series, and in Game Two he grabbed game-best 14 boards. Pippen jumped into the starting lineup for Game Five, the first playoff start of his career, and rose to the challenge, shooting layups and dunking all over the Cavs. His 24-point performance electrified the crowd in Chicago Stadium, with the fans rooting as loudly for Pippen as they used to do for Jordan. He was named Miller Lite's Player of the Game. While he had every right to celebrate, nobody was prouder than Krause. Not so much of Pippen, but more so of his decision to pick him, saying: "Scottie showed what he can do, but I know he's just scratching the surface."[13]

Krause was proud of the other Bulls players not named Michael Jordan, saying, "All this stuff about a one-man team. I'm sick of hearing it. Guys like Rory Sparrow, Charles Oakley, Dave Corzine—they played their rear ends off. This is 12 people working together."[14]

After the game Ron Harper again visited the Bulls' locker room, despite being on the losing end of the series. He even hugged Krause, and jokingly promised that next season he would get back at Jordan for fouling him.

In the next round the Bulls ran into the Pistons, who overpowered them, targeted Jordan, and were better on the boards. That elusive big man would come in handy playing against Rick Mahorn and Bill

Laimbeer, who subjected Jordan to a series of hard plays known as "the Jordan Rules," according to which whenever the Bulls player drove to the basket, the big men were to knock him down.

Fellow general managers voted Krause Executive of the Year, ahead of the Nuggets' Pete Babcock and the Lakers' Jerry West. The recognition from his peers meant more to him than the trophy.

Krause left for Colorado Springs to evaluate prospects at the United States Olympic trials, immediately after the Bulls were eliminated by the Pistons in five games. At the same time, he was looking for the big man who could challenge the Pistons' Bad Boys, set a hard screen, and battle for rebounds.

One of the names thrown around was Moses Malone, three-time MVP and one-time NBA champion, who at 33 years old was averaging 20.3 points and 11.2 rebounds for the Bullets. Malone was one the best players in the new, unrestricted free agency. Asked whether he would be willing to sign him, Reinsdorf said: "that's a basketball judgment that Jerry Krause has to make first,"[15] either ceding responsibility, publicly supporting his employee, or both.

Krause, as expected, originally declined to comment and later said that the team did not have the cap space to meet his financial demands, which was a negation of Reinsdorf's statement made just a couple of days earlier about Krause's decisive role in roster decisions. Krause was afraid that the veteran would be another misfire similar to Gilmore, not worth going over the cap space, which the Bulls would exceed, despite the 17 percent spike from the previous season.

Another big man considered by the Bulls was Danny Schayes, whose contract with the Nuggets was up and who at 28 was enjoying a breakout year of sorts, averaging 13.9 points and 8.2 rebounds per game. Both would remain the career highs for the son of the 12-time All-Star, Dolph Schayes.

New Jersey Nets general manager Harry Weltman was willing to consider trading the fourth pick of the 1988 draft in exchange for the Bulls' 19th pick and the 1989 first-round pick originally acquired by the Bulls from the Nets as part of the Orlando Woolridge trade.[16] Three top centers in the draft were Rik Smits, Rony Seikaly, and Will Perdue. Smits would not have been available at fourth, as he was drafted by the Pacers with the second overall pick. The same Pacers had earlier offered the Bulls sharpshooter Chuck Person for Charles Oakley. Krause enjoyed that he was receiving offers, bragging, "Two summers ago, I was in a position of having to do things. Now I can sit back and listen."[17]

Smits was one of the players on Krause's radar and he did not want anybody to know that he was scouting him back when Smits was still a junior at Marist College. He said to Vermeil: "I'm not telling anybody, only you and I know that we want him." He sent the conditioning coach to Pittsburgh, to prepare a scouting report from the game Smits was playing in. A year later, he sent Vermeil again.

> Jerry wanted to know what I could do with his body. It's in Baltimore somewhere, I am walking around, the team is getting off the bus and I walk up to him and ask him what's happening, and he tells me there's a basketball game going on. I'll never forget looking at Smits, I'm 5'8", he's 7'2" and I know what's going on, but as he was talking, I was evaluating his frame, looking him up and down. Then I returned home to report to Jerry.

That was one of the scouting missions Krause requested of Vermeil, whom he nicknamed "U-2," after the spy plane.

A couple of days after the Pacers' trade proposal was reported on, Oakley was traded to the Knicks, along with the 19th pick and the 69th pick, for Bill Cartwright, the 11th pick, and the 62nd pick. Krause explained that "the development of forward Horace Grant enabled [the Bulls] to make such a trade. We feel Horace can be a quality player and do an outstanding job in replacing Charles Oakley."[18]

The Bulls traded one of the best power forwards in the league, the best overall rebounder during the previous season, and one of Michael Jordan's best friends for, essentially, two reserve centers, Bill Cartwright, backing up Ewing, and Will Perdue, who was predicted to be a career backup by draft experts. Krause picked Perdue 11th instead of Dan Majerle, whom he wanted to keep a secret from other general managers and select further down the draft.

Majerle played center for Traverse City Central High School in Michigan, where he averaged 37.5 points and 16 rebounds per game as a senior. At 6'6", college coaches knew that he would have to transition to small forward, and some were skeptical about how he would handle it. He ended up playing for Central Michigan, where he earned the nickname "Thunder" for his powerful dunks.

Averaging 23.7 points and 10.8 rebounds per game in his final year for the Chippewas, Majerle was primarily a tough, interior player, and when Krause saw him at one of his camps, he offered to buy Majerle a ticket to Hawaii so that he could rest and not participate in tryouts for other teams. In exchange, Krause would pick him in the third round. Majerle was flattered but he knew that he would be a first-round pick.[19]

Krause praised his toughness, tenacity, and jumping ability, which did not sit well with Jordan, who would remember that in the 1993 NBA Finals, when the Bulls would play the Suns. "Krause thought Majerle was the second coming of Jerry Sloan,"[20] Jordan recounted in Isaacson's book. The team from Arizona picked him 14th overall, with the fans watching the draft in Phoenix booing the selection.

The fans in Chicago were not particularly happy with losing Oakley either, just as they made it known that they would prefer Harvey Grant, Horace's twin brother, or point guard Gary Grant of Michigan, instead of Perdue. The latter was projected to be the starting point guard of the 1988 Olympic team, but his decision to focus on rehabilitating injuries that he picked up during his senior year impacted his stock in the eyes of NBA scouts. Apart from Majerle, Krause also loved 6'6" point guard Brian Shaw, who was picked by the Celtics with the 24th pick. Krause described Shaw as "a very good defensive player," reminiscent of Laker Michael Cooper, with potential of becoming a good shooter.[21]

Bringing in Cartwright and Perdue at the same time was described by Gene Seymour, who would become one of Krause's most vocal critics in the press, as "another Krausism. Meaning, it was an odd approach that the often-irrational Krause took, snaring two players to fill one need, losing the league's premier rebounder in the process."[22] Bulls announcer and former head coach Johnny Kerr defended the move, pointing out that with "[Cartwright], Perdue and Corzine, that gives us 18 fouls at center. Last year, if Corzine fouled out, we were in big trouble."[23] Krause believed that with the two big men, the Bulls were "strong at center for the next 10 years,"[24] adding that Perdue was "the type of player the fans in Chicago [would] like ... a blue-collar, hard-working guy."[25] Vermeil confirmed that opinion, stating that apart from being a hard worker, Perdue was very intelligent and a pleasure to work with.

Furthermore, as great as Oakley was, trading him turned into another case of addition by subtraction, because Krause, Collins, and other coaches were paying attention to how Grant, despite being a physically inferior rookie, was able to hold his own against Oakley in practice. Even though he was the team's second offensive option next to the best offensive player in league history, Oakley continued to complain to Collins about not getting enough touches and not shooting the ball often enough.

Oakley did not hold the trade against Krause, blaming Doug Collins instead: "Everybody thinks Jerry Krause made the deal, but the coach did it.... Doug didn't respect what I did for that team.... I feel I helped the Bulls get respect in the paint, that it gave them more than the great Michael Jordan."[26] The trade would not have occurred without Al Vermeil's input. Krause came to the strength and conditioning coach and asked, "Can you make Horace Grant become strong enough and big enough to play 82 games or more at power forward?" Vermeil said "yes," because he recognized Grant's potential.

In the gym, Horace Grant outworked every Bulls player not named Michael Jordan (1988).

Once Oakley was traded, Vermeil spent the summer working with Grant. "If my memory serves me right, Jerry didn't make Horace go to summer league so he could spend more time training," Vermeil said during our talk.

The coach put him through around 70 workout units during the summer, the most by any Bulls player. Grant reminisced how he had to push Vermeil's Ford Pinto in order to build his strength.[27] During our talk Vermeil clarified: "I had a Ford Taurus station wagon."

Recognized as an innovator, Vermeil considered his training methods to be very basic, mentioning squats, overhead presses, push presses, power snatches, medicine balls, and sprint drills among the exercises he used in his workouts. It was Grant's physical abilities and work ethic that made the difference. Vermeil said: "Horace Grant had the genetics to make me look smart," and while he was trying to replicate the same results with future power forwards, like Dickey Simpkins or Jason Caffey, they simply were not as gifted physically as Grant. When asked why the latter two were not as good as Grant, he used to reply: "They didn't have the same parents."

Apart from Oakley, the Bulls lost an important front office member in Billy McKinney, who worked for two seasons as an assistant coach and a scout until Krause promoted him to assistant vice president of basketball operations for 1987-88. At 33 years old, McKinney became personnel director for the expansion Minnesota Timberwolves.

A native of Zion, Illinois, McKinney first met Krause when he was a 16-year-old two-sport athlete for Zion-Benton High. Krause gave him advice that would influence the rest of his life: "Stick with basketball. You're one of the few 6-footers that I'd recommend to stay with basketball."[28] McKinney attended Northwestern and, despite his short height, became one of the best scorers in the university's history. In the years 1978 through 1985 he played for the Kings, Jazz, Nuggets, and Clippers before retiring with his home state Bulls. He immediately became a member of the coaching staff and soon the front office. There, McKinney benefited from the workroom culture Krause created. Karen Umlauf reminisced that the executive "basically trusted people and allowed them to do their jobs. That always creates a great work environment, a positive work environment."

Krause was happy with the state of the team, and he embraced the competitive aspect of roster building, outsmarting other general managers, stating: "I think organizations are getting better and I think the salary cap is having a real effect on the league. There are two games in this league—the game on the floor and the game in the front office. Each is fascinating in its own right, and I think we're reaching parity in both."[29]

5. A Big Bill

As for temporary absences, the Bulls found themselves without Scottie Pippen during the first month of the season, after he underwent surgery to remove a herniated disk in his lower back. He was playing through pain in the series against the Pistons but made enough of an impression to convince Krause that he was worth investing in and waiting for.

His absence meant that Sellers was again the designated starter, despite losing his spot to Pippen in the playoffs. The Bulls sent Sellers to play in the Los Angeles summer league and work on his post-game. Vermeil worked with Sellers during the summers as well, and while the forward worked hard, "he was a slender player, he did put on some weight, but certain body frames will put on weight and certain won't. The more ectomorph you are, the smaller your bones are, you just won't put on weight. He worked hard, was a smart young man, but simply wasn't a good fit."

As for Bill Cartwright, Vermeil's task was to keep him healthy for two or three seasons. He eventually managed to keep Cartwright playing professional basketball for six more seasons, seven if counting the 29 games he played for the Seattle SuperSonics in 1994-95. Years later the veteran center called Vermeil "the best strength and conditioning coach on the planet."[30]

When the Bulls began the 1988-89 season 6–8, Jordan complained to the executives, the coaching staff, and the press about the roster. Cartwright was second on the team in points per game with 13.8, but his efficiency and defensive play left a lot to be desired. He was also the second-highest earner on the Bulls. When Jordan spoke to Krause about bringing in other players who could help the team win now, Krause replied that Jordan's salary was taking most of the cap space.[31] Nobody doubted that the eight-year, $25 million deal was well deserved, but it limited the Bulls' financial flexibility. In return, Jordan openly criticized Cartwright and the deal Krause made to get him.

To calm things down, Jerry Reinsdorf spoke to the press about the 1989 expansion draft as a chance to free up cap space, expressing hope that "We might be able to move somebody. We'll lose some players and that will free us up. At least we don't have a whole team on guaranteed contracts."[32]

In the middle of December Krause traded forward Ed Nealy, cash, and a 1989 second-round pick to the Phoenix Suns for long-range shooter Craig Hodges. The shooting guard was the reigning league leader in three-point field goal accuracy, making 49.1 percent of his shots in the 1987-88 season. Hodges was brought in because Jordan was again playing big minutes and felt overworked, the only player in the

NBA to average 40 minutes per game or more for the third season in a row.

Oftentimes Pippen played next to him in the backcourt, and Hodges's presence allowed Pippen to be moved to his more natural position at small forward. Krause had talks with the Suns about Hodges in February, and later in June 1988. Now, finally, Krause got his man. Hodges was more than a shooter—he was a locker room presence, a veteran whose opinion Jordan respected, but didn't always agree with. Hodges was very generous with his time, regardless of whether the teammate was first or 12th on the roster. For example, he worked out daily with Brad Sellers on his three-point shooting, but in games Sellers was hesitant to utilize the abilities he acquired during these workouts.

Around the same time, while Krause was still meddling with the roster, perfecting the formula, he had to address the demands of the global market, as European cities, one of which would become the host of the annual McDonald's tournament—Athens, Barcelona, Milan, Moscow, and Paris—all wanted to host the Chicago Bulls as the representatives of the NBA in the four-team exhibition.

Just a year earlier the Boston Celtics had made the trip to Madrid and played great basketball against great teams, such as Yugoslavia and Real Madrid. The tournament was competitive, it was fun, and since the Celtics had made the trip, other NBA teams lacked a reason not to. If approached with the proposition, it would be only common courtesy to participate.

In typical Krause manner, the general manager politely informed the cities interested in bringing in the Bulls that at this moment the franchise had different things on its mind, and participation could hurt its chances of reaching that goal: "Your team has to start too early, it throws training camp off, there's too much pressure on your team. It's disruptive. Our first concern is to win a championship."[33] The NBA eventually went with the Denver Nuggets.

The pressure was on the Bulls, and not everybody in the organization was handling it well. Doug Collins reacted to Sellers complaining to the press about playing time by throwing him out of practice. However, the coach did not see a problem with complaining to the press himself about the pressures of his job: "I don't think people understand how hard it is to win a game in this league. When you put yourself in the position of head coach, you assume all of the responsibility. Basically, everything is placed on your shoulders, and that's a terrific burden to carry."[34] Collins was deflecting pressure, and he soon found himself at odds with Krause and Reinsdorf.

The more success the team had, the less he wanted to listen to their advice. Making players buy into the triangle required a proper salesman, because, as Winter said, "it requires attention to fundamentals, to things like two-hand overhead pass, chest pass, things like that"—things that professional basketball players found basic and boring.[35] And Collins followed that way of thinking as well.

The Bulls won three fewer games than the previous season, 47, and lost eight of their last 10 games. The momentum was not on their side when entering the playoffs. After the season-ending loss, Collins once again dodged responsibility for the overall performance, saying: "I can't make [the players] ready to play. The coaches will do their job, but those 12 guys in the locker room have to be emotionally ready to play."[36]

Jordan was once again doing everything, playing 40 minutes per game and averaging close to a triple-double with 32.5 points, eight rebounds, and eight assists. He was also open to moving permanently to the point guard position, as it allowed him to control the game more. He added: "It would be a change. But it is easier on me. It's just up and down, and I feel a lot better after games. It's something I'll be thinking about, but I could do it."[37] Considering the Bulls' inability to find a point guard who could play alongside Jordan, it was an enticing prospect.

The newspapers were filled with criticism of the team as a whole and Krause specifically as its architect, even as the Bulls were progressing in the playoffs. During our talk, Vermeil called Jerry Krause "one of those basketball historical figures whose historical image is never going to change." He compared him to Generals Douglas MacArthur and George Patton—although with proper proportions—as a historical character whose perception was tainted by incidents which, in Vermeil's opinion, were insignificant and whose legacy deserves a second look. He added: "the press, they paint you with one brush, one color, either positive, negative or neutral, when you did not mean anything. History may treat Jerry Krause a lot kinder when they look at the fact that he was the second winningest general manager of all time."

At the time, though, *Northwest Herald*'s Chris Juzwik eviscerated this incarnation of the Bulls and hoped that the team would be eliminated from the playoffs early, so that it could be broken up,[38] while the *Chicago Tribune*'s Bernie Lincicome mocked Krause's stature by comparing him to team mascot Benny the Bull.[39]

Disappointment with the roster, amid the team's best playoff run in over a decade, shifted the discussion from this year's postseason to the offseason. The Bulls held the pick in the draft from the Nets, which they acquired in the Woolridge trade. The Nets were bad, so the pick was going to be good. So good, in fact, that the Nets were willing to buy it back from the Bulls for their sole star, Buck Williams, but Krause came back to the Nets general manager, Harry Weltman, with a counteroffer of Sellers and the 20th pick that the Bulls also held. Weltman, who was not particularly fond of Krause in the first place, hung up on him and traded Williams to the Blazers. One Bull who was not pleased by that turn of events was Jordan, who wanted to play alongside another fellow Tar Heel.

Unfortunately for Krause, the player who would be perfect for his team, Glen Rice, saw his stock rise after the NCAA tournament, in which his Michigan Wolverines won the title. Krause praised him, saying: "He might be the best pure jump shooter in the draft."[40] The small forward, who could move without the ball, could blossom in the triangle offense. At 32, when Rice finally got to learn the triangle as a third offensive option behind Shaquille O'Neal and Kobe Bryant on the Lakers, he was not as receptive as he would have been had he been taught the system earlier in his career. Phil Jackson, who introduced Rice to the offense, said that he "thought there was a lot of growth area in [Rice's] ability to play without the basketball."[41]

The Bulls went on an almost improbable run, considering the criticism they endured—sans Jordan—throughout the season, beating the Cavaliers 3–2 and then eliminating the New York Knicks 4–2 on their way to the Eastern Conference Finals. Putting out the Cavs took an incredible shot from Jordan in the last seconds of Game Five—eventually dubbed "The Shot"—to win the series for the Bulls. Jordan averaged 39.8 points per game and dished out 8.2 assists, with sharpshooter Craig Hodges as his backcourt partner. After the game Jordan spoke up against his individual performance being presented as the sole reason the Bulls won, stating: "We can't beat Cleveland with a one-man team" and adding that he paced himself through the first part of the game in order to get everybody involved.[42] He scored 30 of his 44 points that night in the second half of the game. Krause struck a similar note, speaking to the press after Game Four about how diversified this new Bulls team was.

At the center of the coverage of the series against the Knicks was the Oakley-Cartwright trade. In the series against the Cavs Grant averaged 13 rebounds per game. In Game One against the Knicks, he scored 19 points and had nine rebounds, while Oakley had three rebounds, two points, and left the game early due to fouls. Cartwright scored 18 points and grabbed 14 boards on Patrick Ewing.

Suddenly, after a whole season of almost unanimous criticism, Krause became a genius. For allowing Grant to become a starter. For getting Cartwright. For keeping enough cap space to fit in Hodges, whose long-distance shooting was hard for the Knicks to contain. Even though Oakley out-rebounded Grant, and Ewing did the same with Cartwright, the Bulls emerged victorious from the series, for the time being putting away the criticism Krause had to endure for making the trade.

On Friday May 19, the Bulls eliminated the Knicks. During the team's stay in New York, it was reported that Jordan's suite cost the Bulls $2,500 per night. The press reacted to these revelations with outrage.

If the team would not win the series in six games, it would have to fly back to New York for the Sunday rematch. Instead, only Krause flew there for the draft lottery, in which the Bulls got the sixth pick. He told the press that Jordan would get a voice in deciding what to do with the pick and who to draft.

The rumor was that the team would once again pick a big man, after ... picking a big man in the previous draft. Will Perdue was not playing much, but he was informed before the season what he was getting into. He might not have anticipated appearing in a mere 30 games in his rookie year and playing a total of 190 minutes, but he was patient; he knew his time would come.

Krause wanted him on the roster, because he was convinced, as he said numerous times, that for two years there would not be an interesting big man in the draft. Krause held him so dearly that when the Timberwolves picked up Pistons starting big man Rick Mahorn in the expansion draft, Krause refused to trade the center for Perdue. He offered Sellers and a second-round pick, but the expansion franchise was not interested. Mahorn's agent even wrote a letter to Krause, asking if he really liked his client. He did, but not enough to put out a package that would work for the Timberwolves. The Sixers did, and Mahorn eventually moved to Philadelphia.

The same day the Bulls drew the sixth pick, they won Game One of the Eastern Conference Finals in Detroit. Krause complained about the Pistons' physical style of play, which he characterized as "contamination and prostitution of all basketball," complaining that basketball "used to be a finesse sport."[43] While the Pistons eliminated them in six games, it was becoming clear that the Bulls were finally surrounding Jordan with proper talent.

After leaving small forward Charles Davis, big man Jack Haley, and point guard Sam Vincent unprotected in the 1989 expansion draft, and with Craig Hodges being a free agent, the logical thing to do was select a guard to play alongside Jordan. Among the players available to them in the draft were two native Chicagoans, point guard Tim Hardaway and shooting guard Nick Anderson. The latter was a declared Bulls fan, and prior to the draft, he said: "If it is the Bulls it would be nice, but wherever I go, I'll be a happy person. I just hope to go as high as I possibly can."[44] Both Hardaway and Anderson would cross paths with the Bulls later in their careers.

Jordan reportedly wanted George McCloud, a 6'6" guard who could play both backcourt positions, which would suit Jordan perfectly; he was still considering playing at point guard. Following his pre-draft visit to Chicago, McCloud was optimistic and looking forward to playing with Jordan: "I am sure he has a lot to say in that organization. It would be great for me to play next to a player like him."[45] Krause was, as always, mute regarding the pick, calling the draft the "weirdest he has ever seen."[46] There was no consensus number one pick, which put all the pressure on the teams picking in front of the Bulls.

They were able to find their point guard of the future in that draft, but it was not with the sixth pick. With their 18th pick the Bulls selected B.J. Armstrong, a 6'2" playmaker from Iowa, a player who was eager to learn and work on his game. His size would prove to be a subject of constant debate and the team would look for a replacement for him almost annually, just like it did with Paxson. Armstrong was a lifelong fan of the Detroit Pistons and his family was rooting for them, even when they played the Bulls.

With the sixth pick Krause selected Stacey King, a center, which in the light of the GM's declaration that there were no interesting big men in the draft made for another smoke screen, the amount of which was already overclouding the executive's status among the press. King was ecstatic about moving to Chicago, saying that playing with Jordan was "a dream come true because he is one of my idols."[47] The University of Oklahoma standout hoped that playing next to the best basketball player in the world would allow him to get the ball more and score.

With the 20th pick, which the Bulls were able to acquire for Sellers from the Sonics, Krause picked small forward Jeff Sanders. Krause was so happy that he said: "If you would have told me we'd get B.J. and Jeff Sanders, I would have kissed everyone in this room."[48] Armstrong would turn out great, King was OK, but Sanders would suffer a foot injury and miss training camp, which would hamper his development and prevent him from playing a significant part with the Bulls.

Brad Sellers's time in Chicago ended after three seasons and 242 games. Sellers learned about being traded on the phone, as he was eating at Olive Garden. Jordan, who never was a fan of Sellers's game, called the restaurant and asked to talk to his soon to be former teammate. He told him: "They're trading you to Seattle tomorrow. Good luck, B."[49]

Prior to the draft, Krause was welcoming the praise bestowed upon Coach Collins, because he could bask in it as well. Interviewed for a

In suits from left: Doug Collins, Johnny Bach, Phil Jackson, Tex Winter, four coaches who shaped the Bulls dynasty (1988).

profile piece on Collins for the *Philadelphia Daily News*, Krause said: "I had scouted him in college, I knew him as a pro player. He had a mind I respected, and I was impressed by what he turned in. He was an outstanding communicator, and I wanted a young guy.... I also wanted someone I thought could relate to Michael. It was a gut feeling."[50]

6

You Always Remember Your First

Phil Jackson should have been one of the candidates for the New York Knicks head coaching job when Rick Pitino left to work at the University of Kentucky. General manager Al Bianchi wanted Jackson, just as he reportedly wanted John MacLeod, Fred Carter, and Mike Dunleavy. MacLeod turned him down. He preferred to stay coaching the Mavericks, which were far from a stable and respectable organization. Carter was an assistant for the Sixers, Dunleavy for the Bucks. Jerry Krause reportedly prohibited Jackson from auditioning for the job before the draft concluded. Krause said that he did not get any calls regarding Jackson. Doug Collins supposedly intervened, but to no avail. He did not know that Krause had already settled on Jackson as the new head coach of the Bulls.

Krause's trust in Jackson was so big that he told the players that whenever they had a problem, they should go to their coach first, and whatever he decided, Krause supported. He would then tell them the story about when he was a child and would ask his father for something. Instead of giving a definite answer, the father would respond: "What does your mother say?" If she said "no," then the answer was "no." Unknowingly, Krause was putting a lot of power into Jackson's hands, which would hurt him in the long run.

On Thursday, July 6, 1989, Collins was invited to a morning meeting, at which he was informed that despite a year remaining on his contract with the Bulls, he was fired. Originally he was asked to resign, but he refused, so he was let go. The meeting supposedly lasted only a couple of minutes. Both Krause and Reinsdorf spoke about "philosophical differences" as the reason for the dismissal, with the latter adding that he appreciated Collins, but he prioritized the "health and welfare of everyone in our organization."[1]

Collins was 37, and during his three seasons as head coach the Bulls continued to improve, but he continued to have issues with Krause. The head coach refused to play Will Perdue, even though he promised to give him around 10 minutes per game, and was especially tough on Brad Sellers, who he never wanted on the team in the first place. Collins's attorney John Langel pushed the narrative that Collins was fired by Krause, adding that "Doug is extremely popular,"[2] although he did not specify in what circles. Krause said that he had no issues with Collins. During the interview with Wojnarowski he said that he would love having him as a neighbor, but not necessarily as the head coach of his team. Jordan, for his part, washed his hands of the matter, refusing to take any responsibility for the firing.

People like *Philadelphia Daily News*' Bill Conlin called Collins "one of the brightest, most intense coaches in the NBA, a future Bill Walsh in his sport," while referring to Krause and the Chicago White Sox's Larry Himes as "two of the worst general managers in sports."[3] Kurt Begalka of the *Northwest Herald* suggested that Krause and Reinsdorf "envied the young coach's stamina" and criticized their roster decisions, while misspelling Karl Malone's name.[4] The *Daily Tar Heel*'s Doug Hoogervorst claimed that unlike Krause and Reinsdorf, "Collins has the idea that team isn't spelled with an 'I,' and that it takes five players working together to win consistently in the NBA,"[5] ignoring the fact that Collins was playing Michael Jordan for 40 minutes per game and relied on him to bail out the team in crucial moments of games.

In his autobiography, Scottie Pippen wrote that "by favoring Michael, Doug [Collins] stunted the growth of everyone else, including me,"[6] adding that there was a different set of rules for Jordan and the rest of the team.

The *Chicago Tribune*'s Bob Verdi argued that "Collins probably would still be the Bulls' coach if he had been more obedient and less popular, but Collins is into winning, not heeling. He's a leader, not a lap dog."[7]

Sam Smith reported that part of Collins's leadership was not listening to criticism, like when he didn't allow Tex Winter to attend practices because he spoke his mind about certain of Collins's coaching decisions. It was soon revealed that Collins lobbied to get Krause fired and for Reinsdorf to give him his job. This offended Reinsdorf, who had a deep sense of loyalty and who saw Collins turning on Krause, his biggest advocate, as the ultimate betrayal.[8] Collins wanted to influence roster decisions and was constantly looking for a proper point guard for his offensive system. The issue was that he seemed to change his mind on what he wanted the team to play.

Collins presumably always saw Phil Jackson as an adversary, somebody who was constantly banking on his mistakes and would jump on the first possibility to take over the team. Winter was seen by him and many others as Krause's man, but, as David Halberstam pointed out, "he was no one's man but his own, and he was always completely honest. That was what appealed to so many people about Tex—he was simply so straight, and he played no political games."[9]

Jackson was six years older than Collins, a less accomplished player, but a two-time NBA champion. Krause said that "Phil's primary asset is his brain. He has great curiosity. The brightest people I've been around know they don't know it all."[10] Jackson had more experience as head coach than Collins but had collected it in the CBA, which was a plus, because he got to be closer to the game and was exposed to various approaches to keeping the players accountable and in check. In Melissa Isaacson's book on the Bulls, Jackson recounts: "I've been on clubs where trainers would wake players up for practice, where they would wash players' clothes and become babysitters."[11] He decided to do the opposite, introducing rules but giving the players certain freedoms within them.

This approach would be developed on the Bulls within a year or two. For the moment, though, Jackson was grateful for finally getting the opportunity to be the head coach: "It was a long process. At times, I wondered if anyone up there was watching, but Jerry Krause was and I was given the opportunity."[12]

As Jackson did scouting on rival teams, in his place Krause employed the son of his old friend, Clarence Gaines, Jr., who also got to serve as assistant to the general manager. One of the lessons the son got from his famous father: "remember that teachers and coaches don't make any money."[13] He did not care; the calling was too strong to ignore.

To fill Jackson's spot as assistant coach, the Bulls picked Youngstown State's Jim Cleamons. The two hirings allowed Jackson to focus on building team chemistry. And he was not the only one.

Al Vermeil used to organize a golf tournament for the players, called the BSF Open, in Lincolnshire. The whole team was invited, but Jordan did not participate. Vermeil recounts that he invited him once, "but he was a good golfer and he did not want to play with us hackers." He laughs and adds that the best player during the tournaments was usually Ed Nealy, a 6'11" power forward who would return to the Bulls prior to the 1989-90 season, after Krause traded him mid-season to the Suns.

The usual BSF Open participants were Grant, King, Perdue, Cartwright, Paxson, and later on Toni Kukoč and Steve Kerr. Vermeil credits the competition with getting Kukoč hooked on golf. The tournament was an annual tradition and ended along with the championship run in 1998, because the young players were not as much interested in golf.

After a promising preseason—in which Jackson got a win over his University of North Dakota head coach, Bill Fitch, when the Bulls beat the Nets 108–82 on October 16 in Ontario—the Bulls got their first official test when they played against the Cleveland Cavaliers on November 3, 1989. The season opener was more of the same, however, with Jordan scoring 54 points, including 10 in overtime, and leading the Bulls to victory. "In a situation like that, it's natural to rely on Michael ... and when it comes to a point that you need to make shots, he's going to put them in,"[14] said Jackson.

Still, the mood around the organization was different, more relaxed and upbeat. Asked about the Collins firing, Krause said: "We took a little bit of pounding, but you know what? We didn't lose one single season-ticket holder."[15] How could they, with Michael Jordan on the roster?

The expectations were high. In the poll of writers covering the NBA, the Bulls were picked to win the league, despite the coaching change. Doug Collins was picked as most likely to be hired as the next head coach.[16] Meanwhile the Bulls were able to remain healthy, with six players appearing in at least 80 games during the season. That was thanks to Vermeil and trainer Mark Pfeil, who Jordan referred to as "magic man," adding: "In the five years I've been here, he's saved me from not playing a lot of games."[17]

Pfeil would resign after the season, following a 10-year tenure on the Bulls. As for Vermeil, he explained to me that during season preparations he focused on two things, power and speed, because "when you have a long season, the first thing to go is your strength, you must maintain that, and if you don't, you put more stress on the joints and the tendons, and then you develop tendinitis."

The Bulls finished the season with 55 wins. The roster remained intact, despite strong rumors of landing Adrian Dantley, the Dallas Mavericks' veteran small forward, who was traded there by the Detroit Pistons just before they won their first NBA championship. Because he missed out on the title with the Bad Boys, he was open to joining the Bulls, who in exchange were supposed to sacrifice one draft pick. However, before anything came of it, Dantley broke his right leg just 34 seconds into a game against the Blazers in Portland, which put an end to his season and any further talks of a potential trade.

Prior to the playoffs, Krause said that the Bulls were ready "to go to war with the people we've got. We've done it all year and have won a lot of games."[18]

The Bulls held the second-round pick in the draft and Krause considered selecting Hank Gathers, Loyola Marymount's 6'7" power forward, whose three games he attended during the 1989-90 season. He would have attended more had Gathers not collapsed during a game against the Portland Pilots. Gathers died because of a heart-muscle disorder.

During the season, five Eastern European players made their NBA debuts: Sarunas Marculionis, Vlade Divac, Drazen Petrovic, Zarko Paspalj, and Alexander Volkov. Sensing that there was some potential there, much to his displeasure, Krause was seen scouting players in Europe. He found one worthy of attention, but as usual, he refused to share the information with almost anyone.

The Bulls once again made the Eastern Conference Finals and once again ran into the Pistons. Asked about his team's chances, Krause said: "We know we're a better team than we were at this time a year ago. Phil has made a huge difference. We think we have the capability to play with anybody at anytime."[19] The Pistons needed all seven games to eliminate the Bulls. In Game Seven they won by 19 points and the Bulls just could not get anything going. Scottie Pippen had a migraine, which caused him to score just two points. Grant made three of his 17 attempts, Hodges went three from 13. There was nobody on the bench experienced enough to step in and help Jordan in such an important game.

Krause destroyed the bathroom door and one of the toilets out of frustration. He probably knew that the blame for the loss was going to be placed on him, because he refused to sacrifice draft picks for tested veterans in the middle of the season. Jordan was the one who started publicly piling on Krause.

"I'm all for veterans. Rookies take too long to develop," said Jordan, adding: "But I'm not the general manager."[20]

He could have just gone to Krause and demanded he bring in veterans, but blame needed to be placed; the public needed to know who was responsible for the loss.

"Within a few days after that loss to Detroit the first two guys in the weight room were Scottie Pippen and Horace Grant. That's when I knew the next season was going to be special," said Vermeil.

The Bulls had $1.5 million under the cap, and while there were murmurs of some players being underpaid and displeased with what they were getting, Krause was hoping to bring in an established free agent. One of his targets was Sam Perkins, whom Jordan wanted and who wanted to play with Jordan. Purposely or not, the best player on the

Bulls was refusing to acknowledge the bigger picture, as well as refusing to understand how much cap space was needed to bring in Perkins, who was considering leaving Dallas for either Chicago or Los Angeles. The Bulls were rumored to be willing to part with Grant, as well as the 22nd and 29th draft picks. Perkins reportedly wanted a six-year deal worth $18 million, which would limit the Bulls' cap flexibility for that time period.

In the summer the Bulls would sign Grant to a three-year deal worth around $2 million per season. Perkins got his wish with the Lakers and became one of the highest-paid players in the NBA.

Krause indicated that no big trade was coming, saying: "We don't need to make a lot of changes. If we'd had the home-court advantage on the Pistons, I believe we'd be in the Finals now."[21]

The criticism was not falling on deaf ears and Krause exchanged the 22nd pick, as well as two future second-round picks with the New Jersey Nets, for shooting guard Dennis Hopson. The Nets had drafted Hopson third overall in 1987, and in his third year as a pro he finally became the starter. At 25, he was about to enter the role of backup to Jordan. The trade was made solely with the Pistons in mind, as Krause commented: "We feel Detroit has eight players who can start, and in adding Dennis, that's a starting player who will come off the bench. He can shoot the ball and put it on the floor with any of our guards."[22]

Hopson turned out to be a one-season rental exchanged for the first-round pick, unlike the second-round pick that Krause decided to keep. With it, he picked a 6'11" left-handed playmaker out of Croatia, Toni Kukoč, who he considered to be better than his compatriot, Drazen Petrovic. Krause learned about the Croatian prospect from Leon Douglas, who at the time was playing in Pistoia, Italy. The way Krause told the story to Wojnarowski years later, Douglas approached him during a playoff game against the Pistons and told him Kukoč was a special player "who plays guard in [the Italian] league."[23] For a year Krause was checking on him, monitoring his stats, and got to see him on a tournament in Spain. After seeing him in person, Krause was impressed and presumably put him in the top five of that year's draft.

There is a gaping hole in Krause's version of the Kukoč origin story—the Croat moved to Italy in 1991, a year after the Bulls drafted him. Douglas learned of him simply because everybody in European basketball knew who Kukoč was. In 1990, as a 22-year-old, he was selected the best basketball player in Europe for the first time in his career ... and he was there for the Bulls to select him in the second round of the draft.

A month later Yugoslavia won the 1990 Goodwill Games in Seattle, and Kukoč dunked on Alonzo Mourning in the final game of the competition. That dunk and that win put the league on notice—the Bulls had drafted a world-class talent. Driven by doubt, despite being courted by Krause throughout the whole season, Kukoč would sign with Benetton Treviso in Italy. That courtship further soured the tense relationship between Jordan, Pippen, and Krause, extensively described in Sam Smith's *The Jordan Rules*.

The immediate reactions to the pick were largely negative. *Journal Gazette*'s Al Lagatolla wrote that with the pick Krause "proved that he should be locked up on draft day, just throw away the key until he can't do anymore harm."[24] Even in his moment of triumph, following Kukoč's stellar performance in the Goodwill Games, Krause still could not catch a break from the press. *Northwest Herald*'s Kevin Ball wrote that following the win by Yugoslavia, "Krause wiped away a strand of drool from the corner of his mouth."[25] There was nothing new in the way Krause was ridiculed, always with the focus on his *physis*. Even Roland Lazenby wrote a Phil Jackson story about how Krause was in the team bathroom when it was Jordan's "turn" to use it. Jackson told the story to show that Krause did not respect boundaries, but there were undoubtedly better examples of that.[26]

During the Goodwill Games, Jordan participated in batting practice with the White Sox, fulfilling his lifelong dream of experiencing baseball on a professional level. Krause's comments about the workout were good-natured, as he joked: "I've kidded him from time to time, 'Michael, you're going to find things a little faster than you think.' If he hits too well, I don't want Jerry Reinsdorf trying to steal him."[27] Jordan however, always the one to respond to a challenge even when none was issued, recounted that Krause told him beforehand that he "wouldn't hit one out of the infield."[28] Only two people knew whether Krause said that to Jordan.

People expecting a roster overhaul were undoubtedly disappointed, as the GM was not only reluctant to part with Grant, but also not willing to give up on Cartwright. Not yet. Krause's Sonics counterpart, Bob Whitsitt, turned his attention to the Bulls' big man after being rejected by the Celtics, who were not willing to part with Robert Parish. Krause denied reports that Cartwright was on the trading block. Then again, he also denied reports that the Bulls were pursuing veteran power forward Cliff Levingston, and a couple of days later it was announced that the Bulls were signing the 30-year-old former Piston and Hawk. This was his common practice, one that made him so unpopular with journalists, whose job was to report on the trades that Krause was actually making as well as the ones he was attempting to make.

6. You Always Remember Your First

Rick Telander stopped trusting Krause in 1995:

> I won't say he lied, but what he told me was complete bullshit and he knew it. They were playing Toni Kukoč at power forward, and we know he's no power forward, he's a two or a three, not a four. We were looking at the players that were available and there were two players available, one was Jayson Williams, the other was Dennis Rodman. Everybody knows Rodman's crazy, but I still ask Krause: "What about Rodman?" And he's like "No, never, no." And he said that as if it was absolute, instead of saying something like "Rodman would be an incredible reach, but never say never." I reported that "Bulls would never take Dennis Rodman." And when they traded for him, I didn't like that, because Krause was messing with my job. Up to that point I believed him. Then I didn't.

That unpopularity only grew when it was revealed that Krause was lobbying for reporters to be barred from courtside before NBA games. He probably was not the only GM who saw them as a distraction to his players, but he was the most vocal about it. According to a survey conducted by the Professional Basketball Writers Association, the Bulls were the least media-accessible organization in the league.[29]

When there was no way of keeping the negotiations with Levingston a secret, Krause eventually admitted that the two sides were talking. The Bulls were able to get him for half the price that the Hawks were offering him before the previous season, with a year left on his deal. To get Levingston the Bulls sent Jeff Sanders to Miami, even though they had been so big on him the year prior. According to Krause, the move was made with the championship in mind. Prior to signing Levingston, the Bulls were negotiating a sign-and-trade deal with the Clippers for Joe Wolf, who would certainly appease Jordan to a certain extent, making up for not taking him in the 1987 draft. Three years into his NBA career, Wolf was averaging 5.8 points and 3.7 rebounds as a bench player for the other L.A. team.

However, if Krause indeed had a chance to win some of Jordan's goodwill back with getting either Wolf or Levingston, he wasted that opportunity after going public with a statement about Jackson reducing the star player's minutes from 39 to 35 minutes per game, with hopes of Jordan being rested for the playoffs. For Jordan, that was similar to issuing an open challenge, and the statement did initially put Jackson in a tough spot, almost at odds with his superstar. The last minutes restriction issued by Krause, back when Stan Albeck was the coach, had brought about the first crack in their relationship.

Another one would appear with Krause's visit to Yugoslavia in early December, made in order to get to know Kukoč and convince him to move to Chicago. They met again in Italy. Journalists reported that

Krause offered him $27 million for seven years—a highly exaggerated number, which in reality turned out to be $15 million for six years. In case the European star made up his mind, the GM left $1.75 million under the cap.

Kukoč eventually got cold feet and decided to move to Italy, fearing that he was not yet ready for the NBA. He also got handsomely paid there, as Benetton gave him a six-year deal for $24 million.

Disappointed, but not scorned, Krause continued his search for the perfect complementary players to Jordan and Pippen that would allow the team to win now. Hopson's trade did not turn out as planned. Krause offered him to the Sonics for swingman Dale Ellis, whose issues with the law, as well as disruptive behavior, hurt his trade value, but not enough for the team from Washington to even consider trading him for Hopson. Hopson was not playing up to his standards, but he was enjoying the role. Krause recounted: "He told me coming here has taken the weight of the world off his shoulders."[30] Moving from 32 to 12 minutes per game was easy; playing against Jordan and responding to his challenges during the workouts turned out to be much harder. Years later Krause acknowledged bluntly that "Dennis Hopson couldn't handle Michael."[31]

Krause tried to trade him mid-season for the Nuggets' veteran Walter Davis, but the Colorado franchise presumably wanted a first-round pick in return, which the GM refused to part with. Davis went to the Blazers and Jordan went to the media to publicly criticize Krause by saying: "If I were GM, we wouldn't be in this position, we certainly would be much stronger."[32]

While Jordan was disgruntled about the roster decisions, Pippen was dismissive of the praise that Krause was showering on Kukoč. He also wanted to renegotiate his contract, which the management promised it would do before Christmas. With no deal in place in January, he issued an ultimatum: either pay me or trade me. According to his six-year rookie contract he was earning $765,000, with $1 million and $1.25 million for the next two seasons. Jordan agreed that Pippen deserved more money, which was a sound statement for him to make, albeit without taking into account how NBA contracts worked.

Will Perdue was complaining about playing time and so was Stacey King. Perdue was working hard in the gym and in practice, but he could not get big minutes. King found himself playing behind Grant, whom almost nobody on the team could outwork. Hopson was crumbling under the weight of Jordan's abuse. And yet, the Bulls were on track to set the best record in franchise history. With 61 wins, they finished first in the conference and second in the league, behind the Blazers, who were also able to snatch Davis from the Nuggets.

Because of the latter, Jordan refused to speak to Krause, but he continued to speak *about* Krause to the media. And the topics he wanted to discuss did not include the decisions to pick Grant over Wolf or passing on Johnny Dawkins, who was out for the season after just four games. Even when the Bulls were the best team in their conference, Jordan refused to give credit when it was due, saying: "I never said we didn't have the team to win," and adding just a few sentences later that "No one predicted we'd be in the position we are now."[33]

Still, not all journalists unanimously sided with Jordan. *The Daily Breeze*'s Mitch Chortkoff wrote that "Krause could rub people the wrong way ... but his heart is in the right place," and praised the GM for how hard he was willing to work in order to improve the Bulls' roster.[34] The *Los Angeles Times*' Mark Heisler was on to something when he asked the obvious question: "Maybe Jordan's greatness is such that he doesn't require the normal complement of helpers?"[35] Clifton Brown of *The New York Times* also praised Krause, who admitted in late March that "everything we've done in the last six years has been designed to win the world championship."[36]

Indeed, it might have been championship or bust for this particular Bulls team, and when talking to Brown, Krause recognized something that was now evident for anyone who was willing to suspend their bias: "Michael and I have one major thing in common: we both want to win in the worst way. I want to win as badly as he does, if not more."[37] Judging from the abuse he continued to endure in order for the Bulls to keep winning, that was not a far-fetched statement.

The Bulls played in the 1991 playoffs like a team possessed. They lost only one game on their way to the finals, including a sweep of the Pistons in the Eastern Conference Finals. The Bulls were stronger and tougher than ever.

Krause attributed this to his player selection process, which he explained as follows: "We look for resilient bodies that are strong, that can take the rigors of a 100-game season, and look like they'll last for 10 years."[38]

That sounded somewhat impersonal, but it was not the general manager who was responsible for molding the team into a collective. That was the job of the staff and the coaches. Al Vermeil explained: "When I coach, I coach people, not players and I never focus on winning or losing as a strength coach, I focus on the results and keeping their personalities up. They're being already evaluated by everybody, so my role was being positive, talk to them about their families. They're human beings, they're people. And people forget that. Coaches forget that."

Krause was supposed to pick out proper players, who could

physically endure playing in the NBA and function as parts of a team. And in the Eastern Conference Finals they out-rebounded the Pistons, who had been bullying them for three years straight, by over six boards per game.

"The magic number is 15, we've got it down to four. We're getting closer every day. Craig Hodges and I started counting down and we've missed only one beat,"[39] said Krause prior to the finals, referring to the 15 games that the Bulls needed to win in order to get the title.

The Pistons were the gatekeepers that the Bulls had to defeat, but waiting in the ultimate series of 1990–91 were the Lakers, led by that season's MVP, Magic Johnson. And when the Lakers took Game One, the talk about Jordan not having enough support returned. Then the Bulls won four straight and claimed their first title.

"I don't want credit. I want the ring. I'm a Chicago guy, I wanted this for Chicago,"[40] said Krause.

Jordan dominated in the series as he usually did. His greatness should never be taken for granted. However, the rest of the team did not disappoint. Pippen averaged 20.8 points, 9.4 rebounds, 6.6 assists, and 2.4 steals. Grant had 14.6 points and 7.8 rebounds. Paxson was averaging 13.4 points on 65 percent shooting. The players that Krause surrounded Jordan with delivered in their debut on the biggest of stages. In Game Five Pippen had 32 points and Paxson scored 20.

Pippen finally got his contract extension after Game Two: five years for $18 million, coming into effect after his two remaining rookie-deal seasons, which tied him up with the Bulls until the summer of 1998. Pippen felt validated and satisfied with the contract he got.

The Bulls won their first championship on June 12, and two days later the *Chicago Tribune* was already writing about what they needed to do to repeat. Krause had waited six years for the title, but once it came, the pressure was on him to re-sign Cartwright and Paxson. The same Cartwright whose elbows were lethal weapons, who was old and injury prone. The same Cartwright who Krause so defiantly stuck with and defended from media scrutiny could now "resent [the Bulls'] financial conservatism"?[41] It was more of an issue of contract length, as Cartwright wanted a three-year deal; the Bulls were offering two.

Even as the city was celebrating its heroes, first at O'Hare International Airport and then in Grant Park, Krause could not catch a break. Ira Winderman of the *South Florida Sun Sentinel* wrote that "while Jordan & Co. revel in their success, Bulls Vice President Jerry Krause has plenty of work to get done in the next few weeks,"[42] as if the success and the celebrations were not his to participate in, even though it was his city. And it was *his* success.

Patrick Reardon explained: "I did not get any sense of these players being Chicagoans, if you know what I mean. They mostly lived in the wealthy north suburbs or the rich residential towers near the lake. They weren't knitting themselves into the fabric of the city in any way I could tell." Reardon did not mean that they simply cared about winning the title in a different way than the people who were born and raised there:

> I'd say the Bulls' players and organization wanted to win the championship because they were basketball players and wanted to be seen as the best basketball players in the world. For Chicagoans, the championship was more than an athletic victory. In some way, it was an endorsement of the city as something special. It said, in some deep way, that Chicago was a winner in the world. A winner not just in basketball, but in a psychological and spiritual way.

Jerry Reinsdorf recognized that during the championship celebrations, when he said: "I'm happier for Jerry Krause. This is great vindication."[43]

This new NBA championship team became part of something bigger, as it fit right into Mayor Richard M. Daley's program of revamping the image of the city. Sean Dinces writes that the rise of the Bulls coincided with Daley's plan of "transforming downtown Chicago into a world-class leisure and cultural destination for tourists, professionals, and businesspeople."[44] Unlike his father, Richard J. Daley, the 1989-elected mayor could no longer rely on the Democratic machine. Instead, he relied on corporate donations. Daley Jr. entered office following a special election, held because of the death in office of Harold Washington, the first African American mayor of the city of Chicago.

Larry Bennett characterizes Daley Jr. as representative of the post-federal-era mayors of the early 1990s, focused on promotion of their cities as "world-class." Through his years in office, Daley focused on three fundamentals of his program: "promotion of Chicago as a global city, the reorganization of a variety of municipal and independent agency service functions, and social inclusivity at the elite level."[45] One of the ways of showing that a city belonged in this new world was through sports, such as Chicago's hosting of the 1994 World Cup games, including the opening game of the tournament played on Soldier Field, the home of the NFL's Chicago Bears.

Before the World Cup was to take place, there were the Bulls, who were new and fresh. The athletic bodies of the basketball players were physically attractive and aesthetically appealing, with Jordan serving as the perfect salesman to all generations. On the bench was Phil Jackson, an intellectual, who was open and outspoken. Jackson was hip, he seemed to be in touch with the times, a true Renaissance man who had experimented with drugs in the past and was into Eastern philosophy.

But that was just the surface of the organization, the one that the NBA was marketing. Underneath was a group of NBA lifers, whose old-school work ethic gave the team its identity. Krause described the coaching staff as "the best in basketball. They bring to us so much experience and brilliance."[46] Tex Winter, Johnny Bach, and Jim Cleamons were not going anywhere. Jordan, Grant, and Pippen all had long deals. And when the Bulls extended Paxson and Cartwright for three seasons each, it was evident that they wanted to run it back not only this season, but for at least the next three years.

It took some time, but Krause seemed to be convinced that he found the right combination of players and personnel. The Bulls were set for a bright future and Chicago could now be proud of its native son.

Except it never was.

Krause said numerous times that being the general manager was the hardest job to do in sports, because "if you make a mistake, you have to live with it."[47] He ignored or failed to notice that one decision could also make someone the most loathed person in all of sports.

7

Suffering from Success

In 2005, ESPN2 and ESPN Classic began airing a show about the biggest scapegoats in sports. The title, *The Top 5 Reasons You Can't Blame...*, was supposed to describe the nature of the show, which intended to look for forgiveness for sports people in the eyes of the general public by arguing that, well, they were not to blame for something that happened. One of the episodes was devoted to Jerry Krause, who presumably was the person most in need of absolution for breaking up the Bulls dynasty.

While it is somewhat questionable why there is no blame cast on Jordan retiring just before the start of the 1993-94 season, the episode provides a proper explanation concerning how complicated a job Krause had. The introduction, in which some of the smartest, most competent people in sports writing are piling on Krause, shows just how loathed he was, despite bringing six championship titles to Chicago.

And despite him wanting recognition for everybody in the franchise. These were his baseball roots talking, as Lee Lowenfish, in his book on baseball scouting, writes that the most devoted, "pure" baseball scouts "had traditionally avoided using the *I* pronoun."[1] This had been a mainstay of the baseball world since its inception, best expressed by a quote from Paul Krichell, the head scout of the New York Yankees, who said: "scouts should be one hundred percent organizational men," adding that "credit for any player reaching the major leagues should be given to the team's entire scouting system."[2]

However, when Krause thanked everybody in the organization for their efforts back in 1991, he was criticized for not praising Michael Jordan enough.[3]

Jordan did make use of his special status by skipping the customary White House visit, made annually by the reigning champions. Other players were forced to attend the meeting with President George Bush, but to save face of the organization, Krause said that the visit was not mandatory. Jordan found time to host *Saturday Night Live* in New York, but he could not go to D.C. with his teammates two days later.

Horace Grant openly criticized the special treatment Jordan was receiving, and instead of toning down the tensions within the team, at least in the media, head coach Phil Jackson understood that he would be better off siding with Jordan. Jackson said he was not surprised "that Horace would say that because he doesn't get as many shots as Michael and he has to do all the rebounding and the dirty work."[4] Translation: Grant was jealous of Jordan. And it was Jordan who went to the media to inform them that the issue was resolved. He explained that "Horace didn't know exactly what was going on."[5]

He did; he just had to accept the double standard, just like all the other members of the franchise. Grant predicted that if Jackson and Krause let that slide, it would lead to "the death of the team."[6] Publicly, Krause was defending Jordan, as he said prior to the season: "It ain't easy being Michael. Michael has no private life and since we've won the NBA title it's gotten worse. I understand now more than I ever did how tough being him can really be."[7] Whether that was genuine or Krause wanted to keep his star player happy for the sake of organizational success, the statement had little to no effect on his relationship with Jordan or his perception by the fans in Chicago. Whenever he appeared publicly, Krause was booed. His wife told me that it took some time to adjust to this reaction, as she did not understand why the Bulls were so successful, yet the mere mention of her husband's name inside an arena made it feel as if he were managing a failed franchise.

However, when they went out to restaurants people were cordial and nice.

The spirits on the team were not particularly high entering the season, and the banner-hanging ceremony was a brief distraction from what would turn out to be the toughest test for the championship franchise. On November 17 and 18, 1992, the *Chicago Tribune* published excerpts from *The Jordan Rules*, a book written by beat reporter Sam Smith, that provided a unique look behind the scenes of a winning organization. No one was angrier at the publication than Krause, because it revealed a lot of information about him and about the team, information that he considered wrong or inaccurate. Sam Smith reminisced:

> Jerry and I actually had a decent relationship early on in the mid–80s, when I was covering the Bulls after he was hired. We had a few dinners and one time spent an evening together in Portland on a road trip, when he showed me where he used to work there. But relationships deteriorated as the Bulls improved, but not enough, with multiple coaching changes and Michael Jordan's criticisms of Krause and management. Krause viewed media

reports of Jordan's and Scottie Pippen's condemnations of him and management as personal, and basically also blamed the messenger.

More people learned in the *Tribune* about the way Jordan bullied Krause and because he could not go at Jordan, the executive went at Smith and other journalists. When having phone conversations, Krause was writing everything down in hand as he was talking, so that he would have proof of what was said. He also complained about being limited by the constraints of recognizability brought about by team success: "I can't jump up and I can't scream because people are looking. I can't walk in tunnels or hide before the game because there's no place to hide at the Stadium."[8]

Most Bulls players decried Smith's account of the 1991-92 season as fictional, partially because it vilified multiple members of the team, even the image-conscious Jordan. On the court it was more of the same as the Bulls dominated games, as if they thrived on conflict. Midway through the season they were 36–5.

What's more, they were setting an example for the rest of the league. The general manager of the Houston Rockets, Steve Patterson, whose team was involved in a contract dispute with the best center in the league, Hakeem Olajuwon, said: "A star player doesn't have to like the general manager of the team. Look at all the stuff Michael Jordan says about Jerry Krause. All they did was win a championship."[9]

Krause said to the press: "When a writer, in the name of personal greed, writes a book that is mostly fiction and passes it off as fact, that just proves to me we live in the greatest country in the world."[10] Meanwhile, backstage Krause was conducting a private investigation into who had leaked "classified" information to Smith. As Smith recounted in an email exchange with me:

> Jerry was very upset about *The Jordan Rules* and believed I depicted him inaccurately. Phil Jackson arranged a "peace" conference meeting because Krause was so upset, but it went badly as he was angry throughout. He claimed there were dozens of errors in the book, though often his idea of "errors" was characterizations I made about him or the team.

Jackson playing the role of the negotiator was a savvy move by the head coach, since many people believed he was the main source of information for the book.

"It was Phil," said Thelma Krause bluntly, still livid about the hurt that *The Jordan Rules* caused her husband. The book was indeed a turning point when it came to Krause's relationships with journalists, of whom he now became extremely distrustful.

"I think I have a reputation among other teams in the league. If they tell me something, they know it won't show up in the newspaper. They can tell me things in confidence. It goes in one ear and it stays,"[11] Krause said with pride about his secretiveness.

Once, when he saw a journalist interview Phil Jackson on the team bus, Krause allegedly asked: "What are these whores doing on the bus?"[12] It turned out that the journalist in question was David Halberstam, author of numerous acclaimed books on sports, politics, and history.

Halberstam was not on Jerry Krause's reading list. His favorite author was Damon Runyon, a journalist and short story writer who depicted Prohibition-era New York. Thelma Krause referred to her late husband as a "Damon Runyon character." She added that he loved World War II history "because his uncle was in the war and ever since he read anything he could find about the subject. And he also liked Danielle Steel and Nicholas Sparks, romance novels. He was very sentimental." Therefore, Krause could be forgiven for not knowing who Halberstam was.

Contract negotiations had been a recurring theme during the previous seasons, with a prized player supposed to leave, only to be extended just in time for another series of articles and watercooler talks about what a mistake it would be to let them leave. In 1991-92 these discussions were centered around the head coach, who had one more year left on his contract and was one of the lowest-paid coaches in the NBA.

Now he was going to earn one of the highest contracts in the league. Once the deal was signed, Krause praised Jackson and spoke critically about him not being named Coach of the Year, comparing him to one of the best ever: "Red Auerbach was the best coach in the history of basketball, the best motivator and biggest force in history of the game," but he won the ultimate coaching honor only once, "because he had Bill Russell."[13] The award eventually went to Don Nelson, who was able to work wonders with the Golden State Warriors.

The Bulls finished the season 67–15, at the top of the league and with the best record in team history. However, most people on the team could not wait to put the season behind them. Krause reiterated the strategy for the playoffs that had worked a season ago: "This is when we start at 15 and count backward."[14]

The Bulls were not so much title favorites; rather, the championship was theirs to lose. The path to the finals was seen as easy, as the Celtics and the Pistons were rebuilding, while the Knicks were on their way, but Krause preached caution. When asked about which team scared him the most, he provided his signature non-answer: "All of 'em. Every one. They all scare us."[15]

In the first round the Bulls played the Miami Heat, coached by Kevin Loughery, whom Krause had fired in May 1985. Much was made of their meeting, simply because there were no other narratives to cling to, as the teams had no history between them. The Heat were making their first playoff appearance in the franchise's four-year history. Loughery said he would not give Krause a chance to either speak to him or give him the silent treatment, choosing to avoid him altogether. He added that Krause "is the only [person] in the league that I've been associated with that I don't talk to."[16] It didn't matter; the Bulls swept the Heat in three games.

In the next round the Bulls played the tough, revamped New York Knicks, coached by Pat Riley. The series was close, and Jackson blamed the referees for that, publicly suggesting a league-wide conspiracy against the Bulls. He was communicating through the media to his team that they were on their own, against the world, which was a tactic he was already instilling within the locker room. In order to beat the Knicks, the Bulls adjusted their tactics properly, and Krause was upset about their style of play, caused by the refereeing in the series, which forced the coaching staff to decide between winning ugly and losing attractively: "We play 82 games one way and then the playoffs another way. This isn't basketball. Everybody else in the playoffs right now is playing basketball except us."[17]

He was quick to admit, however, that the series against the Riley's Knicks was nothing like the Bulls' previous wars with the Bad Boys: "The Pistons are an out-and-out dirty team, a bunch of thugs. New York didn't try to cripple us, just inflict pain."[18]

During Game Four in New York, Krause complained to Knicks GM Dave Checketts about heckler extraordinaire Robin Ficker, who sat behind the Bulls bench and read aloud from *The Jordan Rules*. A resident of Washington, Ficker usually reserved his heckling for the opponents of his Washington Bullets, but for that game, former Georgetown standout Patrick Ewing gave him a ticket in favor of waging some psychological warfare on the Knicks' behalf. That did not amount to much, as the Bulls withstood the tough test and progressed to the next round, but they needed all seven games to do so.

The Eastern Conference Finals provided another entry in the one-sided rivalry against the Cavaliers, with exceptional performances by "The Dobermans," as Scottie Pippen and Horace Grant were called. The two were growing apart from one another after being very close in their first seasons in the league, but on the court they were in great synchronicity, averaging over 11 rebounds and close to two blocks per game each. While Grant stayed consistent throughout the 1992 postseason,

Pippen rebounded in the series against the Cavaliers following the Conference semifinals, in which he took a pounding from the Knicks.

Some people were openly calling for a trade for Charles Barkley, the disgruntled Sixers star, who was trying to force a move out of Philadelphia. Jordan might have been friendly with Barkley, but Krause was quick to rush to his prized pick's defense, calling Pippen "a special kid with a huge heart."[19]

In the 1992 finals the Bulls played the Blazers. In early December 1991 they were playing in Portland, and nobody had provided a game seat for Jerry Krause, who decided to travel with the team to the West Coast without informing the Blazers beforehand. He went to sit in the press section, but soon the people whose seats he occupied asked for security to escort Krause out. An intervention from a Blazers executive put an end to the proceedings and Krause was given a different seat, which did not stop him from complaining: "This isn't going to do anything to cement relations between these two teams."[20]

As the season progressed, the animosities increased as well, but there was no real rivalry between the Blazers and the Bulls. Even when Chicago won 4–2, the triumph provided no relief for Krause, who was worried about the draft, which would take place a bit over a week after Game Six concluded, as well as the Barcelona Summer Olympics, which were for the first time supposed to feature professional basketball players from the NBA. Both Jordan and Pippen were heading to Spain to market the best basketball league in the world, along with American capitalism and the flashy, fun, and exciting lifestyle it provided. The first post–Cold War Olympics filled a lot of people with excitement, but Krause dreaded the competition and its impact on his two star players: "I'd much rather see Michael on the golf course and Scottie [on his boat] on Lake Michigan. I know that may sound un–American, and that I should be happy that they are playing for the United States. But I've got to be concerned for my team first."[21]

He delivered the statement on the night the Bulls won their second NBA championship in a row, which showed just how much pressure Krause was feeling to keep the team healthy and competitive. Not only for himself, but also for the franchise and the city. To show them how much they were valued, Reinsdorf gave championship rings to all 95 employees of the organization.

Jerry Reinsdorf asked Krause a couple of times to consider a monthlong vacation, as Krause was becoming too closely attached to the fate of the franchise, even though there was no happiness at the end of the line, just less misery. Krause was learning how to vacation at that stage of his life, learning about certain places only when visiting them in his free time, despite having been there numerous times in the past.

Such as when he was in Saragossa, Spain, to scout European players participating in the pre–Olympic basketball tournament. His visit there gave him another chance to talk to Kukoč and convince him to trade northern Italy for midwestern America. He even gave him championship T-shirts, in hopes that they would convince Kukoč to leave Europe. The Croat had more important issues on his mind, as the Yugoslav wars put an end to the myth of a united Yugoslavia. With Croatia drained in conflict, he was worrying about his family and friends.

Kukoč was deemed NBA-ready by the observers of the tournament, and bringing him over made more sense for the defending champions than the rookie selected that summer with the last pick of the first round. Krause said: "It's no fun drafting 27th but drafting 27th means you have the ring on your finger and that's fun."[22] The 6'5" power forward Byron Houston, selected by Krause in 1992, would not even suit up for the Bulls.

Kukoč would not do as well at the time. The T-shirts might have been nice, but he wanted to stay close to home, just in case.

Ian Thomsen told me that when he was at an assignment to write about the EuroLeague Final Four, he saw Krause talking with Kukoč's agent, Luciano "Lucky" Capicchioni, at a hotel restaurant. He reported about the encounter and the GM was unhappy, because he knew that the news would reach Jordan and Pippen, and the latter would be seriously agitated. That assessment proved to be true.

At the Olympics, during the game between Croatia and the U.S., Jordan and Pippen took turns guarding Kukoč and they limited the European incarnation of Magic Johnson to 2/11 shooting from the floor.

"I'm pretty sure that he won't take the film [of the game] and send it to Jerry,"[23] said Jordan.

"I did this because I can't put Jerry Krause on the court,"[24] added Pippen.

Both were ignorant of what their prospective teammate was going through in his home country. One of the more important reasons for his reluctance to move across the Atlantic was the proximity of his family, members of which stayed in Croatia, with the country being involved in a war against Serbia. The Croatian national team was preparing for the tournament 20 miles from where the battles were still going on, yet it was able to reach the final and play the Dream Team for the second time. In that game Kukoč had 16 points and nine assists.

With the forward still unwilling to join the NBA, Krause continued to look for a reserve swingman who could step in for either Jordan or Pippen, fearing the toll that the number of playoff games in recent years, plus the Olympics, could take on their bodies. Krause considered trading for veterans Anthony Bowie and Gerald Wilkins from Eastern Conference rivals the Orlando Magic and the New York Knicks, respectively. B.J. Armstrong and Stacey King were reportedly appearing in trade talks with the Mavericks, as the Bulls were trying to get either point guard Derek Harper, small forward Rodney McCray, or both. The Bulls had just waived reserve guards Craig Hodges and Bob Hansen, two veterans happy to be in Chicago, under the pretense that they wanted to give more playing time to younger players.

Hansen was a pickup from the Sacramento Kings and he initially was ecstatic about joining the Bulls. When the team was able to repeat as champions, Krause spoke with pride about how "when we got Bobby Hansen, he said he felt like he was going to heaven."[25] After the season, though, Hansen said that at times it "was misery. There were times when I was the only guy who wouldn't get into a game."[26] When Krause wanted Hansen to try out before the new season, the veteran felt offended and refused to participate.

In his book Hodges wrote that Krause called him personally and thanked him for mentoring the players he was now being released to cede minutes to. Hodges did not buy that argument, writing: "I knew management thought I was corrupting the minds of the players and compromising relationships with corporate sponsors. Certainly Michael wanted me gone."[27]

Finding a proper backup for Jordan was not easy, as Krause needed to factor in not only physical capabilities, but also character: "The bad thing is to have to play against him every day in practice—and he really takes it out on you in practice. For a kid, it's a good learning experience. For a veteran, it's bad because you know you're not going to get a lot of minutes. You need someone whose ego is not too big but big enough because of the tough time in practice."[28]

The reasoning behind the releases was put into question by Krause himself: "There's going to come a time when we'll look to get younger, but when you're winning you have a tendency to say you want to win another. One thing you don't do while you're winning is to disturb something just to get younger."[29] The Bulls brought in 32-year-old Trent Tucker and 31-year-old Rodney McCray to replace Hodges and Hansen.

The Bulls eventually got McCray for two second-round picks and Byron Houston, who was sent to Golden State. The Warriors' Don Nelson really liked Houston and had been working on a deal to get him since the draft. McCray had been the third overall pick of the 1983 draft, selected by the Rockets the same year they selected Ralph Sampson. A year later they were joined by Hakeem Olajuwon. McCray was a great defender but failed to develop into anything more than a complementary player in the shadow of the two giants. Upon his arrival in Chicago for his 10th season in the NBA, Jerry Krause described him as "a fine defender, passer and ballhandler and a proven unselfish team player,"[30] who he had been pursuing for three years.

Adding McCray made the roster bigger, as the Bulls were able to keep King and Scott Williams. The latter was particularly important for their first championship runs. The former North Carolina Tar Heel went undrafted in 1990 and in three seasons had progressed from the end of the bench to serving as the Bulls' power forward/center off the bench. Phil Jackson called him "a great utility player" who was still a work in progress, but who would eventually become a starter somewhere in the NBA, although "not this year or very soon."[31] This led to a disagreement between Williams and Jackson, with the player hurt that he learned about not having a chance of starting for the Bulls from the newspapers and not directly from his coach.

Al Vermeil spoke of Williams with admiration: "He was a really good player for us and he had a very difficult background … very difficult." Williams and his brother and mother suffered domestic abuse at the hands of his father. When Williams was at college, his mother left his father, who found her where she lived and shot and killed her before killing himself.

Williams continued to play and had a good career at Chapel Hill, but fell from a projected lottery pick to missing the draft altogether because of issues with his shoulder. The Charlotte Hornets passed on Williams because of it. During a camp organized by Michael Jordan's friend, Fred Wilmington, Williams made such an impression that Wilmington called Krause and recommended the big man to the Bulls executive. Three years later he was still on the roster and his role was increasing with each season, despite the growing number of big men on the team.

Two of them, Williams and Perdue, were in contract years, and the season would determine whether they would remain on the team. Williams, Perdue, Cartwright, Grant, and King were battling for two starting spots. Asked about the in-house rivalry, Jackson simply replied: "That shouldn't be my concern. I've been able to play 11 and 12 guys in the past and I think it will work out."[32] At the beginning of the season Perdue and King demanded to be traded.

Speaking of working out, in September 1992 the Bulls became the first NBA franchise to open its own practice facility, the Berto Center. Through the years they had trained either at Wheaton College, Angel

Guardian Gym, or the CSO Multiplex, but now they had a home, named after Sheri L. Berto, Jerry Reinsdorf's assistant since 1974, who died in 1991.

It was located near Lake Cook and Waukegan roads in Deerfield, around 25 miles from the Chicago Stadium, and cost $3.6 million. Team headquarters were moved there from Michigan Avenue as well, less than 40 miles north. Berto Center was supposed to face its first front-office test when the facility became the Bulls' 1993 draft center.

"Jordan lived nearby, in Highland Park, so I assume that was part of the reason why they decided to settle there," said Wojciech Michałowicz, the man synonymous with NBA basketball in Poland, during our talk. When reporting on the Bulls, Michałowicz was a frequent guest in Deerfield. He spoke to me about how media visits were organized, that the members of the media had a special room available to them, where they would wait behind the glass and a gray curtain, which was lifted during the last 30 minutes of every workout. After it concluded, the journalists could interview the players in the hallway or on the track. People hated the curtain and considered it another representation of the GM's paranoia.

"Everyone here thinks I'm responsible for the curtain at the Berto Center. That wasn't my idea. It was Phil's,"[33] Krause explained in 1997.

The first floor, where Jackson, Krause, and other coaches and scouts had their rooms, was off limits to visitors. The rooms overlooked the court and it was easy to record every aspect of every workout so that they could be later analyzed.

"The building was not particularly impressive on the outside, humbly branded," Michałowicz continued. "But the court was beautiful, with the championship banners hanging there. There were also replicas of jerseys, Bulls logos were brightly lit."

The see-through aspects of the facility reflected how Jordan was feeling about his life. With recognition came exposure, which the player saw as constraining his everyday activities: "You miss doing the things most people can do—like walking around a mall or going to a movie. I would love for that to happen. I'd rather be able to give something back and be normal again."[34] And Jordan, feeling the pressure for the team to win, was further pushing his teammates in workouts to play harder and better. He spoke like a true Chicagoan when he said that the early seasons, in which the Bulls were not very good, "developed in me this attitude of broad shoulders, of having to carry the load."[35] He no longer had to do that in the equal-opportunity triangle offense, with Pippen and Grant next to him and a competent playmaker in B.J. Armstrong, yet he still felt the responsibility to take over whenever things were not going right.

7. Suffering from Success

Krause spoke about the system with pride, saying that the Bulls were "the only team in the league that does not run set plays, and it's also not a passing game," bragging about how complicated the offense was and how intelligent players needed to be in order to understand it.[36] Therefore, finding the proper personnel was a chore, which was why keeping the core of the roster intact was so crucial. However, the constant replacing of the players on roster spots eight through 12 was disrupting the learning process and hurting the fluidity of the offense.

The Bulls finished the season atop the Central Division with 57 wins, behind the New York Knicks in the East and the Suns in the West. For a team that was stale, criticized for its style, its star on the verge of burning out, and various players complaining about either lack of minutes or exhaustion from annual deep playoff runs, the Bulls had done quite well.

In *Transition Game*, Melissa Isaacson estimates that during the last four seasons, the Bulls averaged around 100 games, more than any other team in the league. Later Jordan complained that numerous players were injured, resting, or tired. For the first time, basketball stopped being fun to him.[37] Isaacson set out to write her book precisely to describe how the Bulls were transitioning to a life post–Jordan and how Jordan was transitioning to a life post-basketball.

In the 1992-93 season Jordan returned to his war with Krause, relaying to the press that the general manager supposedly said to him "he was going to win one without me," referring to a championship title.[38]

Undoubtedly Krause was hoping for that, as competitive as he was, but he probably knew better than to say so to Jordan, who did not need much to start lashing out at him publicly. Krause later explained that "that was taken out of context. Sure, I want to win a title without Michael. But that's only because I want to keep this thing going."[39]

Jordan was surprisingly mute on talks of Krause's negotiations with Kukoč and unsurprisingly mute on renegotiations with Grant, who was to become a free agent after the 1993-94 season. Despite considering the possibility of retiring a Bull, he simultaneously openly talked about exploring the offers that he could get on the free market. There was no ultimatum for Grant, unlike the one supposedly issued to Kukoč, who had to either buy out of his contract with Treviso or Krause would simply stop pursuing him. By June 10, because of the rules in the Italian league, a decision had to be made. Thanks to a clause in his contract, the Croatian had an opening to leave for the NBA in the summer of 1993. He bought out the remaining $2.1 million of his contract to play for the Bulls and signed an eight-year, $17.6 million deal with Chicago.

In order to not distract from the current playoff run, Kukoč was invited to Minneapolis, where he was monitored by Al Vermeil. The strength and conditioning coach was impressed with how athletic the Croatian was:

> Toni had some experience in strength training, because he had some technique. Years later I was approached by a gentleman in Italy, where I was speaking, and he asked me what we did for him to put on so much weight. I said: "We trained." He said: "Well we trained, for 45 minutes." I said: "We trained two-three hours, five days a week." And Toni was very coordinated, very gifted, much stronger than people think. He could do 150 kilos in a power clean.

Meanwhile the Bulls breezed through the first two rounds and entered the Eastern Conference Finals against the Knicks as if what was going on around the team was just a minor distraction. When it came time to perform, the Bulls handled the opposition like they were supposed to. Until they ran into the Knicks, who were ready to do whatever it took to win. There was no love lost between the two organizations, and when Charles Oakley questioned the Bulls' toughness, even Krause got into the mind games.

"You're not my son anymore. The stuff you said about us in the papers, you're not my son anymore. How could you say that?"[40] Krause said to Oakley when they accidentally met in a hotel lobby.

"We don't like to bring in young backups. Michael just eats up these kids in practice"[41] was how Krause responded to a question about why he did not bring in John Starks, then the shooting guard for the Knicks, back when he was in the CBA and available.

The series was about guts and mental toughness, and when the Knicks opened with a 2–0 lead, it seemed that the Bulls had finally met their match. That was when the aforementioned factors gained special meaning, as the Bulls had to prove that they could rise above criticism that they had had to endure throughout the whole season. It was not only the on-court rivals they were facing, but also the journalists at home, questioning everybody on the team and in the front office who was not named Michael Jordan. Even when reports surfaced that Jordan was up all night gambling in Atlantic City, the press did not make much of it, abstaining from criticism.

The organization grew tired of the harassment and simply refused to talk to the press. The players said that they were OK with being fined by the league, and Krause refused to speak to journalists during the playoffs as well. The only member of the Bulls willing to talk was Jackson. That was until after Game Four, in which Jordan scored 54 points in a memorable performance and once again all was well with the world.

Krause probably believed in Toni Kukoč more than in any other player he scouted (1994).

The press were welcomed back in the Bulls' locker room. Role players on the Bulls were even in the mood for jokes.

"It was a good day for the Tar Heels, I think we combined for 55 points," said Scott Williams, who had four fouls and one point.

Jordan, Pippen, and Grant were still not talking to the press, not after it was reported that Jordan had lost $1.25 million gambling on golf games he was participating in. Regardless of his private opinion, Krause supported Jordan publicly, talking about separating personal matters from team issues. Again, all the chatter was not an issue for the Bulls, who progressed to the finals and took a 3–1 lead over the Charles Barkley–led Phoenix Suns, but when they lost Game Five, no one was more frustrated than Krause, who refused to talk to the press and did not allow players to take their wives to Arizona for Game Six.

In the final seconds of that game, Krause's trust in his players paid off. Horace Grant declined to shoot a layup, instead passing outside to John Paxson, who drained the three-pointer and set the score at 99–98. The Suns had less than four seconds to answer back, but Grant blocked Kevin Johnson's off-balance shot.

The Bulls had won their third championship in a row. And with Kukoč about to come in and have an immediate impact, there was no reason to doubt they could make it four.

Or five.

Or six.

8

Good, Not Great

It happened in Berto Center, the house that Jordan built or at least largely contributed to building. A house he was supposed to inhabit for a number of years, but now wanted to escape. Jerry Reinsdorf, the man who had funded the house, was visibly shaken, uneasy with the words, uncertain of what to say. On October 6, 1993, a month before the new season was about to start, Michael Jordan decided to retire from professional basketball. The chairman was doing his best to deliver the news but was too shocked to make any sense of it. Few people did.

"He's living the American Dream. The American Dream is to reach a point in your life when you don't have to do anything you want to do..." said Reinsdorf during the press conference, and immediately corrected himself: "...you don't want to do, and everything that you do want to do."

The excitement with which that offseason started was gone. Now there was only confusion.

The years of courting Kukoč were about to conclude with a contract, and Krause was excited for the player he had scouted to show the fans in Chicago exactly why he valued him so much. Before that could happen, he was on the hunt for the next piece of the puzzle to fit next to Michael Jordan.

The year 1993 saw the beginning of a certain tradition, as during the days (and long nights) leading up to the draft, Krause would order buckets of rib tips from Carson's Ribs. As recounted by Karen Umlauf, "during draft time Jerry would order Carson's Ribs ... he would eat a bucket of these rib tips and we'd be laughing: 'Must be draft time, Jerry and his rib tips.'" And in late afternoon, when not a lot of people were at the facility, Krause would put on a T-shirt and walk around the track. Umlauf continued: "Exercise wasn't his thing, but he would walk and tell us: 'I know I got a bad body.' He was funny like that."

One of the players Krause personally scouted during the season was the 7'7" Romanian giant Gheorghe Mureșan. Always on the lookout for big bodies, Krause attended not only his games, but also his workouts, aware that Mureşan had one more year left on his contract in France. Various mock drafts predicted the Bulls taking the center with the 25th pick. Mureşan turned out to have a personality that fit his frame and became a beloved NBA presence ... just not on the Bulls.

Instead of picking another European prospect for whom the team would have to wait, Krause decided to play it safe and went with Corie Blount, a 6'10" power forward from the University of Cincinnati. He was able to convince the Bulls with his workout. Scout Clarence Gaines, Jr., praised the young big man for the ability to rebound and defend, which were two things the team was looking for in power forwards.[1] Blount was another big body added to the front line of Cartwright, Grant, King, Perdue, and Williams.

The training camp started on October 8, with Cartwright injured, Pippen recovering from wrist and ankle surgeries, and Jordan mourning the death of his father. On July 23, 1993, James Jordan was murdered by two men while sleeping in his car along a highway.

Burned out, dealing with gambling allegations, and in mourning, Jordan, at 30, was about to call it quits. Still, the Bulls were hoping he was going to change his mind when given time and space. On October 5, during the day, Krause told the press that Jordan would miss at least two weeks of training camp because of toe surgery. He was once again lying for the sake of loyalty, to buy some time for the organization, hoping Jordan would reconsider. A couple of hours later, "Dateline NBC," the *Denver Post*, and the *Chicago Sun-Times* all reported that Jordan was going to announce his retirement the next day.

For loyalty's sake, Reinsdorf decided to honor Jordan's contract and pay him the money he was owed. Despite his deep sense of loyalty and the respect with which he treated his employees, Reinsdorf was lumped together with Krause as the two of the most hated people in Chicago sports.

"What (angers) me is that I know what a good person Jerry Reinsdorf is. I've never met a more honest person or a smarter person. And I've never met anyone who was more loyal. Very few people know him or understand him, but his morals are impeccable,"[2] said Krause.

The low-income families who were displaced back when Reinsdorf demanded a new stadium from the city of Chicago, lest the White Sox relocate to Florida, felt otherwise. Reinsdorf was able to redeem himself in the eyes of the city when along with NHL's Chicago Blackhawks owner Bill Wirtz they redeveloped the surroundings of their indoor teams' new arena, the United Center. Sean Dinces writes that "Reinsdorf and Wirtz not only provided millions of dollars in resident-designed replacement housing for those displaced by the arena; they also contributed to a new nearby library branch and park renovation, and they provided no-interest loans to the local community development corporation for additional revitalization efforts."[3]

During the conference Krause was sitting between Jordan's agent, David Falk, and head coach Phil Jackson. A lot of people had tears in their eyes, including Krause.

"There will be some grieving, that's very natural," said the GM to the reporters, adding that he understood Jordan wanted to move away from the limelight.

The next day at the Berto Center it was business as usual, with Kukoč expected to step in and have an immediate impact on the team. The expectations for him were high, higher than for any other second-round pick in league history. And a large part of that was blamed on Krause, who talked about the Croatian as if he were the second coming of Magic Johnson. Pippen was especially skeptical of the European, because he assumed the Bulls were now *his* team.

Jordan was replaced by Pete Myers, the Bulls' 120th draft pick in 1986, who had left the team after just one year. He bounced around from team to team, and for the last two years had been out of the league, playing professionally in Italy. Then, at 30, he got a call from Jerry Krause and was tasked with playing the same position as Jordan, starting for the three-time NBA champions.

The start of the new season filled Krause with dread, as it was going to be uncharted territory for almost everybody in the organization: "Most of our players have never played a game without Michael. Phil has never coached a game without him. I've never general managed without him. There's no way of knowing what this will bring."[4]

The fear of the unknown motivated Krause to look for trades to strengthen the guard rotation, but the Sixers turned down his offer for Jeff Hornacek, as did the Mavericks for Derek Harper, and the Knicks for Greg Anthony. He had to settle for guards Steve Kerr and JoJo English. Kerr would become an integral part of the second incarnation of the championship Bulls, but at that point he was coming off a season in which he averaged a bit over nine minutes per game for the Magic.

The Bulls began the season 8–8 and the critics were piling on, writing about how they were lost without their star player. Jordan was not the only one absent; a lot of other players were missing too due to injuries. And then there were the conflicts that were tearing the team apart. Horace Grant was in the final year of his contract, and he wanted to earn $4.5 million per year. The Bulls were offering $3.5 million. According to Grant's agent, Krause said that A.C. Green was a better player.

Green, a true professional, would become the league's ironman, setting an NBA record with 1,192 straight games. But he was not on Grant's level.

Soon afterward Grant went public with his contract demands, a New York–based magazine published a picture of Grant posing with nude women in a Chicago gym. Krause defended the player publicly. Grant apologized. There were no consequences.

Grant continued to have the best season of his career, and used his first All-Star appearance as justification for his contract demands: "If Jerry Krause's leg was long enough, he'd be kicking himself right now ... the price definitely went up."[5] By February, when no deal was reached, Grant said: "I will never play for the Bulls again. It's very disappointing to leave, but this is a business."[6]

Will Perdue wrote critically in the local newspapers about Krause traveling with the team, adding, "So often, it seems most general managers stay away from the spotlight and work behind the scenes, but not Jerry."[7] The assessment was unfair and wrong, just another example of punching down by a player frustrated with his position on the team. Perdue openly spoke about regretting signing a six-year contract worth $10.7 million and he attacked the GM, who wanted to trade him, but could not find any takers. Krause did not want the publicity, he wanted to focus on his job—that was why he was so secretive about everything concerning his business and the way he conducted it.

In Roland Lazenby's *Blood on the Horns*, Krause explained, hopefully putting the issue to rest: "I came here out of baseball, all baseball general managers travel with their teams. That's very normal.... I find that to be effective at what I do, I have to see players on the road, OK? I don't have to visit with them every day or talk to 'em. But I have to watch 'em on the road, because I judge our team a lot by what goes on on the road, OK?"[8]

In the middle of all the turmoil, the Bulls were able to turn the season around and Krause was once again praised for the way he was able to find the players who would eventually lead the Bulls to 55 wins, just two wins short of the previous season's total.

Newsday's Shaun Powell wrote that "maybe the real story behind the Bulls is the astonishing production from a bench of nobodies. Bill Wennington? Jo Jo English? Steve Kerr? GM Jerry Krause's fanatical scouting of talent has paid off."[9] Pippen did not think that way and in January took a page from Jordan's book, criticizing Krause in the press for the lack of trades.

In late February he struck again, this time going after not only Krause, but also the fans and one of his teammates: "I've been here seven years. I've never seen a white guy get booed in the Stadium. But

8. Good, Not Great

it seems like when things go bad and the ball is in your hands and you don't score, the fans tend to take over on you. Toni was 0-for-whatever tonight and I never heard one fan get on him."[10]

Pippen apologized publicly the next day.

The lack of roster moves was disappointing, since the Bulls had the cap space to sign a free agent shooting guard, like Byron Scott, who eventually joined the Pacers after Krause passed on him. Scott was a three-time NBA champion with the Lakers and was happy to settle for a bench role behind Reggie Miller.

Playing the long game, Krause wanted a player who could serve as a fill-in for Jordan, now dabbling in baseball. That was why he decided to wait for soon to be free agent, Ron Harper, who had participated in some of the Bulls' battles with the Cavaliers over the years before he was traded from Ohio to California. Pippen also wanted the team to get Harper's teammate on the Clippers, soon to be free agent Danny Manning, although adding another forward to Pippen, Grant, and Kukoč would require some work on the coaches' part.

Coming back to Perdue's argument, the only time when Krause enjoyed taking public positions was when he was asked to evaluate talent. He just could not help himself; his whole career depended on picking the best people and putting them in the positions to succeed. It did not matter whether it was on the court, on the field, or in the front office, he wanted to have the satisfaction of identifying talent before everybody else.

In the 1994 draft, even though the Bulls had no shot at picking first, he praised Purdue's small forward Glenn Robinson, who according to Krause had great hands, shooting range, and the will to win necessary to validate the number one selection. Krause was right in that prediction, because Robinson was the first overall pick, but when it came to that draft class, two players chosen immediately after Robinson, Grant Hill and Jason Kidd, enjoyed better professional careers. Krause liked Robinson, though, to the point that he attended his games without the fear of being seen.

The Bulls would end up picking 21st and would select another big body, hopefully to fill in for Grant. Krause picked power forward Dickey Simpkins from Providence. When I asked Al Vermeil about Simpkins, he said that he tried doing the same things with him as he had with Horace Grant, and to his credit Simpkins worked hard, but he did not have the same physical capabilities as Grant. Vermeil said the same thing about Jason Caffey, another power forward selected by the Bulls with the 20th pick a year later, in 1995. Neither lived up to the expectations that the team put on somebody supposed to step in for Grant.

During the 1994 trade deadline Stacey King was traded to the Minnesota Timberwolves for their backup center, Luc Longley. The general manager of the Wolves was an all too familiar foe of the Bulls, the man responsible for constructing the roster of the Bad Boy Detroit Pistons, Jack McCloskey. Now working in Minnesota, he contacted Jerry Krause with the intention of trading King for Longley, the 7'2" Australian. Longley, the seventh pick in the 1991 draft, lost his position in the starting lineup to a 30-year-old Mike Brown, whose NBA career started in 1986 with the Bulls. After just two and a half seasons the Timberwolves were giving up on Longley. Only 25 years old, Longley was not a scorer, but he could rebound, block, and, most importantly, pass, which could make him a functional part of the triangle offense.

Krause was careful with his prediction: "This is a young man with some growing to do. He will have to learn to fit into the system, but he'll get intense individual teaching."[11] With Cartwright still on the roster and in the last year of his contract, Longley would have half a season to learn in relative peace, backing up a more established player.

He was the fifth center on the team, but the only reliable presence out of the five throughout the season was Bill Wennington, another pickup from the Italian league, who appeared in 76 games. Perdue played in 43 games, Cartwright in 42, and Williams in 38. Come playoff time Perdue was the odd man out, left out of the playoff roster. He reacted with frustration, doubling down on his criticism of the GM, who was, ironically, one of his biggest supporters. Jackson was the one who made that decision.

Perdue demanded a trade. Again.

The Bulls swept the Cavaliers in the first round and were playing the Knicks in the Conference semifinals. The Knicks had eliminated the Nets 3–1 in the previous round; their coach, Chuck Daly, resigned after the series. Always dapper, the accomplished Daly was reportedly wanted by the Philadelphia Sixers, and local journalist Stan Hochman for some reason thought he would increase Daly's chances of considering the job by attacking Krause, describing him as "a pudgy, rumpled, demeaned little guy in clothes Daly wouldn't wear to wash his car."[12]

Krause read and heard much, much worse, even from his own players. However, as the Bulls were engaged in a tough, ugly battle with the Knicks, interrupted by a beautiful Kukoč game winner in Game Three, Krause decided to vent his frustration by filing a tampering charge against the Orlando Magic, whose president had praised Grant during a TNT broadcast. The charges were dismissed by the league, although later events proved that there was a lot to them.

Throughout the series Grant continued to be the consummate

professional he always was, unlike Pippen, who took issue with Kukoč taking the final shot and refusing to enter Game Three with 1.8 seconds left. Pippen refused to acknowledge that Kukoč was brought to Chicago precisely for these moments, as he proved during the regular season, making three game winners as a rookie.

Krause did not criticize Pippen publicly, instead deciding to leave the issue to be resolved by Phil Jackson and his coaching staff. Jackson then left the issue to be resolved by Pippen's teammates. He chose to stay out of it.

The man who took it upon himself to let Pippen know how disappointed the teammates were with him was Cartwright. When talking to Isaacson about the moment, he said it was a culmination of the actions exhibited by Pippen through Kukoč's rookie season: "When a new guy comes in, go over and introduce yourself. Help him out. That's what Scottie should have done with Toni. The better Toni is, the better the team is. That's what he didn't understand."[13]

Despite all this, Krause had Pippen's back, like when referee Hue Hollins made a foul call on the small forward with 2.1 seconds left in Game Five, which gave the Knicks three free throws, allowing them to win the game 87–86 and take a 3–2 series lead. Fifteen minutes after the game concluded, Krause was heard screaming at the referee, "You're never going to be able to live with yourself the rest of your life."[14]

The Bulls were able to win Game Six, partially thanks to Longley, who played tough defense on Ewing and made two important free throws late in the fourth quarter, exhibiting surprising toughness in the first NBA playoffs of his career. Cartwright was also doing his best against the Knicks' center, but the Knicks overpowered the Bulls and progressed.

"I don't like not working on Memorial Day. If you ever find yourself not wanting to work on Memorial Day, then it's time to get out of this business,"[15] said Krause, as the loss came on a Sunday. Memorial Day was the next week.

His point was that the season was over. John Paxson and Bill Cartwright were openly talking about retirement; Scott Williams wanted to become a free agent and test the market. So did Grant, whom Krause still wanted to keep. In an article about Paxson and Cartwright, Sam Smith wrote: "Talent can be replaced. Class cannot. And so they'll depart, which in effect ends the championship era the Bulls have enjoyed. This doesn't mean the Bulls cannot compete for a championship soon, even next season."[16] Further in the piece Smith pointed out that Pippen and B.J. Armstrong could be the only two players remaining from the championship seasons. Surprisingly, Will Perdue would be the third and final champion, back on the 1994-95 team.

The first decision of the summer was getting rid of assistant coach Johnny Bach, who Krause had long suspected of being the "leak" who provided secret sacred information for Sam Smith's book. Smith himself criticized the move in the *Chicago Tribune* and called Krause "mean," revealing that the GM "even got to the point of making Bach leave the room when team plans were being discussed or whispering to other assistants while Bach sat nearby."[17] Krause said that the firing was Phil Jackson's decision and he supported it. According to Roland Lazenby, Jackson played a crucial part in justifying the firing, as the writer recalled in an article published on *Medium*:

> Both Reinsdorf and Krause said they agreed to allow Jackson to fire Bach only because Jackson persuaded them to do it by telling them Bach was a major anonymous voice in *The Jordan Rules*.
> Reinsdorf said on the record that he only learned of Jackson's deceit after Sam Smith discussed with him the sources for the book. Reinsdorf said he had learned from Smith that Bach had little to do with the book and that Jackson himself had provided anonymous information for the book.[18]

Bach, 68 at the time of the firing, was shocked. He had suffered a mild heart attack in May 1992, but wanted to continue coaching the Bulls.

"My health is fine, and my age doesn't mean a damn thing,"[19] he said to Melissa Isaacson.

For a man with a military background, the accusations of betrayal must have been especially painful. The fact that Jackson purposely lied to get the Illinois native fired from his home state team did not influence his position in the NBA, as he continued to coach the Bulls and later the Los Angeles Lakers, guiding them to multiple championships.

By all accounts, this was the hardest offseason of Jerry Krause's career as general manager. In late June reports surfaced that Pippen was on the trading block because of his behavior during Game Three against the Knicks and the negativity he continued to spread around the team. One rumor had Pippen going to the Kings for Mitch Richmond and the eighth pick in the draft. Another possibility was trading Pippen for a top-three pick to either the Bucks, the Mavericks, or the Pistons and the chance of landing Glenn Robinson, who Krause really liked, but all bottom-three teams were happy with whoever they would pick. The Washington Bullets and the Miami Heat also wanted Pippen, the latter presumably willing to offer Glen Rice and their 12th pick.

Then there was the infamous Pippen-for-Shawn Kemp offer, which was rejected by the Sonics' owner, Barry Ackerley, who refused to trade the beloved power forward, fearing that the people in Seattle would be

Scottie Pippen buried the hatchet with Krause only after the executive retired from the Bulls (1988).

unhappy. According to the Sonics' coach George Karl, it was he who shot down the offer after being contacted by Krause. Krause said the Bulls did not contact anybody about a trade, but he also did not provide information as to who specifically inquired about Pippen. The reported deal not only disgruntled Pippen, but also hampered the chances of re-signing Grant, who could now see himself as a second-choice power forward, now that Kemp was unavailable.

"I never comment on anything regarding matters of that respect. We try to improve our team and will improve any way we can,"[20] said Krause, hesitant as always to tip his hand.

However, he did not dispel the notion that no offer was off the table: "The last time I looked, we didn't win a championship, so we have to look at every situation presented to us."[21]

That did not do much to shake off the narrative of the ungrateful executive looking to get rid of his star players. His response was that there was no chance of Jordan coming back, and so the Bulls needed to do whatever necessary to either stay competitive or rebuild. One could say that this was the biggest vote of confidence Jordan got from Krause, but he clearly was not going to acknowledge it as such.

When the Celtics' new GM M.L. Carr asked Krause for permission to talk to Jordan—still on the Bulls payroll—in exchange for a draft pick, Krause refused, not because he did not like the offer, but because he was so surprised by it.

Scott Williams was the first to leave Chicago, getting a seven-year guaranteed contract from the Sixers. Williams said the Bulls did not appreciate him and did not do their best for him to reach his full potential. Krause did not even approach him with an offer; instead, he waited for Williams's agent to reach out to the Bulls.

Grant signed with the Magic, getting more than he would have got, as well as more than he wanted, from the Bulls. Sam Smith pointed out that Grant's proposed five-year deal for $21 million that he presented to Krause and Reinsdorf was worth more annually than the annual salaries of Jordan and Pippen, and the Bulls simply could not agree to it without further damaging the relationship between the front office and both players.[22] After moving to Florida, Grant continued to trash Krause in the media, blaming him for the atmosphere on the team, while praising the laid-back attitude of the Magic organization.

After his first season in the NBA, in which he *just* made the All-Rookie Second Team, Kukoč was signed by the Bulls to a six-year deal worth $26 million. Krause was not making new friends within the organization by refusing to pay the third-best player on a championship team, only to shell out more money to a sophomore foreigner. During the Olympics in Atlanta Krause was seen attending games of the Croatian national team, closely monitoring his prized possession and admiring the big man's passing skills.

Pippen, Armstrong, and Perdue were the only team members left who remembered hoisting up the first championship trophy in franchise history back in 1991. Looking at the 1994-95 roster, that moment seemed more distant than it really was.

Ron Harper had averaged 19.3 points, 5.2 rebounds and 4.9 assists in eight NBA seasons prior to signing with the Bulls that summer, but unlike the Cavaliers and the Clippers, the Bulls saw Harper primarily as a defender. Harper welcomed the change, speaking with appreciation about the structure that seemed to be lacking in Cleveland and Los Angeles: "Other teams I've been on tried to find out what style of basketball we were going to play. The Bulls know what kind of style they want to play. Any time you come to camp on the first day and they tell you this is what you have to learn and this is what you have to do, that's good."[23]

When Harper became a free agent, he demanded a five-year deal worth $20 million from the Clippers, while for the Knicks or the Bulls he was willing to take a pay cut. He signed for around $2 million per year, which showed how much he valued winning.

And that was the kind of player Krause valued.

Robert "Corky" Meinecke of the *Detroit Free Press* put forth the insane proposition that the Bulls should consider trading for.... Dennis Rodman and his expiring contract with the Spurs. In an act of incredible foreshadowing, Meinecke wrote that "Rodman respects Phil Jackson. He respects Scottie Pippen. And you know he'd love returning to the Eastern Conference, especially in the same division with the Pistons. He is motivated by fame and money, and he can get plenty of both in Chicago."[24] Meinecke predicted that getting Rodman was Krause's last chance at a championship, and in a way he was right. However, Krause was not yet ready for the gamble.

Before the new season could start, it was time to cut ties with the past. And what better way to do that than by turning the player who elevated the Bulls (and the NBA) like no other in history into a statue in front of their new arena? Suspended and motionless, the statue served as a reminder that Jordan was not returning to the floor. Undoubtedly a hero, but a hero from a time long gone.

The Bulls moved from Chicago Stadium to the United Center, just across the street. Roger B. Brown of the *Fort Worth Star-Telegram* characterized it best when he wrote about "a brand-spanking new building with luxury boxes and movie seats, a state-of-the-art structure that sticks out like sore thumb in a drug-infested, ghetto-like neighborhood."[25]

Bill Savage told me that as of the writing of this book, almost 30 years later, it still does: "When you go to Google Maps and look up the United Center, it is surrounded by vast parking lots. Those parking lots had been densely populated Black neighborhoods that were in decline because of deindustrialization, that were devastated during the Martin Luther King riots. The area is still depopulated."

In preparation for the 1996 Democratic National Convention, which was planned for late August, Mayor Richard M. Daley spent $60 million to beautify the streetscape, but as Savage pointed out, "he didn't invest in affordable housing or businesses, so the United Center still sits in an island of parking, which in American urbanology is really a suburban thing."

Michałowicz, who started extensively covering the Bulls in 1995, reminisced that he was urged by a man who presented himself as a security guard—although there was no proof of him holding such function, let alone being associated with the Bulls in any way—to park his car in a particular spot just to "keep it safe." The price for that service was $5.

"On a normal day your car wouldn't survive the day here," was what the security guard told him. Back then there was rubble everywhere and the parking was not regulated in any way. Last time Michałowicz was in Chicago, for the 2019 All-Star Weekend, he had to pay $50 just to park his car near the arena.

Coming back to November 1, 1994, first Jordan's statue was revealed, and then his jersey was retired, stopping midway to the rafters, like the player who seemed to hang in the air whenever he jumped to attack the basket. The ceremony was not held mid-game, as these things usually are, but was a separate event, and from a Chicago standpoint made very little sense. Apart from few basketball-related personalities, like coaches Dean Smith and Bobby Knight, the ceremony had also little to do with the sport.

Jordan's statue was revealed by journalist Larry King, who like Jordan was born in Brooklyn. King was dressed in a Bulls jacket. Fellow Brooklynite Spike Lee, Michigan comedian Sinbad, Texan Woody Harrelson, and Philadelphia group Boyz II Men all were present, heard, and applauded by the crowd.

Chicago columnist Bernie Lincicome was on point when he wrote that "the night was pretty much a series of people Jordan didn't know telling him how glad they were to finally meet him."[26]

When the host of the event, Ahmad Rashad, asked Krause a question, the people in the arena started booing. Rashad even paused for a couple of seconds, confused. To save the situation he then turned around to Spike Lee and joked: "Spike, would you sit down?" before turning back and explaining his joke, "They're booing Spike over there, he's a Knicks fan."

The people continued to boo even when Krause was talking about Jordan's family and the qualities that made him so special as a player, his words of respect for his mother and late father bouncing off the listeners because of who was saying them. When they booed Bobby Knight, he took it as a true heel, a bad guy who wanted to be bad, but for the crowd to boo one of their own, the most prominent Chicagoan in that organization, was particularly telling about the fans' attitude toward the people in the front office.

The person most affected by it was Thelma Krause, who cried as her husband was being booed and whose tears in turn affected Krause, who said: "The night I saw her crying at Michael's thing really bothered me because Michael had said some things over the years that he didn't need to say."[27] It was Jordan who was cruel to Krause, yet Krause was the bad guy.

The new, revamped Bulls sure did not play like the old ones. At the halfway mark of the season they had 21 wins and 21 losses, and risked missing the playoffs. The atmosphere in the organization was awful and only one man was to blame for this.

"He lies about everything. He's one of those guys who can look you in the eye and lie," Pippen said about Jerry Krause, criticizing the executive for not trading him and not re-signing Grant.[28]

He later complained to the media that the Bulls needed a power forward in order to compete and he was willing to be part of a trade to bring one in, alluding to the failed move for Kemp. Rising NBA salaries made Pippen angry about his contract, and Kemp felt the same way about his deal with the Sonics. Both became top players, yet both sacrificed their negotiating positions for long-term security.

Pippen was making the situation in the locker room unbearable. Phil Jackson used it to paint himself as the voice of reason, further cultivating the myth of the Zen Master. He said to the press: "I'm going around with a fire extinguisher and there's a forest fire."[29] He added that in the first two years of his contract Pippen had been overpaid and now, because of inflation, he was suffering the consequences of a long-term deal.

His behavior was getting more and more erratic. Apart from picking up 12 technical fouls during the first half of the season, he threw a chair during a game against the Spurs.

Reserve center Bill Wennington defended his teammate, saying:

"We're all human. We've all thrown things around the house. It's unfortunate, in his case, that half the world got to see him do it."[30]

Pippen described his relationship with Krause as "beyond hate" and doubled down on his trade demand. It seemed that wherever the Bulls played, Pippen was telling the local journalists that he wanted to play there. Whether it was Milwaukee or Oakland, he would be happier than in Chicago.

Meanwhile, trade rumors continued. The Golden State Warriors were reportedly offering Latrell Sprewell and two first-round picks, while the Houston Rockets were willing to part with Robert Horry, Sam Cassell, and two first-round picks for Pippen.

When Vernon Maxwell of the Rockets ran into the stands to punch a fan who made fun of his stillborn baby, and got a 10-game suspension, Pippen commented: "Better him than me. I'm glad I found out what it costs to go into the stands after Krause."[31] The journalists, who usually sided with the players in these arguments, almost unanimously called Pippen's actions embarrassing.

Eventually, Pippen decided to continue playing for the Bulls until the summer and consider his options afterward, choosing to focus on making the playoffs first. And the rumor was that when time came, one of the first teams Krause would contact was going to be the Timberwolves, who had power forward Tom Gugliotta and shooting guard Doug West, both of whom Krause had targeted in the past.[32]

The situation changed in the middle of March, after reports of Michael Jordan attending Bulls workouts leaked to the press. Krause, per usual, downplayed the rumors. Even when people in league offices called him, he still refused to admit what was transpiring, presumably afraid of being fined.

Pippen had some fun with the rumor and when the camera was on him during a game against the Cavaliers, he pointed at the sole of his shoe with the Jumpman logo on it, suggesting that Jordan was going to soon make a comeback. Other teammates were careful to not get their hopes up, especially Kukoč, Kerr, and Wennington, who had joined the team a year and a half earlier hoping to play with Jordan, only to learn about his retirement a month before the start of the season.

The 10 days of speculation, with seemingly every sports journalist in the country weighing in on whether Jordan was going to return to basketball or not, ended on March 19, 1995, with Phil Jackson confirming that yes, Jordan was indeed back on the Bulls and he was going to suit up for the game against the Indiana Pacers. The Bulls were 34–31 at the time, yet the announcement immediately turned them into title favorites. And not everybody was happy about that.

"When Michael left, I had no advance warning. Now when he comes back, I have no advance warning. I was totally convinced we were never going to see Michael again. I would not have signed Harper if I had known that,"[33] said Krause with palpable anxiety.

His hands were tied at the moment, and he could not make any roster moves. The team was in transition, between staying competitive and rebuilding, and that summer was going to be crucial for its future. All of that had to be scrapped and players had to be evaluated differently, the main criteria being whether they could play next to Jordan during games and against him in practice.

And yet soon, in the first round of the playoffs with the Bulls facing the Hornets, Krause's vision of Jordan, Pippen, and Kukoč playing together on fast breaks, in synchronicity, came to fruition. The Bulls progressed to the next round rather easily, but they fell to the Orlando Magic—a young, brash team, which hugely benefited from Horace Grant's mentorship. When the Magic eliminated the Bulls, Chicago fans booed Grant, who first pointed at Jerry Krause, sitting in the stands, and then mockingly waved to the crowd. A year ago he was one of their favorite players, now he was on the shoulders of their rivals, celebrating the Bulls' loss.

"He was our MVP in this series. This win was for Horace. He was the key to this team,"[34] Shaquille O'Neal said of the Magic.

9

Tough Guys Don't Dance

The first order of business was assuring Pippen of his worth to the Bulls and putting an end to his trade demands. Keeping him on the team would guarantee keeping Jordan there as well. Jackson and Krause put their differences aside in order to convince one of the best defensive players in the league that he should stay in the only NBA franchise he had ever played for.

However, that did not mean that the Bulls were not listening to offers, with Jordan being the only untouchable member of the roster. With the NBA about to extend beyond the borders of the United States, to Toronto and Vancouver, an expansion draft was coming up and some hard choices had to be made.

Krause opted for freeing cap space by making guards B.J. Armstrong and Ron Harper available, along with Corie Blount, who did not turn into the predicted replacement for Horace Grant. Harper was a disappointment, struggling to learn the triangle offense and averaging career lows in minutes (19.9) and points per game (6.9, almost nine less than his previous career low). Armstrong was the best player among all made available to the expansion teams. His $2.5 million salary was supposed to be the main reason for leaving him unprotected.

"So much for all the Bulls' talk about being a family and about appreciating loyalty,"[1] said his agent, Arn Tellem.

Krause needed the cap space because he was looking for a more conventional power forward than Kukoč. Apart from Armstrong's salary, Krause was also looking for a taller playmaker, now that the 6'7" Anfernee Hardaway of the Orlando Magic was supposed to be the top point guard in the NBA for years to come. When the expansion draft concluded, the Bulls still had somebody like that on their roster—the 6'6" Ron Harper, whom neither the Raptors nor the Grizzlies picked.

"Obviously, if we had not been prepared to lose B.J., we wouldn't have put him on the list,"[2] Krause said cryptically.

9. Tough Guys Don't Dance

As for the power forward, the Bulls were interested in versatile restricted free agent Anthony Mason. At 6'8" he was able to overpower bigger players, like Hakeem Olajuwon, whom he guarded during longer periods of the 1994 NBA Finals, and later in his career would play as point guard for the Milwaukee Bucks. Instead of Mason, who clearly had an attitude problem and was openly challenging his coaches, the Bulls brought in somebody else, equally as far as possible from the criteria players in previous years had had to meet to be qualified as O.K.P. (Our Kind of People).

The Spurs had had enough of Dennis Rodman, who had been clashing with authority figures ever since coach Chuck Daly left the Pistons in 1992. On the Spurs, Rodman experienced a mental breakdown and came out of it changed, more confident than ever before. He titled his autobiography *Bad as I Wanna Be* for a reason. During the 1995 playoffs, with the Spurs having the best chance to win the NBA championship at that point, Rodman seemed out of it. He did not pay attention in the huddle, sometimes not joining it at all. He took his shoes off before one of the games concluded. But when he was focused and motivated, he was by far the best rebounder in the NBA. Keeping him that way would be the ultimate test for the Zen Master, who welcomed the challenge.

When the trade was announced, Jackson said: "I guess this is on my shoulders, I was left room to make this choice."[3]

Rodman was traded for Perdue, after the center's only season as a starter following seven years on the Bulls. He was brought in to come off the bench behind the reigning league MVP, David Robinson. Still, the move was criticized by the beat writers in Detroit, who knew Rodman and remembered the ugly way he left Detroit for San Antonio. Corky Meinecke, who a year earlier ago put forth the proposition that Rodman should join the Bulls, now wrote that Rodman was "vulgar and repulsive," calling the trade "too funny. But this happens when great teams try to resurrect their glory days.... The thing is, it's already too late."[4]

The Chicago journalists were not fans of the deal either, partially because of how well liked Perdue was, with his blue-collar work ethic relatable to the people in the city, but they wrote about the move with careful optimism, apart from the *Chicago Tribune*'s Bob Verdi, who called it "the smartest move by the Bulls since their response to Michael Jordan's sudden retirement."[5]

During our talk, Telander reminisced that "signing Rodman was seen as crazy. Good luck. The guy did not respect David Robinson! And David Robinson is in the Hall of Fame. Rodman was a very nice guy at heart, but a very strange person."

Accused of lying by Rodman's soon to be teammate, Scottie Pippen,

Krause surprised Rodman with his honesty. He did not guarantee him anything, instead talking about expecting the power forward to play hard, tough, and stay away from trouble.

"Holy shit, that sounds cool,"[6] was Rodman's reply.

Krause complimented his rebounding ability the only way he knew how—by comparing him to other players. Jordan got offended by Krause's comparisons to Earl Monroe and Elgin Baylor. Rodman did not care all that much that the GM likened him to Paul Silas and Charles Oakley, who like Rodman were not leapers, but used "their brains or heart" to grab the ball.[7] In fact, Krause was so sold on Rodman that he criticized the power forward's not making the 1996 All-Star team. Krause also spoke out against the six-game penalty issued by the league after Rodman head-butted a referee who gave him his second technical foul during a game against the New Jersey Nets.

Rodman was 34 years old and writers with the knowledge of his off-court exploits predicted that his career would soon be over. I asked Al Vermeil whether he did something to prolong Rodman's NBA lifespan like he did with Cartwright, and the answer was surprising:

> I did not interfere with Dennis. When you have a player who played as long as he did and has a unique personality, and I don't mean that negatively, I told him if I could help him I would. I remember telling him: "Dennis, you've been in this league a long time and you've been successful without me, but if you want my help, I will help you." He was looking at the stuff we were doing, asking questions, but he did his own stuff. I basically let Dennis be Dennis. And it worked for us.

Krause played his part in building a safe environment for Rodman, bringing in his former Pistons teammates James Edwards and John Salley (in a mid-season trade with the Raptors) and his close friend Jack Haley, who would end up playing just one game for the Bulls that season. When I asked Vermeil whether Haley's function during workouts and games was purely ornamental, he quickly denied it:

> Jack had a good training background before we got him. He'd been at UCLA and he had trained hard. He was a good person, a big, strong, good-looking California surfer. As far as him being Rodman's caretaker, it was always implied they came as a package deal, but I didn't involve myself in the things I didn't need to know. Jack wasn't a hanger-on, he wanted to work, he came with the intention to play. Obviously, there was something to that companionship, but he didn't just come in to pick up his paycheck. He worked hard.

By losing Perdue, the Bulls found themselves in need of strengthening the center position. However, it turned out that the perfect center for

Dennis Rodman meshed with the rest of the roster, including Michael Jordan (1996).

their system was already there, he just needed more minutes. Similarly to Ron Harper at point guard and Horace Grant at power forward in the past, trading away Perdue and sticking with Luc Longley was another case of addition by subtraction.

In January 1996 the Bulls had flown freshly retired Sam Bowie to Chicago for talks. When healthy, Bowie was one of the best passing big men in the NBA. In the end he preferred to remain retired and spend time with his family, despite Chicago's proximity to Lexington, where he lived, and the Bulls being OK with him having his own practice schedule.

Krause was not constructing the roster for the 1994-95 season with Jordan's return in mind, yet the players he was able to acquire during the summer of 1994 turned out to perfectly complement Jordan's game to an extent that nobody had expected, with the Bulls dominating the opposition and finishing the 1995-96 season with an unprecedented record of 72 wins and just 10 losses. Jordan was named MVP, Rodman Defensive Player of the Year, Kukoč Sixth Man of the Year, Jackson Coach of the Year, and Krause Executive of the Year. It was the second time he had won the award, at the moment one of only four executives to achieve that feat, and two trophies short of the only front office worker to win the award more than twice, his mentor Jerry Colangelo. Krause got 11 votes, with the Spurs' Gregg Popovich coming in second with six.

"What makes you real proud is what an honor it is to be voted on by your peers, but it makes me feel good for the entire organization,"[8] said Krause, praising the work of everybody involved in allowing the players on the team to just focus on playing basketball.

"I think the second championship run was even more impressive than the first, just because Krause was able to build the team so quickly, with just Jordan and Pippen from the previous dynasty," said Wojciech Michałowicz, who had tried being a general manager, so he knew how hard a job it was to run a basketball organization.

During the 1996 championship celebration at Grant Park, Krause wanted all the members of the organization to feel appreciated. He took it upon himself to introduce people to those Chicagoans who were oblivious to such knowledge: scouts Jim Stack and Clarence Gaines, Jr., international scout Ivica "Duke" Dukan ("who travels all over the world looking for players to help you people celebrate"), Karen Stack ("my left arm"), and statistician Pam Kunkel, as well as strength coaches Al Vermeil and Erik Helland.

Krause was basically saying the same thing he said a year later—that organizations win champions—but at the time he was cheered by

9. Tough Guys Don't Dance

the city of Chicago, a rare instance when he was appreciated for his work. Even Jordan had to admit: "As sadly as it might be to say it, you have to give him some credit. I'm pretty sure he's deserving of some."[9]

In the summer, despite the success of the team, Krause was considering replacing Phil Jackson with a new head coach, Tim Floyd. Their relationship had begun in 1988, when Krause was scouting Louisiana Tech's power forward, senior Randy White, who he considered taking with the sixth pick in the 1989 NBA draft. Krause would pick Stacey King, and White would be selected eighth overall by the Mavericks. Floyd was coaching Louisiana Tech's opposition during that game, the New Orleans Privateers.

"We had the smallest team in the country at the University of New Orleans, we had a 6'4" center, and he watched us play them three times that year. He walked up to me after the third time we played them and he said: 'Look, I'm Jerry Krause from the Chicago Bulls and I just want to let you know I'd like you to be the next head coach of the Bulls.'"[10]

Krause had called Floyd a week later, and continued to do so more or less once a week. He wanted the coach to learn the triangle offense, but Floyd refused, thinking it did not fit his team at the time. Yet they continued to talk after Floyd took over Iowa State University in 1994, and around that time the calls intensified, became more of a daily than a weekly thing. They talked mostly about basketball. But Krause wanted to know whether Floyd was O.K.P., so he visited him and the two went fishing. According to Floyd, Krause did not know how to fish, but after Floyd taught him how to do it, he became hooked.

Thelma Krause confirmed that fishing became Krause's hobby somewhere around 1994, but told me that it was not Floyd but Bulls assistant coach Jimmy Rodgers who had a house at Lake Geneva and, along with his brother, taught Krause how to fish. She continued:

> When we bought our house, it had a pond, which we called a lake, but it's a pond. And it had a lot of fish in it and that was it, that was his relaxation. He loved to fish. And when we bought the house in Arizona in 2009 it was also on the water and he had hoped to fish there, but it was more of a waterway that really wasn't stacked and he was disappointed, because he didn't get to fish there much.

Asked why he liked fishing so much, Krause replied: "I really enjoy it. I never had a hobby because my vocation was my avocation. Some guys bowl, some hunt. But Jack Brickhouse had the best line about that. When the deer gets a gun, then it's even, it's a sport. I couldn't kill an animal."[11]

Rick Telander described the affinity for fishing as the most surprising thing about Krause: "I mean, the guy grew up in Chicago, fishing is not in your culture. That was the first time the guy was seen as human."

With Phil Jackson's deal expiring on July 1, 1996, Tim Floyd was presented as one of three candidates for the head coaching job only after he was seen during the finals, both in Chicago and Seattle. If not for that, the relationship between Krause and Floyd would have stayed secret. The coach, 42 at the time, was renegotiating his deal with Iowa State after amassing the 46–20 record in his first two years at the job.

Reinsdorf had grown distrustful of Jackson, who started undermining Krause publicly and privately. After Game Three of the 1996 finals Krause was still giving interviews, while the team and the coaches were ready to head back to the hotel, waiting for the bus. Jackson ordered the team bus to leave without the GM. The next day, after the team was leaving practice, Jordan asked: "Can we leave? Is the fat guy here yet?"[12]

Jackson's approach worked on the players, who sided with their head coach. However, the man who signed the checks sided with Krause, because they shared the same vision for basketball. As pointed out by Sam Smith in an article on the issue: "Jackson's requests for personnel control and reins on Krause began to strike Reinsdorf as Collins-like. Reinsdorf saw Krause as having saved Jackson's career. For Jackson to reject Krause was unholy."[13]

When Pippen was abusing Krause in the press, the latter took it like a champ, not for a moment letting it be known that he had no authority to renegotiate deals, which was Reinsdorf's common practice. If you signed a deal with Reinsdorf, you had to honor it, just like he was going to honor his part. That was true in the case of Jordan's contract with the Bulls, which Reinsdorf paid out even after Jordan's first retirement, but it worked the other way around as well.

In the summer of 1996, the most important contracts were out of Krause's hands, as both Jackson and Jordan negotiated directly with Reinsdorf. The latter, for years underpaid, got a one-year deal worth $30 million. His salary alone exceeded the league-imposed cap by close to $6 million, undermining Krause's annual efforts of staying under it.

The Bulls were able to bring back almost all members of the championship roster, including Rodman, who during the early stages of negotiations complained to the press about the Bulls' initial offer of $6 million.

"This isn't personal, and I know Jerry Krause is just doing his job, but the offer that's on the table just isn't fair. It isn't about the money, it's about respect," said Rodman's agent, Dwight Manley. "Money is not the issue here, he'll play somewhere else for $1 for the sake of pride."[14]

Reinsdorf and Krause presumably thought that they could get Rodman to sign for a lower price because thanks to being in Chicago he was making more money off the court through his various TV and movie deals than in San Antonio. Terry Armour of the *Chicago Tribune* hoped that Rodman did not "hold a grudge from contract negotiations,"[15] which could lead to him behind unhappy, unmotivated, and behaving the way he did on the Spurs.

The veteran center spot, vacated by 40-year-old James Edwards, was taken by 43-year-old Robert Parish, whom Krause had been coveting since 1994, when he was a free agent ready to leave the Celtics. The Celtics wanted to move on after the Big Three Era, of which Parish was the last remnant, following retirements by Larry Bird in 1992 and Kevin McHale in 1993. And now, after he'd spent two years in Charlotte playing behind Alonzo Mourning, Krause finally had Parish. When I asked Vermeil about his plan to keep Parish healthy, he answered that a player like that knew exactly what he needed to do to stay in shape.

In order to keep the roster spot for Parish free, Krause did not sign his draft pick, center Travis Knight, who was picked up by the Los Angeles Lakers instead. Krause was certain that he was going to land 7'4" Chicagoan Priest Lauderdale with the pick, but he was snatched up from underneath his nose, with the Hawks trading their three second-round picks for the 28th selection with the Sonics. Krause was angry, because he wanted Lauderdale to remain his secret.

"That Jerry Krause, he's a smart fellow, but he really wants things his own way,"[16] said Lauderdale. He did not elaborate on the topic, but knowing how secretive Krause was with Pippen and Majerle in the past, it was clear what Lauderdale was alluding to. The center played in the 1996 All-Star Game of the Greek basketball league, so he was not much of a secret anyway.

The 1996-97 season was filled with speculation regarding what was going to happen with the roster, with Krause and Reinsdorf being associated more than ever before, and the team and the head coach being on the other side of this inner battle. The narrative was that the "Two Jerrys" wanted to break up the team and start rebuilding, with Tim Floyd on the bench and Toni Kukoč as the focal point of the offense. Sensing that something was going to happen, Jackson negotiated with the Orlando Magic during the playoffs. The team from Florida reportedly proposed a five-year deal worth $30 million. It was no secret that Jackson was also monitoring if an opening came up with the Lakers, who had Shaquille O'Neal, a cast of young guards in Nick Van Exel, Eddie Jones, and Kobe Bryant, and an esteemed executive in Jerry West.

In a sense, West was everything Krause was not: a former player who enjoyed a Hall of Fame career and a respected front office presence. The man was the logo of the NBA. Krause could never compete with that. And yet West, as beloved as he was in Los Angeles, lost the power struggle with Jackson. When West quit as the vice president of basketball operations after the Lakers won the 2000 championship, he wrote a farewell note in which he thanked the people in the organization by name, but made no mention of Jackson. It was later revealed that Jackson saw West as an adversary. In his biography of Jackson, Lazenby calls Jackson's hastening of West's resignation "a virtually bloodless coup to clear up the team's management picture."[17]

If Jackson was able to alienate one of the most respected players and executives in the game, his inability to get rid of the 5'5" Jerry Krause may very well be considered one of the bigger failures of what Lazenby calls Jackson's "mind games." In Los Angeles no reasonable journalist would side with Jackson against West; in Chicago it was hard to find any reason to side with the unapproachable and shifty GM. And yet Jackson lost. This was a testament to Reinsdorf's understanding of loyalty, something becoming much harder to come by in the world of professional sports.

The whole 1996-97 season was a power struggle over whether Jackson would go or stay. In a sense he held Krause and Reinsdorf hostage because of the attachment Jordan felt toward him. Jordan refused to re-sign with the Bulls if Jackson would not be there next season, and the pressure to keep the roster together was immense. Yet the same people who appreciated Jordan's loyalty to his coach scoffed at Reinsdorf's loyalty to Krause or Krause's attachment to Tim Floyd.

Asked about his relationship with the former, Krause replied: "Somebody asked me if I'd take a bullet for [Reinsdorf] and I said I probably would because I know he'd save me. I know damn well he would because he's stood up for me before."[18]

Jackson's agent, Todd Musburger, played a huge part in building up the public pressure for the Bulls to re-sign Jackson, stating to the press that "Michael's support was a statement of tremendous loyalty from a superstar to his coach."[19]

The roster stayed intact throughout the season, despite rumors of trading Ron Harper for Golden State Warriors icon Chris Mullin, who at 32 was willing to move on and join a championship contender. He would join the Indiana Pacers and cause some problems for the Bulls in their quest for their third consecutive championship.

With nine games left in the regular season, the Bulls signed Brian Williams, the 10th pick of the 1991 NBA draft, who had had a breakout year on the Clippers, averaging 15.8 points and 7.6 rebounds. He demanded too much money, however, which caused the Clippers and the Sonics to sign other players. Both teams would regret their decisions. During the season various teams courted Williams but were reluctant to sign a player who had to undergo knee surgery because of something he did off the court—reportedly he was injured while skydiving.

The Bulls decided to give him a shot after he was evaluated by Vermeil: "He was a character, I liked him. I remember one day he comes in the training room at 4 PM and the players are gone, it's only me. And he said he had to put ice on something, because he went down to the soccer field and played soccer with a bunch of kids."

Professional basketball players are contractually obligated to abstain from non-work-related activities that may cause injuries, so it is somewhat understandable why the Clippers were afraid to give Williams the seven-year, $101 million contract that he demanded.

Krause, never missing the opportunity to stock up on big men, was happy about the signing, even though he gave the press a rather generic answer about how "the addition of Brian Williams gives us a proven NBA rebounder, scorer and defender to help us in our quest for another championship."[20]

The relationship ended bitterly, as Williams claimed that Krause promised to pay him the double playoff bonus for his contributions. Because he was signed for only $27,500, according to Williams the GM wanted to compensate him for his contributions by giving him $260,000. Williams eventually got $130,000. Playoff shares were traditionally decided on by the players, and one of them did not need much to jump on the opportunity to criticize the GM.

"We didn't get approached, and I think it was unfair of Jerry to make a promise to a player knowing he has no control over how the playoff shares are divided with the players,"[21] said Pippen, taking Williams at his word.

"It's a total falsehood," replied Krause, willing to take a lie detector test.

There was no chance for Williams to return after these accusations. He did not have the status of a Pippen or a Jackson, let alone a Jordan, to call Krause out publicly. They were "allowed" to disrespect Krause because of their contributions to the team through the years.

The negotiations with Jackson and Jordan made for another tense summer, filled with criticism for the GM. Krause and Reinsdorf were described as plotters, who wanted to deprive the people of the pleasure of watching Michael Jordan. When he said that his conditions to re-sign with the team were that the Bulls keep Jackson and Pippen, Krause and

Reinsdorf found themselves stuck. Both wanted the team to rebuild instead of being stuck with veteran players on high contracts and thought that 1997 was the right time to do it. But public opinion wanted Jordan and the NBA needed him too, so there was this surrounding pressure for the Bulls to be the same team they had been a year ago.

Krause and Jackson hit an impasse just like they had the year earlier, when negotiating the head coach's salary. Krause was offering him $3 million, Jackson wanted $6 million. Reinsdorf had to go to Jackson's home in Montana and personally negotiate the deal with the head coach.

Jim Litke of *The Associated Press* criticized how "for the second consecutive year, the Jerrys made Jackson wait for an offer and then threw him a lowball. At another juncture, Jackson was reportedly thrown out of his office at the training center while Krause worked out a potential draft pick."[22] If that indeed happened—and it is hard to understand why Krause and his scouts would be in Jackson's office deciding on who to draft, since they had offices of their own—Jackson took a page from that book with the Lakers and threw Jerry West out of the locker room, saying: "Jerry get the fuck out, I'm not finished here yet,"[23] disrespecting the general manager in front of the whole team.

Asked in Deerfield whether the Bulls were now going to sign Jordan, after Jackson was taken care of, Krause replied that he first wanted to sign Jackson's assistants; only then would he start re-signing players. This year Jordan was not negotiating with the Knicks, as he had a year earlier, demanding a better deal than the one-year, $25 million contract the team from New York was offering him. This year he was certain that if the Bulls met his demand to keep Jackson, he was going to get his contract. He signed a one-year deal for $36 million, the biggest single-season contract in professional sports at the time.

In comparison to what was happening with contracts in the NBA in late 1990s and taking his contributions to the game of basketball into account, it was still seen as a reasonable signing. On October 1, 1997, Chicago native Kevin Garnett would sign a six-year deal worth $126 million with the Timberwolves. It was the first time that a basketball player was paid so much based on potential. Other members of the 1995 draft class also signed contract extensions, the most notable being Rasheed Wallace's six-year deal with the Blazers, worth $80 million, and Bryant Reeves's six-year deal for $65 million with the Vancouver Grizzlies. These contracts, as well as the deals signed during the previous summer by Shaquille O'Neal with the Lakers ($120 million for seven years), Alonzo Mourning with the Heat ($105 million for seven years), and Juwan Howard with the Bullets ($105 million for seven years), would have serious consequences after that season was over.

That summer the proudest moment of Jerry Krause's life occurred, and it had nothing to do with basketball. On September 27, 1997, Krause walked Thelma's daughter, Stacy, down the aisle.

"Even now he would tell you that this was the proudest he ever felt. At home he was Dad and he loved it," said Thelma Krause.

Nobody covering the Bulls wrote about Krause giving away the bride and the bond he was able to build with her. Instead, the focus was on Phil Jackson not getting an invitation to the wedding and Tim Floyd's appearance at the ceremony, as if anybody would want to celebrate one of the most important moments of their lives with a person who was undermining them privately and publicly.

The 1997 draft brought about another generation of promising players. According to Scottie Pippen, Rick Pitino of the Celtics was willing to trade for him and Luc Longley in exchange for the third and the sixth picks in the draft, as well as the 1999 first-round pick.[24] Another option was trading Pippen for the ninth pick in that draft, Tracy McGrady, with the Raptors. The promising swingman was predicted by the Bulls' medical staff to have a career filled with knee injuries, which was exactly what happened. That did not prevent McGrady from emerging as one of the top scorers of the 2000s and entering the Hall of Fame. He rarely experienced postseason glory and never won an NBA championship.

The roster from the previous two seasons was once again brought back, with the singular goal of winning an NBA championship. Anything else would have been considered a disappointment. Instead of praising the Bulls for their ability to be able to keep the roster together despite the constant tensions, there was only criticism. Jackson decided to make that the theme of the season and called it "The Last Dance."

The worst instance of criticism came from Craig DeVrieze of the *Quad-City Times*, who wrote a column titled "Jerry Krause Deserves a Slap for His One-Last-Run-and-Done Attitude." The fact that the editors approved it shows their approach to the standards of journalism.[25] Skip Bayless of the *Chicago Tribune* wrote that "dozens of other GMs could have done equally brilliant jobs building around the mighty river Jordan," while referring to Krause as "the Penguin."[26]

Even Dennis Rodman eventually gave into the narrative and complained to the press in early February 1998 that Krause was not willing to bring the team back next season. The same Rodman continued to have disciplinary issues and, in the playoffs, lost the starting spot to Toni Kukoč, who was not a power forward.

Interestingly, the Croatian, who became Phil Jackson's whipping boy and had to endure hard play from Jordan and Pippen during workouts, was also at odds with the decision, saying: "There's no reason to split a team that is winning and doing an incredible job on the court."[27]

For the Bulls, just reaching the 1998 finals was difficult, as they needed all seven games to beat the Pacers in the penultimate series of the season. To lighten the mood, when during the series Jordan found himself behind the driver's seat of the team bus and he saw Krause in front, instead of making the usual pig sounds, this time he yelled to Pippen: "Five bucks and I'll hit the gas."[28]

The Bulls won their sixth championship. The last game of the finals was the highest-rated single game in NBA Finals history, watched in around 18.3 million homes domestically. The series was transmitted to 175 countries, and it largely contributed to the development of the NBA's website, with highlights and statistics made available to the fans during halftime of each of the games. The popularity and expansion of the website were made possible by Jordan, and their growth relied on him as well. The upcoming financial drop-off was inevitable.

More than 400 people were arrested in Chicago for acts of vandalism after Game Six of the finals, but the city did not utilize 6,000 police officers and 200–300 National Guard members like it had the year before. As far as championship celebrations went, this one was bittersweet.

To nobody's surprise, Krause and Reinsdorf were booed by the crowd in Grant Park. Unbeknownst to most of the fans there, Reinsdorf gave in to the pressure and tried to convince Jackson to stay for one more season. The coach declined. In a farewell interview following the celebrations, before getting on his Harley and riding off into the sunset, Jackson said that it was liberating to leave, and it was simply his time to go.[29]

For Krause there was no relief, no break, even though the league was about to take one.

10

Footwork and Chemistry

By 3:00 p.m. on June 30, 1998, the Bulls' roster hopefuls left Deerfield. The five-day mini-camp had just concluded, and the four players left on the roster were Ron Harper, Toni Kukoč, Keith Booth, and Randy Brown. The four did not have to attend, and the most prominent of the players from the previous season at Berto Center was Rusty LaRue, who admitted: "Jerry wanted me to use the time to come in and work a little bit ... because, with the lockout, it may be two or three months before I get back up here."[1]

LaRue was a three-sport athlete at Wake Forest, playing shooting guard, quarterback, and pitcher. Undrafted in 1996, he played basketball for a year in France and the CBA and got called up by the Bulls from Idaho Stampede because of an injury to Steve Kerr. LaRue was one of the final cuts by the Bulls prior to the 1997-98 season, but Krause promised him that if something happened to Kerr, he was going to give him a call. He kept his word once Kerr went down with an injury and liked LaRue so much that he left him on the championship roster. Now he wanted to bring him back as a part of the rebuilding team.

On July 1, the lockout officially began and the Bulls had 10 roster spots to fill, as well as a coaching vacancy, with four potential candidates. They could not sign players, trade them, or allow them to use team facilities, but a new coach could be brought on at any time.

Scott Skiles and Paul Silas were the two biggest names among potential Bulls head coaches. Both were former NBA players, but Skiles was 21 years younger than Silas, and perhaps too ambitious and intense for his own good. Silas was a more accomplished player, but at 55, he had only three seasons of head coaching experience, collected back when the Clippers still played in San Diego.

Another potential head coach was Frank Hamblen, Bulls assistant coach during the last two seasons, who according to Phil Jackson was instrumental in developing the gameplan to beat the Jazz in the

1998 Finals.² The downside was Hamblen's age. He was already 51, well respected and established as an assistant, not so much as a head coach. This left the 44-year-old Tim Floyd as the only candidate possessing the desired combination of age and experience to become the head coach.

Jordan complained to the press that the Bulls were "pushing him out of basketball" by hiring Floyd, adding that he did not want "any input in the coaching."³ He just wanted to play for Phil Jackson and nobody else. It was reported that Floyd had second thoughts about taking the coaching job because he did not want to be the man who chased away Jordan from basketball.⁴ He even contacted Jordan's friend Buzz Peterson and informed him that if Jordan would return under the condition that Jackson would be back as head coach, Floyd would not stand in his way.

One of the people to be first to react to Floyd's hire was Kirk Hinrich, a senior high school basketball player, who committed to Iowa State during his junior year at West High School in Sioux City. Instead of continuing to play in his home state, Hinrich would eventually decide on Kansas.

"I committed to Iowa State because of Coach Floyd. I knew this was a possibility. I'm real disappointed he left, but I understand. He had the opportunity of a lifetime, and you've got to take that,"⁵ said Hinrich, justifying his decision.

Hinrich would enter the NBA draft in 2003 and with the seventh overall pick join the Bulls in their first offseason without Krause, a year and a half after Floyd resigned as the head coach.

With the fear of the NBA 1998-99 season's not taking place, the fans were not only stripped of the pleasure of watching the Michael Jordans, but also the Randy Browns and the Rusty LaRues. Six months of speculations and rumors were officially over on January 6, 1999, with the National Basketball Players Association and the NBA reaching an agreement on the new collective bargaining agreement, which was supposed to come into effect that season and apply for six years. Soon came the details regarding the new season. It was supposed to be shortened to 50 games, but the schedule was more packed.

On January 13, Jordan officially retired for the second time.

On January 15, the Bulls officially named Floyd as their head coach and Krause was extremely supportive, asking for time and patience for his new hire during their first joint press conference: "No other coach has had to step into a situation quite like this one. It will be tough following a coach and a team like we've had and beginning a career under the odd challenges of this season."⁶

Ian Thomsen described the dynamic between Floyd and Krause:

"Jerry had a situation when the coach was relying on him, because Tim Floyd had no NBA experience. I think Jerry wanted a coach who would take direction from him."

Floyd was coming off his first losing season during his 12 years of work in Division I, but he entered the situation with enthusiasm and humor. It was revealed that his contract was for five years and $2 million per season, which showed the faith that Krause had in him and his abilities. Floyd had two requests to the press: "Don't call me Jerry Krause's boy, OK? And don't call what Jerry Krause does fishing."[7]

The players were not as enthusiastic, as they knew that what awaited them were losses. A lot of losses.

"I will be playing for a team I don't know, for a coach I don't know. I'm just waiting for opening night to grab my third championship rings,"[8] said Ron Harper.

Coaches and executives could not talk to the players until January 18, but the players could use team facilities. Among those seen in Deerfield were Kukoč, Harper, Longley, and Kerr, but not Pippen or Rodman.[9]

Krause was orchestrating sign-and-trade deals for most of the players, with no intention of bringing back the troublesome Rodman, the injury-prone Longley (missed 24 games the season prior to knee issues), or the disgruntled Pippen. The small forward reportedly wanted to earn $17–$20 million per season to make up for the money he had "lost" because of his long-term deal with the Bulls, but because of the new CBA he could make only around $10 million.[10] Longley signed a five-year deal for $30 million and was immediately traded to the Suns for Mark Bryant, Martin Muursepp, Bubba Wells, and a conditional first-round pick. Rodman started the season without a team and would be picked up by the desperate Los Angeles Lakers, who were hoping for a championship run with him in the fold. Steve Kerr signed a five-year deal for $11 million and was traded to the Spurs for a draft pick and veteran Chuck Person.

Jud Buechler, who left for Detroit, and Kerr were both reached out to by the GM, who thanked them for their contributions to the NBA championships. "I was very appreciative," said Kerr. "Jerry should make a practice of that kind of communication. It really helps."[11]

Pippen re-signed with the Bulls for five years and $67.2 million only to be immediately traded to the Rockets for a second-round pick and power forward Roy Rogers. The Bulls released him before the season. In order to afford Pippen's salary, the Rockets re-signed Charles Barkley for $1 million. The power forward took a huge pay cut in hopes of winning an NBA championship alongside Pippen and Hakeem Olajuwon.

During his introductory press conference in Houston, Pippen said he called Krause, thanked him, and wished him well.[12]

With their three stars gone, the Bulls were no longer attractive for TV. They were absent from the TNT and TBS schedules, and NBC showed only one of their regular-season games. That was before the team even completed its roster. The first day of camp was canceled because the Bulls had only six players under contract. The league-wide salary minimum was set at $25 million, and the Bulls needed a substantial signing, if only to meet it.

The biggest names the Bulls were targeting were the Timberwolves' Kevin Garnett and the Pistons' Jerry Stackhouse. Chicago-born Garnett cited the Bulls' treatment of Pippen as the reason why he was not even considering joining them.[13] He had just signed a huge extension and the Timberwolves would not make it easy on him to leave anyway. Stackhouse was a shooting guard who came out of North Carolina in 1996 and was being compared to Jordan. He did not want even more pressure stepping into the position of Jordan's "successor" in Chicago, so he stayed in Detroit.[14]

With Stackhouse out of the picture, the Bulls began courting Brent Barry, who the Miami Heat brought in just before the 1998 trade deadline from the Clippers, and who was wanted by better teams than the Bulls, like the Warriors and the Suns. Despite a disappointing second half of the season with the Heat, in which he was averaging just 4.1 points per game, the Heat also wanted him back, if only to trade him for a different shooting guard. Krause was working on a deal to re-sign Scott Burrell to trade him for Barry, but eventually renounced his rights. Burrell chose the Nets and Barry signed with the Bulls for six years and $27 million. He was the biggest name acquired by the reigning NBA champions during that short offseason.

"Jerry Krause saw me play in college—he saw me more times than my dad did. He knows my game, they wanted me on draft day three years ago, so I know I'm wanted here,"[15] said Barry. The Bulls needed more statements like that if they were to land a big-name free agent after the 1998-99 season, as they were openly planning to do.

The 6'6" Barry was the son of NBA great Rick Barry, drafted 15th overall by the Denver Nuggets in 1995 and traded on draft day to the Clippers for the 2nd overall pick Antonio McDyess and small forward Rodney Rogers. In his rookie year Barry won the Slam Dunk Contest, performing the same dunk from the free throw line as Michael Jordan did in 1987. Nobody was expecting him to replace Jordan in Chicago and Barry was fine with that, as he saw himself as a complementary player: "I'm part of a plan and a piece to the puzzle. They're going to try

10. Footwork and Chemistry

to put together a championship team again within the next three or four seasons."[16]

Before the first preseason game, Bill Wennington, who returned on a one-year deal worth $1 million, speaking for the organization, asked the fans present in the arena for patience: "Last year was dubbed the last dance. This year is a lot like a first dance. And like a first dance, our footwork and chemistry might not be there at first."[17]

Harper, Barry, and Randy Brown were the most important backcourt players on the roster. Kukoč was a surefire starting small forward and the focal point of the offense. Potential starting power forward Jason Caffey was signed by the Warriors for seven years and $35 million. The Bulls were left with Dickey Simpkins, Mark Bryant, and Andrew Lang to fill the other two big-man positions. Priest Lauderdale, the 7'4" native son whom Krause really wanted in the 1997 draft, attended the Bulls training camp but did not make the roster.

"Jerry was excited," said Karen Umlauf, after I had asked her about the changes within the organization. "To just have a new coach and not being sure who your star players are going to be, that was a big challenge. But there was no difference in his work ethic and the hours he put in. I was the point person to transitioning the new players in and I was busier for sure, but Jerry continued to work hard like he always did."

Al Vermeil saw the change in the players who were brought in:

> I found that this later group wasn't as committed and that's why they didn't last long in the league. Some of them had a hard time focusing. It's not like college when you play two games per week. You're always playing against someone who's as good as you. There's more intricacy to what you're doing. A lot of the young kids had a hard time learning our offense. They were good people, just not as attentive to what they were doing.

Krause understood that the atmosphere surrounding this team was different, as he dismantled the championship roster in a couple of weeks, instead of the Bulls gradually becoming less and less of a factor in the Eastern Conference. The Boston Celtics, the Los Angeles Lakers, and the Detroit Pistons were taken down brick by brick, while Krause immediately brought a wrecking ball and destroyed what was left. The thinking was that if the Bulls had started the rebuilding process sooner, they would have been able to return to the top more quickly. They were tanking before tanking was a thing. Not many people understood and appreciated that forward-thinking approach, so Krause abandoned the traditional ring ceremony and instead handed the rings out in Deerfield, before practice.

"I think we had a good, fun time. I got a little personal about some of them and the appreciation we have for them and the appreciation we have for past teams,"[18] said Krause, adding that he showed the championship rings to the younger players to motivate them to win their own one day.

The decision to not hold the ceremony also spared them the boos that otherwise might have met them and their more established teammates as they were collecting their rings. After the first two games, played outside of Chicago, the Bulls were 1–1, after losing by eight to the Jazz and beating the Clippers by five.

"The effort has been great, and I'm really proud of this team. They're going to play hard,"[19] Krause said before the Bulls home opener against the Hawks, which was preceded by the banner-hanging ceremony.

Then they lost seven straight games. There was nothing Floyd could do to stop the losses from piling up. Jerry Reinsdorf even said that he should be named Coach of the Year, and Krause Executive of the Year.[20] But when the NBC wanted to interview the owner and the executive about their short-term and long-term plans, they refused to talk to the TV crew.

The Bulls were also costing the NBA money, with only around 6,000 fans on average attending their road games. A bad Bulls team was bad for the whole league apart from Chicago, because at home, they were somewhat surprisingly first in attendance in the whole NBA.

The Bulls finished the season 13–37, third from the bottom. During halftime of the last game of the season, the team honored Phil Jackson with a banner ceremony. Krause and Reinsdorf did not attend, and both were booed when Jackson thanked them. The Bulls lost by 20 points to playoff-bound Magic. According to the lottery odds, the league-worst Grizzlies had 250 chances out of 1,000 of landing the first overall draft pick. The second-worst Clippers got 200 chances. The Bulls had 157 chances, and the Raptors, holding the pick from the Nuggets, who were better than the Bulls by one win, had 120. Krause needed some schooling on how the lottery worked, because as a GM he never was involved in picking so low.

"We felt at the start of the season there was a realistic chance we'd wind up in the lottery," he said, downplaying the low expectations for the season, "We had lost so many players and then the injuries hit. By midseason we were like, 'Oh boy. So this is how it's going to be.'"[21]

Many players had a hard time reacting to the way Krause was trying to control the team. The young players were intimidated by his presence, not because of his stature, but because of his status as the league's top evaluator. The Sleuth was watching them all the time.

Corey Benjamin, the Bulls' first-round pick in the 1998 draft, who

10. Footwork and Chemistry

appeared in 31 games in his rookie season, averaging 3.8 points on 37.5 percent shooting, said:

> When your GM or owner is around all the time, the team isn't comfortable. You're always looking over your shoulder. At the end of the day, you report to the coaches, but now you're thinking, "Okay, well, I have the coaches' boss here too." For us, we were very uncomfortable having Jerry around all the time—riding on the bus with us, riding on the plane with us, walking around at practice.[22]

With averages of 11.1 points and 3.1 assists, Brent Barry was the third-best player on the Bulls, behind Kukoč and 35-year-old Ron Harper.

Prior to the lottery it was rumored that the Bulls were interested in Chicago native and Duke shooting guard Corey Maggette. That was until they got the chance to pick first in the 1999 draft. Grizzlies coach Brian Hill was present at the lottery, as was Krause. Hill said: "I thought he was going to fall out of his chair next to me. He was shaking like a little kid. He had his lucky pennies in his hand that was shaking, so I guess he carried all his trinkets with him today."[23]

And why shouldn't Krause be happy? Just one year into the rebuild the Bulls had the top selection and the cap space necessary to sign a big-name free agent. It was reported that the Raptors wanted to trade their fifth pick and Tracy McGrady to the Bulls in exchange for the first pick and select Steve Francis.[24] The energetic guard definitely was not going to be available at fifth. Raptors GM Glen Grunwald confirmed that the Raptors wanted to trade for the number one pick, but McGrady was off the table. Instead, the Bulls could get the fifth and the 12th picks, both held by the Raptors.[25]

Another rumor was that Krause wanted Wally Szczerbiak, an athletic long-distance shooter, similar to Dan Majerle or Brent Barry.

"It could be true. I saw Jerry Krause at quite a few of my games. He wasn't very secretive. He was right smack in the front row,"[26] said Szczerbiak, which shows that he either did not know how the Sleuth operated or was well aware of his methods and understood he was not going to Chicago.

Szczerbiak, just like Corey Maggette, was considered not worthy of being selected so high. Trading down may have been the Bulls' best option if they did not like Steve Francis or Elton Brand, the two headliners of the 1999 draft class. Two years later the Bulls would offer their 16th pick in the 2001 draft and the 2000 fourth pick, Marcus Fizer, for Szczerbiak, but the Timberwolves would demand more for the sharp shooter.

NBA's director of scouting, Marty Blake, identified the reason behind the number of potential draft trades and the main issue behind the status of this class: "It's not that it's a weak draft, the problem you have is there are no Tim Duncans."[27] The 1997 first overall pick became the focal point of the San Antonio Spurs in his second season and the main reason behind their 1999 championship.

Tim Floyd spoke in favor of keeping the pick: "My gut feeling right now is I'd like to keep it, because I see some guys who can help. But I don't know what Jerry's options are either."[28]

Whatever they were, Krause was also going to follow his gut.

The timing during the 1999 offseason was off. Krause wanted a transformational player, but the 1999 draft did not have one.

Krause had $20 million in cap space to spend, but there were no transformational free agents to sign.

Building around Jordan, Krause had been patient. This year he wanted to have the same approach. In the end, Krause kept the pick and played it safe by selecting Duke power forward Elton Brand. Brand and teammates Corey Maggette and William Avery were the first Blue Devils who were allowed by Coach Mike Krzyzewski to enter the draft without graduating. It was a sign of the times that even "Coach K" needed to loosen up some of his rules in order for his program to remain competitive in the NCAA.

Brand was the logical choice, the college player of the year, a 6'8" power forward who had "the biggest, softest hands general manager Jerry Krause ever [had] seen."[29]

For the 16th pick the Bulls went with Brand's friend, small forward Ron Artest out of St. John's. On the night preceding the draft, the two sat in the hotel hallway and talked about their experiences, which included playing against each other numerous times in games between their high schools. Artest was so happy about finally playing together with Brand that he started crying when he was selected by the Bulls.

"At St. John's, Ron sacrificed much of his individual game to fit the specific needs of the team. His ability and willingness to sacrifice his own game will make him an excellent NBA player,"[30] said Krause with appreciation.

With the 32nd pick, their first in the second round, the Bulls picked another power forward, Michael Ruffin from Tulsa. Ruffin endeared himself to the fans and the coaches by talking about his love for playing defense, adding: "My dream is to play like a Dennis Rodman ... active, aggressive and a great rebounder."[31] And just in case Brand and Ruffin did not pan out, Krause selected Lari Ketner with the 49th pick. With four picks, the Bulls picked four power forwards, as Artest was capable of playing the four position as well.

10. Footwork and Chemistry

Krause had the number one overall pick for the Bulls only once. He decided on Duke's Elton Brand (2000).

On July 16 came the biggest blow that Krause would suffer in his post–Jordan years on the Bulls. Tex Winter, the offensive mastermind behind the triangle offense, was leaving Chicago after 14 seasons. Winter, 77 years old, was moving to Los Angeles to work under Jackson and with Cleamons, Hamblen, and trainer Chip Shaefer. Hamblen had been passed over for head coach of the Bulls because of his age. Cleamons had tried his hand at head coaching with the Dallas Mavericks, but the triangle offense with as talented a point guard as Jason Kidd turned out to be a huge mistake.

"We wish nothing but the best for Tex. His presence has been special. He has made a tremendous impact on the game itself,"[32] said Krause, who for years had been pushing for Winter to enter the Basketball Hall of Fame.

Now Winter was leaving him and joining the Lakers to win multiple championships while working with such generational talents as Shaquille O'Neal and Kobe Bryant. That was way more than the Bulls could offer him. The same could be said of Ron Harper, who was sending subliminal messages through the media about where he wanted to sign now that his deal with the Bulls was up: "I'd like to play someplace I can have some fun. It's not a cash thing. I'd like to go someplace nice and warm, where I'm not going to play a lot."[33]

He soon signed a two-year deal for $4.2 million with the Lakers.

Floyd handled the departures like a champ, joking: "I was gone for 10 days. I decided I better get back or I'll be coaching by myself next year."[34]

Bill Cartwright, and Floyd's old college teammate, Jim Woolridge, were the remaining assistant coaches, and the three of them got to work during the training camp. A vital absence from the preparations was Elton Brand, who was with the national team, playing in the Olympic qualifying tournament in Puerto Rico.

Before joining the Bulls during the summer league in Salt Lake City, Brand had signed a three-year, $9.95 million contract. This did not impact the team's salary cap, and Krause wanted to free up even more money by making Kukoč available. Free agent veterans Mark Bryant, Andrew Lang, and Bill Wennington were as good as gone. The rumor was that Krause wanted enough cap space to lure in Grant Hill and Tim Duncan, who would be available next year. That was despite Hill's unfavorable comments about the organization and the way it treated its players a couple of years previously.

Krause remained hopeful: "The free-agent crop, at this point, looks like it will be better in the future than this year. We're in a situation that if there were somebody this year we felt was outstanding or who we felt would merit us going full-blast after, we would certainly consider doing it."[35]

A fair assessment, considering that the best players the Bulls could get were the 5'11" Terrell Brandon and 6'7" Anfernee Hardaway, two point guards, who were age-wise supposed to be entering their primes, as Brandon was 28, Hardaway 27. Hardaway suffered a knee injury at the beginning of the 1997-98 season and at that point was no longer the exciting and efficient player he had been when he was younger. Brandon would succumb to knee injuries after turning 30.

On August 12 the Bulls made their first post-draft acquisition, trading Brent Barry to the Sonics for 32-year-old shooting guard Hersey Hawkins and 23-year-old James Cotton. Just like Krause, Hawkins was born in Chicago and attended Bradley University, where he was coached by, of all people, Stan Albeck. While complimentary to Barry, Krause said that he wanted a veteran player. A shorter deal was also a factor, as Hawkins could be waived after the season, freeing up even more cap space for the free agents Krause wanted to bring to Chicago.

Hawkins was three years into his five-year extension with the Sonics, which he signed in the summer of 1996, following a deep playoff run at the end of which the Sonics ran into the 72–10 Bulls. Three years later Hawkins was moved to the bench and Krause brought him in to be a character guy and mentor younger players. There was no better player for that than the winner of the 1999 NBA Sportsmanship Award.

"You got me five years too late," Hawkins told Krause after the GM called him to tell him about the trade. Hawkins joked that he would have preferred to come to Chicago back when Jordan and Pippen were still there.[36]

The two stars from the championship team were gone, but Krause was able to bring back two role players from the first championship run, Will Perdue and B.J. Armstrong. Perdue, 34, got $5.2 million for a one-year deal, while Armstrong, 32, signed a $1 million contract.

It was going to be the last season of the veteran point guard's professional career. Armstrong had kept close ties with Chicago and the Bulls organization in the four years he was away. "When B.J. wasn't with us, I still trained him in the summer," said Vermeil. "And when he came back it was great. He was a great guy."

Following his retirement after the season, Armstrong was named special assistant to Krause.

Perdue had won his fourth NBA championship on the Spurs the previous season, backing up David Robinson and/or Tim Duncan, but did not feel valued in San Antonio and wanted to play more minutes.

After spending the 1999-2000 season in Chicago, Perdue would sign with the Blazers before ending his NBA career.

The biggest free agent signing for the Bulls that summer was Fred Hoiberg, the Indiana Pacers shooting guard, who had previously played for Floyd at Iowa State. Hoiberg appeared in 139 games during his four seasons in Indiana, which made for around 42 percent of all possible contests he could play in. The fact that Hoiberg was the biggest name (with no previous ties to the Bulls) that the team was able to sign shows how bad the organization's reputation among NBA players was and how bad the upcoming season was going to be.

The players coming to the NBA were getting younger and they needed more attention, preparation, and, most importantly, patience. Brand was 20, Artest was 19. They were in for some growing pains, as the Bulls were yet to develop a program that could best accommodate such young players. Karem Umlauf explains:

> The dynamic and the demographic of the team was changing so with time we decided it would be more beneficial to move closer to the United Center, downtown. One of the reasons we were up in our practice facility in the suburbs was because of the school system and players with children and/or their families. But a lot of times the players we got did not have children or families.

At the moment, though, Armstrong, Hawkins, and Perdue were tasked with helping the rookies adjust to the life in the NBA on and off the court. Ron Artest was particularly impressed with how Krause was running the franchise, predicting that at the end of the process would be a championship title: "I feel something happening here. I don't know how long it's going to take, but it's definitely going to happen. Jerry Krause knows what he's doing."[37]

Out of the two rookies, Artest was the enthusiastic and spontaneous kid while Brand was the level-headed gym rat, impressing everybody in the organization with his maturity. If they could enjoy even half the success of the forward duo drafted by Krause in 1987, there would be much to look forward to and the process would be worth it.

However, there was also pressure to show immediate improvement. Entering the new decade with a 2–25 record, the team of the '90s proved that it had no place in the new millennium. The best player on the Bulls, Toni Kukoč, appeared in only four of these games due to injuries. Hawkins also went down with an injury, ending his series of 527 consecutive NBA appearances.

There was understandable frustration on Krause's side with all these issues when he said: "I've never seen six guys sitting in civvies and

10. Footwork and Chemistry

nine guys dressed. We've never had the team we thought we were going to have together. If we get healthy, I think we're competitive."[38]

The Bulls' only two wins came by three points in total, as they won 92–91 against the Celtics, then lost the next 10 games, then beat the Nets 71–69, and then lost the next 11 games. The first game of the year was Scottie Pippen's first game back in Chicago. Pippen's first excursion to a different territory ended in disappointment, as he found it hard to adjust to a new system of play, one in which he was supposed to play more off the ball—something he was safely shielded from by the egalitarian triangle offense. Pippen was not a spot-up shooter. After half a year in Houston, he forced a trade to Portland, where he could play more to his abilities. The Blazers were a stacked team, with 10 players on the roster being capable of playing a starting role on most NBA franchises. Pippen called the team the most talented he had ever played for. After the game, he clarified that he did not mean the Blazers were the best team he had ever been on—that distinction went to the 1995-96 Bulls.

After the inevitable Blazers win, despite Pippen being honored by the franchise with a video tribute and getting a warm welcome from the fans, he had some harsh words for Krause and Reinsdorf: "It's kind of funny. It gives you a laugh to see how they destroyed something that was great for the city of Chicago and very entertaining for a lot of people's lives."[39] He also added that in his opinion no big-name free agents were going to come to Chicago, because they lacked the complementary pieces necessary for the team to be successful.

The Bulls won their next two games, at home and away, both against the Wizards. In the first game Kukoč had 18 points and 11 rebounds, but he made just seven of his 26 shots. It was his first game back following a back injury that forced him to miss 24 contests. After the performance, while praising the Croat, Krause was also openly shopping him.

Less than a month after the Bulls won two games in a row against them, the Wizards brought in Michael Jordan to serve as president of basketball operations. He said: "I'm going to have my imprints and footprints all over this organization. I look forward to turning this thing around. Right now we're an underachieving team."[40] Jordan's first decision was to fire the head coach and bring in his old Bulls teammate, Rod Higgins, an assistant on the equally underachieving Golden State Warriors. The move was announced before a compensation fee was agreed upon with the Warriors and the deal fell through. Jordan hired Darrell Walker as interim head coach. The first blunder was quickly forgiven because it was Michael Jordan, the cultural icon.

Douglas Jemal, real estate developer, spoke with excitement about how Jordan's arrival was supposed to attract numerous companies and businesses to Washington's downtown area because "This is all contagious. Jordan is a nightclub, he's fashion, he's Nike, he's everything."[41]

One thing he turned out not to be was a decent judge of basketball talent, someone whose ability to recognize potential could rival Krause's. He never reached out to his former GM asking for advice, nor did he admit to him or the press how hard a job Krause had, and how good a job he did, annually finding complementary players to surround Jordan with.

Now it seemed like Krause had finally found some solid foundations for the future in Artest and Brand. Thanks to their play, dealing Kukoč was easier to imagine. The 31-year-old forward was struggling with his shot, making 33 percent of his shot attempts and 66 percent of his free throws in the seven games he played in the second half of January. He was able to build himself up in February, and the Bulls were 8–12 following his return from injury, but this team was about future triumphs, not short-term gains.

The ideal deal would be to trade Kukoč's expiring contract for Tracy McGrady's expiring contract. The shooting guard had no wish to stay in Toronto and wanted to move closer to home—he was born in Bartow, Florida, an hour's drive from Orlando, and was raised in nearby Auburndale. Despite the physical assessment, which predicted an injury-filled career for McGrady, Krause continued to be infatuated with him. He could be stubborn like that.

"Jerry had strong opinions. I've never been around a good leader who didn't have strong opinions and was a little stubborn in their ways. I've never seen a good wishy-washy leader," said Al Vermeil. "During the draft, trades, and free agency, Jerry would ask me about a specific player's physical abilities, how trainable they were, and potential injuries. He took those assessments, along with others, into his decision-making process."

On February 16, the Bulls officially moved on from Kukoč, trading him to the Sixers in exchange for small forward Bruce Bowen and a first-round pick, as well as shooting guard John Starks from the Warriors. The Sixers also traded promising guard Larry Hughes and veteran Billy Owens to Golden State. The Bulls waived Bowen, missing out on a player who in two years would become one of the best defenders in the NBA.

Kukoč was essentially traded for the first-round pick, which the Warriors acquired from the Wizards as part of the 1994 trade for Chris Webber. If the pick landed in the top three, it would be left unprotected in 2001. Krause was sad, but optimistic: "This is a very hard day for me. But my job here is to rebuild this franchise to the point where it was....

10. Footwork and Chemistry

With two additional free agents and the youngsters that are here … we think this is going to be a very good team in a fast way."[42]

The Sixers, who had gone to the finals the season before, were sixth in the Eastern Conference and needed a serious boost, which Krause was convinced that Kukoč could provide: "I believe Toni and Allen Iverson and Eric Snow and those guys are … a very, very good basketball team."[43] Kukoč went from the egalitarian triangle to Philadelphia's hero ball, with Iverson doing whatever he pleased and the rest of the team forced to adapt. Just like Pippen, Kukoč did not enjoy the same level of success as he had on the Bulls.

The Bulls had only a couple of days to move Starks before the trade deadline. The Heat and the Timberwolves were open about their interest in the veteran shooter, but Krause was not willing to accept any offers that might limit the team's financial flexibility in the summer. He wanted a draft pick and a player on an expiring contract. If no satisfying offers came, Krause was hoping that Starks would remain a professional and give his all in every game, as he had up to this point in his career.

"I used to hate your guts playing against you because you're so tough. Now I love your guys because you are here playing for us,"[44] Krause told Starks.

Starks appeared in just four games for the Bulls. On the day of the trade deadline he played against the Pacers in Indiana and had an abysmal performance, making just five out of 13 shots. The Bulls lost by 17 points. Starks wanted to be released; Tim Floyd wanted to keep him.

"He's not being released and not being traded. He's on our team, and he's going to be playing,"[45] Floyd said emphatically.

In order to be signed by a contender (or any other team), Starks had to be released before March 1. Because the Bulls would have to pay him $900,000 for the rest of the season, Krause said he would allow him to go if the NBA would free the Bulls from paying him what he was owed. The payment would not impact the salary structure during the free agency, so there was no reason to not allow Starks to leave and play where he wanted.

Yet Krause was not willing to do that. The way he justified his decision made it even worse: "I understand that he's in the twilight of an outstanding career and he would like to have a chance to win a championship. And I'd like to have a chance to be 7 feet tall."[46]

In the light of the upcoming free agency, the hopes Krause had for it, and players getting more of a say as to where they wanted to play, as well as demanding better treatment from organizations, the statement was further proof of why interest in playing for the Bulls was so scarce.

Starks took his case to two arbitrators and returned home to

Tulsa to wait for the verdict. He was allowed to waive his salary to join another team, but according to NBA rules, he was not eligible to appear in the playoffs. There was no reason for him to do that. He wanted to be compensated. The Bulls released him anyway and paid him the rest of his salary.

The situation would have been easily avoidable, and the reputation of the organization could have been salvaged with a simple apology to the player. Instead, Krause said: "Our young players are the future of this organization. John certainly isn't."[47]

That was the opposite of the approach taken by Starks, who said: "If they were in the hunt for a playoff spot, I would have loved to been there because it's a great organization and a great city."[48]

The Bulls finished the season with 17 wins, two more than the league-last Clippers, yet still were number one in home attendance. Elton Brand was named the co–Rookie of the Year, alongside the Rockets' point guard Steve Francis. Ron Artest made the All-Rookie Second Team.

And in the summer of 2000, the Bulls had three first-round picks and the cap space necessary to sign the players that the rookies could either complement or at least learn from, so that they could make the franchise their own over the next couple of years.

The 2000 draft would turn out to be one of the worst in NBA history.

11

Baby Bulls

The Bulls had the fourth pick, the seventh pick they got from the Wizards, and the 24th pick from the Spurs. They also had the 32nd, 33rd, and 34th picks. That meant they could get up to six players who could complement their free-agent acquisitions.

In other circumstances, that would have been something to look forward to.

Garry St. Jean, the GM of the Golden State Warriors, said: "They are in a terrific situation. We don't have any picks. They have multiple picks and a terrific cap situation. That's terrific for the Bulls."[1]

The Bulls were hoping to get the Blazers' Jermaine O'Neal, a power forward/center who was growing frustrated with his lack of minutes, playing behind Arvydas Sabonis, Rasheed Wallace, and Brian Grant. Just 22 years old, O'Neal was about to enter his fifth NBA season. Initially he was brought along slowly, until it became evident that the win-now Blazers wanted to get an instant contributor in exchange for O'Neal.

Because of that, they rejected Krause's offer, centered around the fourth overall pick. They needed a veteran, ideally one who could stand up to Shaquille O'Neal and Tim Duncan in case Sabonis was injured or in foul trouble.

The Bulls had the time and the patience to get a big man and develop him, yet Krause complained to the press about how disappointed he was by the workout of rookie big man Chris Mihm. *The Boston Globe*'s Peter May pointed out that Krause's criticism of the player was unprecedented, as through the years the Krause had remained secretive about who he was going to pick.[2] The journalist predicted that the Bulls were going to pick Mihm precisely because they needed a center. That, and Mihm was heavily scouted by the Bulls throughout the whole college season, to the point that he was confident that they were going to pick him. The 7'0" center said: "I think I tested real well," adding that the triple-post run by his Texas Longhorns would allow him to learn the triangle offense rather easily.³

Another possible draft pick was 6'9" Darius Miles, an athletic swingman, who was just 18 years old and would require even more patience than the previous players drafted by the Bulls. The team had no experience drafting such young prospects, let alone knowing how they were supposed to be handled on and off the court. Miles was touted by Michael Jordan as the best player available in the draft, and the sponsorship deal with Nike that came after he was drafted was proof of his belief in Miles's potential.

The Bulls wanted Miles too, although under certain conditions, one of which was Miles getting rid of his signature cornrowed hairstyle, as recounted to the press by Miles's mother. Miles's agent, David Falk, fired back that Krause should not be talking to others about appearance.⁴ This led to serious anxiety in the organization about whether they could recruit young players, whose style tended to include cornrows, headbands, and tattoos. And who refused to respect the league-wide tradition of rookies carrying the veterans' bags. According to Miles's mother, her son was too good for this rite of passage.

Once Miles was snatched up by the Clippers with the third pick, the Bulls decided on Marcus Fizer, a 6'8" power forward from Iowa State. Fizer was recruited there by Tim Floyd and played for him for a year before Floyd left for Chicago. Despite both Floyd and Krause stating that the pick was not made to appease the coach, it was hard to think otherwise, because the Bulls had enough power forwards. Then again, Krause drafted Grant and Pippen despite having Oakley and Sellers on the roster. Maybe he was onto something, or maybe he was hoping for lightning to strike twice during the process of constructing the Bulls' frontcourt.

At 21, Fizer was the father of two children by two different women and was engaged to a third one. After being drafted, he credited his children with giving him a reason to get out of bed, which was an alarming statement coming from somebody who was about to land the dream position for everybody who ever picked up a basketball. The season Fizer and Floyd collaborated in Iowa State was the only losing season of Floyd's 12-year career as a college coach.

"It has always been my desire to come here and try to make up for that and do the best I can to help him win here," said Fizer.⁵

With the seventh pick, Krause decided on Chris Mihm, as predicted, only to trade him to the Cavaliers for the 6'5" guard Jamal Crawford, whom the Ohio team picked eight overall, and cash. Crawford appeared in 17 games at Michigan because he was suspended for 14 contests for breaching the rules of amateurism in high school. The small sample size of Crawford's NCAA career did not scare Krause away, nor did the breach of rules. Even the fact that Crawford had broken his promise to the Wolverines' coach to return for his sophomore year did not impact the Bulls' overall assessment of the player.

That was because Jamal Crawford was a basketball historian and Krause would immediately warm to him. When he came into Krause's office, he identified Earl Monroe and Wes Unseld in a photograph that also included Krause. That showed the GM that the rookie knew his history, while also catering to Krause's vanity.

For the 24th pick, Krause selected 7'1" Dalibor Bagarić, a 19-year-old big man, whose big hands had impressed the GM a couple of years back. He continued to scout him, either personally or through Ivica Dukan, who originally told Krause about the Croatian talent and gave him regular updates about his progress. Bagarić did not fare particularly well in the NBA, as it still did not know how to handle big men with a shooting touch.

The Bulls found themselves involved in a free agency battle with the Orlando Magic. The team from Florida invited Tim Duncan and Grant Hill for a visit. Duncan was originally supposed to be in Orlando for a day, but he extended his stay to spend time with Hill. The Magic had $20 million of cap space, better weather than Chicago, and no state income tax. They prepared special T-shirts with an image of Duncan and Hill wearing Magic jerseys. Krause was not particularly appreciative of their recruitment of the two superstars, calling it a "dog-and-pony show," adding: "We're an organization of substance, not flash."[6] A couple of days later, when McGrady visited Chicago, he was met at the airport by Benny the Bull and fans holding banners asking McGrady to play for the Bulls. In his hotel room there was a tape with a personal message from Oprah Winfrey, trying to convince McGrady to join the Bulls. He also threw out the first pitch during a Cubs game.

An unlikely ally in the Bulls' recruitment of star players was Phil Jackson, who referred to Orlando as a "plastic town" while describing Chicago as more cultured. Krause's former boss, Magic's senior vice president Pat Williams, responded: "Look, Florida is meant to be fun. We're about lakes, bass, fishing, sunshine. Mickey Mouse, Shamu and fun. We just wanted these guys to have fun. And you could tell they were impacted."[7]

Not enough for both to sign with the Magic. Hill was certain that he wanted to play in Orlando, but Duncan decided to stay in San Antonio. After his decision, the Magic increased their efforts to recruit McGrady. The Bulls clearly wanted him more, but McGrady had recently built a home in Florida, and having a chance to be close to his family, he settled for the Magic.

Krause's big gamble did not work; the three big names were off the market.

A day after the Bulls were rejected by McGrady, Krause and Floyd (and Benny the Bull) welcomed Eddie Jones at O'Hare Airport. The 6'6" guard was traded by the Lakers to free up space for Kobe Bryant's development—a case of addition by subtraction that would make Krause proud. After two seasons in Charlotte, Jones wanted to leave. Because of the new CBA, it made more sense for him to sign with the Hornets and immediately be traded, because he could get a seven-year deal for $86 million, not a six-year deal for $67 million.

Though raised in Florida, Jones did not complain about the weather when he came to Chicago. He said all the right things, praising the city, the fans, and the organization, adding that he would prefer to see some veterans joining the team first because he wanted to win. He was the guest of honor at Comiskey Park, where the White Sox were playing the St. Louis Cardinals.

Jones joined the Miami Heat in a sign-and-trade.

Time was running out and the Bulls were below the salary cap. By league rules, they needed to sign somebody to meet the quota agreed upon in the CBA.

They talked to Tim Thomas, offering him a six-year, $67 million contract, but he decided to stay in Milwaukee. Thomas was the sixth man on the Bucks, a 22-year-old 6'10" small forward, who was drafted seventh overall in 1997 and had already been traded two times in his three-year career. As explained by Thomas's agent, Arn Tellem, "he was happy in Milwaukee and it was a good team, so why change for something that is unknown."[8] Especially for the same money.

What followed was the usual and expected ridicule. Sam Smith wrote: "It must be a lot like when the kids in Krause's neighborhood were choosing sides for the sandlot game ... everyone was getting picked and Krause still was standing there."[9] *The Courier-News*' Ian O'Connor wrote about Krause having "so much money and so few friends," getting in the mandatory reference to his appearance, in this case Krause's "stubby little hands."[10]

Ron Mercer was not a big-name free agent. At 24, the University of Kentucky player was three seasons into an NBA career, during which he had switched teams three times, including half a season as a placeholder for Tracy McGrady on the Magic.

Mercer was the biggest name signed by the Bulls during the summer.

11. Baby Bulls

They were also able to get center Brad Miller, a reserve on the Hornets for two seasons, who entered free agency as a restricted free agent. In order to get him, the Bulls had to give Miller more than the mid-level exception the Hornets could match. Anything higher would be over the salary cap limit for the Charlotte team, which opened the door for the Bulls to try to get the center.

With $5.5 million owed to Mercer ($27 million for four years) and $4 million to Miller, the Bulls met the cap space minimum for the season. No new acquisitions were necessary.

Mercer remained hopeful for future roster moves during his introductory press conference, saying that the recruiting process was ongoing and "something could happen tomorrow, something could happen a couple of weeks from now."[11] Krause left the conference early, citing the number of phone calls he was getting at the moment as the reason for his exit. He did not specify who or what they concerned.

Meanwhile, Mercer was saying all the right things, like when he was asked about Jordan's and Pippen's issues with Krause: "It's not any of my business. That's the way I look at it. That's those guys and when they were here. I have no comment on that because it has nothing to do with me."[12]

Mercer was from Tennessee, and he was highly recruited by his home state universities, the University of Tennessee and Vanderbilt, but he picked Kentucky. After two years there, he entered the NBA as the sixth pick of the 1997 NBA draft, joining his college coach, Rick Pitino, on the Celtics after his sophomore season and reuniting with fellow Wildcats Antoine Walker and Walter McCarty. Their comradery did not translate to on-court success.

Mercer was an inefficient scorer, and average defender, and he presumably expressed no willingness to stay in Boston.[13] Prior to the 1999-2000 season he was traded to the Nuggets, who then traded him to the Magic. Now he was supposed to be the starter on one of the worst teams in the NBA. He could either redeem himself or diminish his value.

Meanwhile, Randy Brown, the reserve point guard on the championship Bulls and the starter during the rebuild, was not brought back. "I'm bitter because I didn't hear from Jerry Krause and this is home,"[14] said Brown after signing a deal with the Boston Celtics. Apparently only selected players got a parting call from the executive. After five years, Brown was leaving Chicago.

The 2000-01 season turned out to be the worst of the rebuild so far. The Bulls' biggest triumph came in a home game against the Magic on November 9. The team that spoiled the Bulls' free agency lost to them 95–90. Mercer made nine of his 18 attempts and grabbed 10 rebounds.

It was the Bulls' first win of the season, one of six in the first 48 games. Among those 42 losses came a series of 16 defeats in a row.

Somewhere around this time, the press started speculating that Elton Brand might either demand a trade or be dealt by Krause, whose answer to stagnation could be to reset the whole process. Brand refused to admit defeat: "I'm not a quitter. I don't want to bail out or leave this team behind. I help make this team what it is. And I want to build something and build it here."[15] The power forward added that retiring as a Bull "would be an honor." Brand was just 21 years old, yet had the demeanor of a much older and experienced player.

He stood out even more on the youngest team in the NBA. The overall record was bad, and Floyd decided to give more minutes to guards Bryce Drew and Fred Hoiberg instead of Jamal Crawford, hoping to win some games. Krause understood that and defended the decision: "He's trying to win and that's what he should be doing. I don't have any problem whatsoever with the people he's choosing to play."[16] The team was not winning. It was not showing any progress either. It was a hopeless situation for Floyd, but more so for the franchise.

The Times' George Castle proposed something that more and more people were talking about—in order for the Bulls to finally improve, there was need for a change in management. The newspaper even asked the Heat general manager, Randy Pfund, if he would be willing to take over the Bulls.[17] As long as Krause did not want to leave, that was not going to happen. He stubbornly believed that he could salvage the situation.

The inexperienced team needed a veteran, somebody who could show the Bulls how to win and take over games in crucial moments. Instead, by Krause's own doing, a group of players who lacked NBA experience was being coached by somebody who also lacked NBA experience. Instead of resilience, they had bad habits; they were frustrated and disappointed with playing in the league. They were in need of a reset just as much as the whole organization.

With no trade assets and free agents steering clear of Chicago, Krause once again looked with hope to the draft. The players he coveted the most were Yao Ming, a 7'6" Chinese center, and point guard Jay Williams out of Duke. Either would fill one of the two most urgent vacancies on the Bulls, yet both decided to wait a year before entering the draft. That meant that if Krause picked a center with the top-four pick that the Bulls were sure to land in the lottery—and it was almost certain he would—he would be forced to settle for a high-schooler, as four of the best big men in the draft decided to skip college and jump immediately into the NBA. Kwame Brown, Tyson Chandler, Eddy Curry, and DeSagana Diop were underclassmen.

11. Baby Bulls

"We're like baseball scouts now because the draft has gotten so young. The only difference is we're throwing these players right into the major leagues. We have no minors for them,"[18] said Krause.

The player most scouted by Krause was Thornwood High School's Eddy Curry, the Illinois big man, whose 6'11", 300-pound frame was reminiscent of a much older and stronger athlete. For a team in need of players who could make an immediate impact, the Bulls sure were taking their time. And with the fourth pick, there was little chance that they would be able to pick an NBA-ready player. The first pick went to Michael Jordan's Wizards, and again, when it came to Jerry Krause's fate, the ball was in Jordan's court. These two were seen talking during the rookie training camp in Chicago, reportedly discussing a potential trade.

Players were openly asked whether they would prefer to play for Krause or Jordan. One of the top prospects, Rodney White, said: "I do want to play for the Wizards. I think me and Mike have a little relationship. I like him. He likes me."[19] White was picked ninth by the Pistons.

Eddy Curry, the local boy from Chicago, had grown up a Bulls fan, but said he was hoping that he would not be around for the team to pick him fourth: "Hopefully I'll be in that top two or three. I want to be the first one. And to be drafted by Michael Jordan, that would mean a lot."[20]

Simultaneously to roster decisions, Jordan was also supposed to make a decision regarding his playing career, as the rumors continued to circulate about him working on a comeback to the NBA.

Meanwhile, 10 days before the draft, Sam Smith published a piece about the possibility of trading Elton Brand to the Clippers for the second overall pick. The journalist wrote that with the fourth pick the best available players were power forwards, and the Bulls already had one in Brand. Smith explained that the move made sense because "on a good team, he'd be a wonderful fixture," but that "the Bulls are not a good team."[21] They needed somebody who could turn the franchise around.

According to Smith, Shane Battier, Tyson Chandler, and Kwame Brown could be such players, with only the first of the three seen as a ready-made NBA player following his college years at Duke. Teaming up Brand with Battier would actually make a lot of sense, but it was uncertain whether Battier would still be there at number four, with reports that the Hawks, holding pick number three, really wanted him. Plus, at 23, his talent and potential were considered well known. Battier, like Brand two years earlier, was a safe pick. The Bulls could no longer play it safe.

Meanwhile, Eddy Curry had an individual workout at Berto Center. He came out of it more willing to join the Bulls. "People have the wrong idea when you think about the Bulls and Jerry Krause," he said. "It's a bunch of nice people who want the best for the organization. I cleared a lot of things up by coming here."[22]

The player that would turn out to be the best in the draft, Spaniard Pau Gasol, had little chance of landing in Chicago. Krause had a policy of not selecting players who did not attend the workouts at Berto Center. They needed to be examined by Al Vermeil and have the projected durability and endurance of their bodies estimated. Gasol did not attend; all the Bulls had was tape. Even though they liked what they saw, that was not enough for them to pick the big man from Barcelona. Krause told the press that DeSagana Diop also did not work out for the Bulls. The GM saw his games in person but did not see enough in him to invite him. Later it was revealed that the Bulls had worked him out along with Curry.

"I was sick at first,"[23] said Tyson Chandler after finding out on draft day that he had been traded to Chicago. He wanted to stay in Los Angeles, simply because he was born and raised in California. Moving to the other side of the continent would be intimidating to anyone, but for a teenager who had never known life outside his home state, it was especially hard.

On draft night there was no consensus top pick, nor was there a consensus top five, maybe even top ten of prospects. The player picked first was going to determine the order, and the Wizards went with Kwame Brown. The Clippers, picking second, selected Chandler, a 7'1" 230-pound center from Dominguez High School, Compton. Dominguez, as pointed out by *Los Angeles Daily News*' Billy Witz, "according to the state's academic performance index has long been one of the lowest achieving high schools in California."[24] Chandler was not there for education; he was there to play basketball. And he did that exceptionally well, as evidenced by the averages from his senior year: 26 points, 13 rebounds, and seven blocks per game.

Then Chandler was traded to the Bulls, along with power forward Brian Skinner, for Elton Brand. And when the Hawks picked Pau Gasol third overall, Krause went with Eddy Curry. A high school kid from California and a high school kid from Illinois were about to become the future of the franchise. The fans in Chicago, who were particularly patient with this team and continued to support it by attending games, were now indirectly asked to be even more patient and forgiving of the growing pains of this young Bulls team.

During that season the Bulls would drop out of the top two in overall league attendance for the first time since they had moved to the United Center. In the 1993-94 season, their last in Chicago Stadium, they were seventh, and the main reason was because of the capacity of the dated arena. During the 2001–02 season they would fall all the way to ninth.

Tim Floyd was also against the reset. He made it known that he would prefer the team to think short-term and simply improve the roster: "Maybe in four or five years, Eddy Curry will be the league's best center. But my contract is only for three."[25]

"My ribs are a little sore right now. When we completed some things, I kind of whacked myself. I'm pumped," said Krause, but his enthusiasm was not contagious. He hoped that Chandler and Curry would become a new version of Ralph Sampson and Hakeem Olajuwon or David Robinson and Tim Duncan, the modern-day Twin Towers. Assistant coach Bill Cartwright was a member of a less successful version of the frontcourt tandem, back in New York with Patrick Ewing, and now it was his job to make the two big men work alongside one another.

"The game was slowly changing at the time, they were changing the old rules and you still could win with a dominant big man, like Miami Heat did in 2006 with Shaq, but the perimeter guys were slowly becoming more important," Shawn Fury told me during our talk. "The Twin Towers weren't going to work anyway with Chandler and Curry, two young, unproven guys."

Krause explained later: "We knew taking two of them was a risk but we also felt they were the two best players available at that point. Obviously, we didn't think it was enough of a risk to stop us."[26]

To provide sufficient veteran leadership, Krause traded for a man who, until the memorable series against the Knicks in 1993, he had referred to as "his son": Charles Oakley. Oakley was 37 at the time and his role was to mentor Chandler and Curry. He already served in the role of elder statesman on the Toronto Raptors and was a big reason behind the young team's ascent. Now he was supposed to serve as a starting power forward, helping the young Bulls develop. Jordan was also interested in getting Oakley to play for his Wizards, but Krause was quicker. A year later the Wizards would make up for their slow reflexes and Oakley would again serve as Jordan's bodyguard following his return to playing basketball.

The Bulls also signed veteran point guard Greg Anthony and 25-year-old swingman Eddie Robinson. Always a fan of size, Krause liked Robinson because of his 6'9" frame. Robinson was signed by the Hornets after going undrafted in 1999 and enjoyed two seasons as a bench player. Now he was widely considered to be the Bulls' top priority signing, although it was unclear on what basis. Robinson enjoyed a good 2001 playoff series on the Hornets against the favored Miami Heat, in which he averaged 12 points on 70 percent shooting, but in the Eastern Conference Semifinals against the Bucks he averaged 4.7 points per game on 39 percent shooting.

Krause was again preaching patience and he was buying himself time. *Northwest Herald*'s Nick Hut wrote that "three years from now, they could all be busts, and Krause could be initiating the team's rebuilding phase. But with Robinson, Chandler and guard Jamal Crawford, the Bulls at least have a chance to be a fluid, up-tempo team from the get-go."[27]

Or maybe Krause was escaping an inevitable decision. He had said multiple times that he would leave the game if it stopped being fun. For some people in the organization, it was about to. Krause was 62 years old. He wanted to speed up the rebuild by dismantling the team, but he made the process longer and more painful for everybody involved.

And then Sam Smith suggested that Krause intended to leave the Bulls after two years, turning the team over to his successor.[28] Returning to the finals was no longer a possible goal, but leaving a solid core to build around was more viable. Smith also saw Jordan as the perfect successor in the executive position, as he was collecting experience in the Wizards' front office.

That way of thinking was put on hold prior to the start of the season, with Jordan announcing his return to basketball. He explained his three-year retirement as follows: "You may not remember when I retired the last time, I didn't say I was ready to quit the game. I just didn't want to go through the whole rebuilding process at the time. If the team had stayed intact, I still would've been playing. I constantly said that."[29] Rewriting history was much easier than admitting his mistakes.

Jordan asked Doug Collins to be the head coach of the team, after saying earlier that he was never going to play for anybody other than Phil Jackson.

Twenty-five games into the season, with an overall record of 49 wins and 190 losses, Tim Floyd gave up. He submitted his resignation on December 24, 2001. Krause took issue with Floyd giving limited minutes to Chandler and Curry. Floyd also grew frustrated with not being able to coach the team the way he wanted to.

"The bizarre thing was that after Phil Jackson left, Krause wanted Floyd to run the triangle," said Fury during our talk. "You can't take a coach and make him run a system which he is not used to, which he is not comfortable running, especially when losing the pieces that made it work so well."

After three seasons Floyd decided to depart from the triangle offense, and the team won four of its 25 games playing the coach's offense. The 21 losses included a franchise-worst 53-point pounding by the Minnesota Timberwolves.

After two games with Bill Berry as interim coach, Krause decided to promote Bill Cartwright to the head coaching position. Apart from mutual trust, respect, and the will to return to the triangle, Cartwright was a member of the failed short-lived Twin Towers–like project on the Knicks, so he could at least tell Chandler and Curry what not to do.

"I would like him to be the coach for the next 10 years, that's why we did this. As far as I'm concerned, hopefully this is it,"[30] said Krause, trying to sell the general public on the idea that going with Cartwright was a part of his plan.

Cartwright signed a long-term deal but could be released after the season if the team was not happy with his work. Teaching the triangle offense to young players was going to be a process, but what could be immediately improved was defensive play. The Bulls reacted positively to the coaching change, finishing the season with 21 wins.

Krause made Cartwright really work for that record after trading his team's three top scorers—Ron Artest, Brad Miller, and Ron Mercer—and point guard Kevin Ollie for Jalen Rose, Travis Best, and Norm Richardson. Originally the Bulls wanted to include Charles Oakley in the trade, as he was disgruntled with the team.

Jalen Rose had fallen out with Pacers head coach Isaiah Thomas, as he was unhappy with his role in the offense. At 29, Rose was in the second year of a $93 million deal. Asked about the move to the Bulls a week before it was made, Rose said: "It's something I hope doesn't happen, but we'll have to wait and see."[31] According to Rose, Pacers GM Donnie Walsh promised him that he was not going to get traded. Walsh claimed no such promises had been made.

Artest and Miller were both on the brink of breaking out. In the next few years they would both become All-Stars. This team was supposed to be about patience and player development. Rose, however, was about to enter his prime and Krause was excited about the move: "We feel Jalen is an outstanding all-around player who can play three positions offensively and defensively. He's a very good passer, extremely unselfish, a fine scorer."[32]

In his first game on the Bulls, Rose had 36 points and six assists, and the Bulls won against the Knicks. At 6'8" Rose entered the NBA as a point guard, selected 13th in the 1994 NBA draft. A member of the legendary Fab Five at the University of Michigan, Rose grew up a Pistons fan during the Bad Boy era, so naturally he was rooting against the Bulls. Now he was supposed to lead the inexperienced team.

The Bulls won 21 games, but they were still the worst team in the league, along with the Golden State Warriors. Both teams had the biggest chance of landing the number one pick, which meant the biggest chance of drafting Yao Ming. Apart from being a highly desirable basketball talent, having Ming on the roster also meant more marketing possibilities. Ming was surrounded by enormous hype. His first American workout took place at Loyola University in Chicago, in front of 65 NBA scouts and executives and 150 reporters.[33] Jerry West, Jerry Krause, Pat Riley, and Rod Thorn were among those in attendance.

Despite the biggest odds at the number one pick, the Bulls got the second and the Warriors the third selection, with the Houston Rockets, with the fifth-worst NBA record, picking first. And they were certain to pick Ming, as they already had the backcourt of Steve Francis and Cuttino Mobley, so they had no interest in the player who was considered the second-best prospect of the 2002 draft, Jay Williams.

Williams was one of the leaders of the 2001 NCAA champions, the Duke Blue Devils. His most famous performance came in the regular season game against Maryland, dubbed "The Miracle Minute," because with less than a minute left on the game clock, Williams scored a layup and two three-pointers, changing the score from 90–80 to 90–88. The game went to overtime and Duke won, their comeback ignited by the sophomore point guard. After one more year in college, Williams decided to enter the NBA draft alongside fellow Duke junior, Mike Dunleavy, Jr.

The Bulls missed out on Ming, but their pick was still valuable, with the Cavaliers, the Timberwolves, and the Hornets reportedly inquiring about trade possibilities that could land the Bulls either Andre Miller, Wally Szczerbiak, or Baron Davis. Any one of them would immediately make the Bulls a better team, but so could Williams, given proper coaching and time to develop next to Chandler, Crawford, and Curry.

"I'm not Michael Jordan. I love the fact that Chicago has had great success, but I think this town is past that. Let's move on. It's been a while. I just want to bring it back to where it was,"[34] said Williams, so confident he was getting picked by the Bulls that he had spent the whole second week of June in Chicago.

As predicted, on June 26 the Bulls picked Williams, and Crawford was immediately moved to shooting guard to play alongside Rose, Chandler, and Curry, completing the promising nucleus. Williams even turned down an appearance on Jay Leno's show to arrive at training camp on time. He understood the magnitude of expectations and was willing to do what was necessary to live up to them.

Krause was now tasked with constructing the roster around his

11. Baby Bulls

young players in free agency. He talked with former Bull Scott Williams, power forward Popeye Jones, and small forward Matt Harpring about the possibility of serving as mentors to his younger players. They declined. Krause signed Donyell Marshall to come off the bench behind either Rose or Chandler at forward.

Marshall was looking for a new contract with his team, the Utah Jazz. He was 29 at the time and on his third NBA team. Marshall was selected fourth overall by the Timberwolves in 1994 and was traded to the Warriors after half a season. On the Timberwolves he was not liked because of his nine-year, $42.6 million deal, as well as his supposed lack of enthusiasm. Initially struggling on the Warriors, Marshall was able to become a solid role player, and before the 2000-01 season the Utah Jazz saw him as a missing piece on a championship roster. They orchestrated a four-team trade, in which they traded their 2001 first-round draft pick, backup forward Adam Keefe, and Howard Eisley, the supposed heir to John Stockton, for Marshall.

After two first-round exits, the Jazz offered Marshall a three-year deal worth $21 million. He signed with the Bulls for three years and $15 million instead. After acquiring him, Krause gave the reason why Marshall would decide to sign for less with a worse team: "His averages against Eastern Conference teams were three points and two rebounds higher than against Western Conference teams and he's a natural fit for us."[35]

Other executives appreciated what Krause did with the roster, none more than the Miami Heat's Pat Riley, who compared Curry and Chandler to Robert Parish and Kevin McHale, who "started young and had a 10-year run at it."[36] Such public praise for the Bulls was a rarity coming from Riley. The Bulls stood in the way of his Knicks and his Heat; if it were not for them, Riley would have had more championship titles to his name. He had every reason to hate the organization, but he was able to recognize what Krause was doing.

12

Hall of Fame

"After I met Jerry Krause, I remember talking to Jerry Reinsdorf and he said: 'You saw Krause? There's only half of him,'" Lee Lowenfish recalled during our conversation. "He said he lost so much weight because of his illness."

They met in 2010, during an event held by the Professional Baseball Scouts Foundation. Lowenfish took out his tape recorder and they talked for 90 minutes. He remembered Krause as willing to share his knowledge of the trade and extensively discuss the nature of scouting. He was 71 at the time and still looking for the next big thing.

"His dream was to return to baseball," reminisced Thelma Krause. "He loved scouting high schools, to find talent rather than evaluate what already was there."

When Krause retired from the Bulls at the beginning of April 2003, he cited health reasons. He physically could no longer work at full capacity and there was a chance that he would not have quit if not for his deteriorating health. Living on the road, unhealthy eating, and stress had taken their toll on his body. He could have served an advisory role on the Bulls or simply retired, but nothing filled him with more zest than scouting. He was a hopeless romantic who loved his job more than anything.

During his last season as vice president of basketball operations, the Bulls won 30 games, almost half of the win total from the previous four seasons combined, 66. He was not leaving the new GM, John Paxson, in a position to put out the fires left by his predecessor. Paxson inherited a solid team, one with potential. By all accounts, this was not an ugly exit, but a planned farewell. And he never got enough credit for it.

When he retired in 2003, the waiting period for eligibility to enter the Naismith Hall of Fame was five years. Yet Krause was annually passed over after 2008, despite being an architect of six championship teams.

12. Hall of Fame

"What you're ought to do is find the total number of general managers that have ever been in the NBA," Al Vermeil said during our talk. "Jerry Krause achieved more than 99 percent of them."

Jerry Krause was inducted into the Hall of Fame only after his death, in 2017. In a two-minute prerecorded speech, Thelma Krause gave thanks for the honor bestowed upon her late husband. She joked that Krause would have been happy to work for free and that Jerry Reinsdorf would have probably used that information during contract negotiations.

"The critics of your book will say that he had Michael Jordan," said Al Vermeil. "To that I say: Red Auerbach had Bill Russell. Jerry West had Magic and Kareem."

Krause did not have the presence of Jerry West, or the charisma of Red Auerbach. He did not have the elegance of Pat Riley. He was not R.C. Buford, Sam Presti, or Bob Myers. But he had the broadest shoulders of any GM in league history, despite his small frame.

Prior to the Bulls winning their first title, Krause said: "If I ever leave this franchise, I'd like to leave with us all wearing championship rings. I'm a native of Chicago. I'd like to win for the people of the city and for my father, who didn't live to see me take the job."[1]

From March 26, 1985, until April 4, 2003, the Bulls won 812 of their 1,454 regular-season games under Krause. Despite their magnitude, these numbers are not as impressive as the six forever associated with his name and the city that he loved so dearly.

Chapter Notes

Introduction

1. If not stated otherwise, quotes come from conversations conducted by the author.
2. Alexander Wolff, *Big Game, Small World: A Basketball Adventure*, Durham: Duke University Press, 2022, 16.
3. Scottie Pippen, *Unguarded*, New York: Atria Books, 2021, 264–265.
4. Nick Hut, "Krause No Longer Stirs Bulls," *Northwest Herald*, November 1, 2003, B1.
5. Melissa Isaacson, *Transition Game: An Inside Look at Life with the Chicago Bulls*, Champaign, IL: Sagamore-Venture, 1994, 218.
6. Rick Telander, "The Sleuth," *Sports Illustrated*, March 15, 1993, 62.
7. Phil Jackson, *Eleven Rings*, London: Virgin Books, 2014, 3.
8. Roland Lazenby, *Mindgames: Phil Jackson's Long Strange Journey*, Chicago: Contemporary Books, 2002, 12.
9. S.L. Price, "Bulls' Myers Gets a Daily Dose of Jordan," *The Sacramento Bee*, January 11, 1987, C5.
10. Bernie Miklasz, "As Player, Coach, Sloan Has Been a Take-Charge Guy," *St. Louis-Post Dispatch*, June 13, 1997, 3E.
11. Adrian Wojnarowski, "Jerry Krause Joins Woj," *The Woj Pod* (podcast), February 1, 2017.
12. Roland Lazenby, *Blood on the Horns: The Long Strange Ride of Michael Jordan's Chicago Bulls*, New York: Diversion Books, 2013, 80.
13. Sam Smith, "Seldom One of the Guys, But One of a Kind," *Chicago Tribune*, April 6, 2003, 9.
14. Robert Markus, "After a Long Chase, Krause Finds Dream in His Backyard," *Chicago Tribune*, June 3, 1976, Section 4, 1.
15. Al Hamnik, "Krause Couldn't Win the PR Battle," *The Times*, April 8, 2003, C1.

Chapter 1

1. Sam Smith, *The Jordan Rules*, New York: Simon & Schuster, 1992, 34.
2. Jackson, *Eleven Rings*, 31.
3. Harvey Araton, *When the Garden Was Eden: Clyde, the Captain, Dollar Bill, and the Glory Days of the New York Knicks*, New York: Harper, 2012, 32.
4. Wojnarowski, "Jerry Krause Joins Woj."
5. Bob Ryan, "Title Pledge a Pain—and a Push," *The Boston Globe*, July 17, 1988, 41.
6. Telander, "The Sleuth," 62.
7. John D. Klier, "Russian Jewry on the Eve of the Pogroms," *Pogroms: Anti-Jewish Violence in Modern Russian History*, ed. John D. Klier and Slomo Lambroza, Cambridge: Cambridge University Press, 2004, 4.
8. Telander, "The Sleuth," 65.
9. Chicago Studies, "The History of Albany Park," *Chicago Studies*, https://chicagostudies.uchicago.edu/albany-park/albany-park-history-albany-park.
10. Thomas Aiello, *Hoops: A Cultural History of Basketball in America*, Lanham, MD: Rowman & Littlefield, 2022, 58.
11. Jackson, *Eleven Rings*, 112.

12. Terrence Armour, "Krause Is Silent, but Floyd Wants Immediate Boost," *Chicago Tribune*, May 23, 1999, Section 3, 7.
13. Bob Sakamoto, "Krause Works OT in Pulling Off Coup," *Chicago Tribune*, June 23, 1987, Section 4, 3.
14. Telander, "The Sleuth," 65.
15. Melissa Isaacson, "Why Do People Hate This Guy?" *Chicago Tribune*, February 5, 1995, Section 3, 9.
16. Mike Royko, *Boss: Richard J. Daley of Chicago*. New York: E.P. Dutton, 1971, 62.
17. Bob Sakamoto, "Krause Digs Inside Bulls," *Chicago Tribune*, March 31, 1985, Section 4, 3.
18. Bill Gleason, "Don't Forget Jerry Krause on List of Bulls' Winners," *South Bend Tribune*, June 15, 1992, C1.
19. Mike Conklin, "Odds & Ins," *Chicago Tribune*, June 16, 1993, Section 4, 5.
20. Isaacson, "Why Do People Hate This Guy?" Section 3, 9.
21. John Rohde, "OU Tames This Beast of the East," *The Sunday Oklahoman*, January 24, 1988, B4.
22. Sakamoto, "Krause Digs Inside Bulls," Section 4, 3.
23. Lazenby, *Mindgames*, 114.
24. Telander, "The Sleuth," 65.
25. Wojnarowski, "Jerry Krause Joins Woj."
26. Stan Hochman, "The Builder of the Bulls," *Philadelphia Daily News*, June 13, 1991, 93.
27. Markus, "After a Long Chase," Section 4, 1.
28. Wojnarowski, "Jerry Krause Joins Woj."
29. Mark Montieth, "Leonard Opened NBA's Door to Krause," *The Indianapolis Star*, May 17, 1998, C10.
30. Haize & Pat, "Sam Smith," *Locked on Bulls* (podcast), March 23, 2017.
31. Montieth, "Leonard Opened," C10.
32. Wojnarowski, "Jerry Krause Joins Woj."
33. Jim Hodges, "City of Angels," *Los Angeles Times*, June 16, 1999, D4.
34. Mark Janssen, "It's Not Been the Same Since K-State," *The Manhattan Mercury*, March 17, 1968, 11.
35. *Ibid.*
36. Lazenby, *Mind Games*, 23.
37. John X. Miller, "Gaines's Success Far Exceeds Myriad of Basketball Wins," *The Charlotte Observer*, February 12, 1982, B1.
38. Staff and News Services, "CIAA Coaching Great Gaines Dies," *The Charlotte Observer*, April 19, 2005, C1.
39. Pete Swanson, "Lakers Scout Compares Bird to Jerry Sloan," *Evansville Courier and Press*, December 10, 1978, 5C.
40. Tony Chamblin, "Sloan Likely First-Round Draft Pick," *Evansville Courier and Press*, May 2, 1965, 5C.
41. Sandy Padwe, "Country Cager Has Made Good," *The Times and Democrat*, February 11, 1965, 8A.
42. Bill Robertson, "Jerry Sloan Has a Double Image," *The Evansville Press*, March 9, 1965, 12.
43. Larry Stephenson, "Bullets Burning: Sloan Sits Tight," *Evansville Courier and Press*, July 25, 1965, 1C.
44. Dave Hicks, "Super's Dream Is 7–4 Center," *The Arizona Republic*, June 13, 1971, D3.
45. Bob Frisk, "Kickin' It Around," *Arlington Heights Herald*, October 19, 1961, 32.
46. Edward Prell, "In the Wake of the News," *Chicago Tribune*, June 28, 1966, Section 3, 1.
47. Chuck Swirsky, "Jerry Colangelo," *Timeout Bulls with Chuck Swirsky* (podcast), Episode 23, March 21, 2017.
48. Sean Dinces, *Bulls Markets: Chicago's Basketball Business and the New Inequality*, Chicago: University of Chicago Press, 2018, 8.
49. Royko, *Boss*, 69.
50. Dinces, *Bulls Markets*, 17–18.
51. Associated Press, "Bulls Seek to Break Chicago's Pro Hoop Hex," *Newport Daily News*, January 29, 1966, 8.
52. Riter Collett, "Bighouse Gaines Creeping Up on Rupp," *Dayton Daily News and Journal Herald*, February 11, 1981, 11.
53. Bob Kilborn, "Earl Monroe Shouldn't Quit," *Daily Intelligencer Journal*, December 11, 1967, 14.
54. Dick Weiss, "Michael Jordan Looms Above Mortal Athletes," *The Central New Jersey Home News*, May 21, 1989, E14.

Chapter 2

1. James C. Nicholson, *1968: A Pivotal Moment in American Sport*, Knoxville: University of Tennessee Press, 2019, 18.
2. W.D. Maxwell, "Another Day of Mourning," *Chicago Tribune*, June 6, 1968, Section 1, 11.
3. Nicholson, *1968*, 20.
4. Clayton Trutor, *Loserville: How Professional Sports Remade Atlanta—and How Atlanta Remade Professional Sports*, Lincoln: University of Nebraska Press, 2021, 332.
5. William J. Collins and Robert A. Margo, "The Economic Aftermath of the 1960s Riots in American Cities: Evidence from Property Values," *The Journal of Economic History*, Vol. 67, No. 4 (December 2007), 849–883.
6. Robert Markus, "Do Your Job and Hustle," *Chicago Tribune*, October 31, 1971, 34.
7. Curry Kirkpatrick, "He Rocks the Boat with the Old College Try," *Sports Illustrated*, November 11, 1968, 54.
8. Robert Markus, "Rookie Bulls Learn Life Can Be Tough," *Chicago Tribune*, August 29, 1968, Section 3, 3.
9. George Ferguson, "Motta Likes a Challenge!" *Deseret News*, May 28, 1968, D1.
10. Ernie Accors, "Sixers Seek Rebounding Help," *The Philadelphia Inquirer*, January 13, 1969, 30.
11. Robert Logan, "Klein Out as Bull General Manager," *Chicago Tribune*, August 30, 1969, Section 2, 1.
12. Robert Markus, "The Sports Trail," *Chicago Tribune*, January 27, 1970, Section 3, 3.
13. Jack Malooley, "The 50 Worst Moments in the First 50 Years of the Chicago Bulls," *Chicago Reader*, January 20, 2016, https://chicagoreader.com/news-politics/the-50-worst-moments-in-the-first-50-years-of-the-chicago-bulls/.
14. Bob Logan, "Bull Roar," *Chicago Tribune*, March 22, 1970, 31.
15. Bob Logan, "Klein: My Lineup Took Floor for 1974-75 NBA Playoffs," *Chicago Tribune*, October 9, 1975, Section 4, 2.
16. Bob Logan, "The Court Report," *Chicago Tribune*, January 26, 1971, Section 3, 3.
17. Ben Moffett, "Aggies Eye Midwest Regionals," *Albuquerque Journal*, February 11, 1970, C1.
18. "Collins Unhappy in Bulls' Camp," *Las Cruces Sun-News*, March 2, 1971, 7.
19. Hicks, "Super's Dream Is 7–4 Center," D3.
20. Dave Kindred, "E. Smith, Not Gilmore, May Climb Mt. Alcindor," *The Courier-Journal*, December 11, 1971, B6.
21. Alan Goldstein, "As a Human Being, as a Pro, There's Only One Unseld," *The Baltimore Sun*, March 22, 1981, C5.
22. Mike McGraw, "Lakers Could Easily Six-Peat if O'Neal, Bryant Stay Put," *The Daily Herald*, June 19, 2001, Section 2, 7.
23. Tom Tuley, "Buse Reminds Suns of Sloan," *Evansville Press*, April 15, 1972, 12.
24. Dave Hicks, "Jerry Krause: 'Super Sleuth,'" *The Arizona Republic*, September 27, 1972, 2F.
25. Bob O'Donnell, "Jordan's Air Show Makes Chicago a Bull Market," *Fort Worth Star-Telegram*, March 17, 1987, C7.
26. Dave Hicks, "MacLeod Already Has Had His Hard Knocks," *The Arizona Republic*, September 2, 1973, D4.
27. Dave Hicks, "Scout Hails His 'Find,'" *The Arizona Republic*, September 12, 1973, F5.
28. Norm Frauenheim, "Proski Survives Hot Gyms, Flaky Rookies," *The Arizona Republic*, October 4, 1982, C3.
29. Dave Hicks, "Can Suns Squeeze the Lakers from Playoffs?" *The Arizona Republic*, September 22, 1974, D5.
30. Terrell Lester, "All Stars Orbit Adams," *Tulsa Daily World*, March 19, 1972, Section 5, 6.
31. Trutor, *Loserville*, 281.
32. Phil Jasner, "Sixers Send 'Boy' Scouts After High School Stars," *Philadelphia Daily News*, January 7, 1976, 60.
33. Fred Stabley, Jr., "Pro Scout Calls Furlow a Top NBA Prospect," *The Times Herald*, March 16, 1976, 3B.
34. Bob Logan, "Bulls Are Smelling Up the Joint," *Chicago Tribune*, January 2, 1976, Section 4, 2.
35. Tim Weigel, "Bulls' Dick Motta: Bitterness in Departing," *The Cincinnati Enquirer*, April 17, 1976, B4.
36. Bob Logan, "Krause Tabbed Player

Personnel Director," *Chicago Tribune*, June 2, 1976, Section 4, 1.

37. Bob Logan, "Sloan Wants to Keep Playing—If Possible," *Chicago Tribune*, June 2, 1976, Section 4, 1.

38. Robert Markus, "Krause Faces First Big Decision," *Chicago Tribune*, June 8, 1976, Section 4, 1.

39. David Condon, "Krause Should Get Blame," *Chicago Tribune*, June 10, 1976, Section 4, 6.

40. Joe Mooshil, "Jerry Krause Builds Bulls His Own Way," *The Herald-Palladium*, March 30, 1988, 15.

41. Bill Jauss, "Bulls Should Hire Krause," *Chicago Tribune*, November 28, 1976, Section 3, 4.

42. People in Sport, "Writers Select Vikes' White," *The Daily Breeze*, January 9, 1977, E2.

43. Roger Farrell, "Sikma 1st Round Pick, Wilkins 2nd," *The Pantagraph*, June 11, 1977, A10.

44. Jim Murray, "Laker Rookie Norm Nixon Penetrating Character," *The Cincinnati Post*, March 10, 1978, 30.

45. Bill Neff, "Odysseus Had Nothing on Ex-Terp Brad Davis," *The Baltimore Sun*, December 21, 1980, C5.

46. Michael Janofsky, "Brad Davis: Sits, Watches, Claps… and Learns," *The Evening Sun*, January 30, 1978, C6.

47. Jimmy Claus, "Sporting Around," *The Terre Haute Tribune*, November 29, 1977, 7.

48. Swanson, "Laker Scout," 5C.

49. A.J. Carr, "Steve Spurrier Hoping to Get Devils Off Ground," *The News and Observer*, January 23, 1980, 21.

50. Jack Patterson, "Only Principals Aren't Talking," *The Akron Beacon Journal*, March 1, 1980, D1.

51. John Hillyer, "Why Lakers Don't Panic Sans Magic," *San Francisco Examiner*, November 27, 1980, F1.

52. Rebecca de Schweinitz, "'There is no equality': William E Berrett, BYU, and Healing the Wounds of Racism in the Latter-Day Saint Past and Present," *Dialogue: A Journal of Mormon Thought*, Vol 52, No. 3 (2019), 62–83.

53. Bill Connors, "NCAA Regional Draws VIPs, Colorful Scouts," *Tulsa World*, May 24, 1981, E5.

Chapter 3

1. Chuck Swirsky, "Bulls Chairman Jerry Reinsdorf," *Timeout Bulls with Chuck Swirsky* (podcast), Episode 2, November 1, 2016.

2. "Basketball," *Akron Beacon Journal*, March 24, 1982, D2.

3. Mike Conklin, "Sports World Remembers Arthur Wirtz," *Chicago Tribune*, July 22, 1983, Section 4, 2.

4. Harvey Aaraton, *When the Garden Was Eden: Clyde, Dollar Bill, and the Glory Days of the New York Knicks*, New York: Harper, 2011, 109.

5. Bob Sakamoto, "Reinsdorf Buys Bulls," *Chicago Tribune*, February 9, 1985, Section 2, 1.

6. Bob Sakamoto, "Reinsdorf Gets Big Welcome," *Chicago Tribune*, February 10, 1985, Section 4, 6.

7. Joshua Mendelsohn, *The Cap: How Larry Fleisher and David Stern Built the Modern NBA*, Lincoln: University of Nebraska Press, 2020, 141.

8. Fred Mitchell, "Bulls, Lakers Going 1-on-1 for Jabbar," *Chicago Tribune*, June 17, 1983, Section 4, 1.

9. Bob Logan, "Fat Chance for Bulls," *Chicago Tribune*, April 28, 1984, Section 2, 2.

10. Jane Gross, "The Next Julius Erving?" *The Palm Beach Post*, October 26, 1984, D8.

11. David Halberstam, *Playing for Keeps: Michael Jordan and the World He Made*, New York: Random House, 1999, 152.

12. Jackson, *Eleven Rings*, 59.

13. Bob Sakamoto, "Krause Signals New Bull Era," *Chicago Tribune*, March 27, 1985, Section 4, 1.

14. Smith, *The Jordan Rules*, 35.

15. Jason Hehir, dir., "Episode II," *The Last Dance*, ESPN Films/Netflix, April 19, 2020.

16. Lazenby, *Mindgames*, 118.

17. Wojnarowski, "Jerry Krause Joins Woj."

18. Sakamoto, "Krause Works OT in Pulling Off Coup," Section 4, 3.

19. Wojnarowski, "Jerry Krause Joins Woj."

20. Haize & Pat, "Sam Smith."

21. Lazenby, *Blood on the Horns*, 102.

22. Bill Gleason, "Reinsdorf Adds

Another Chapter to Chicago Ownership Soap Opera," *South Bend Tribune*, January 25, 1987, D9.

23. Halberstam, *Playing for Keeps*, 110.

24. Phil Jasner, "Krause Will Take Time Before Working on Bulls," *Philadelphia Daily News*, April 5, 1985, 101.

25. Haize & Pat, "Sam Smith."

26. Wojnarowski, "Jerry Krause Joins Woj."

27. Haize & Pat, "Sam Smith."

28. Robert Lewis, *Chicago's Industrial Decline: The Failure of Redevelopment, 1920–1975*, Ithaca: Cornell University Press, 2020.

29. Christine J. Walley, *Exit Zero: Family and Class in Postindustrial Chicago*, Chicago: University of Chicago Press, 2013, 57.

30. Marc Doussard, Jamie Peck, and Nik Theodore, "After Deindustrialization: Uneven Growth and Economic Inequality in 'Postindustrial' Chicago," *Economic Geography*, Vol. 85, No. 2 (April 2009), 183–207, 193.

31. Michael Demarest, "Cocaine: Middle Class High," *Time*, July 6, 1981, https://content.time.com/time/magazine/article/0,9171,922619,00.html.

32. Russell C. Crandall, *Drugs and Thugs: The History and Future of America's War on Drugs*, New Haven: Yale University Press, 2020, 159

33. Chris Cobbs, "Widespread Cocaine Use by Players Alarms NBA," *Washington Post*, August 19, 1980, https://www.washingtonpost.com/archive/sports/1980/08/20/widespread-cocaine-use-by-players-alarms-nba/0eb819b3-bd92-412a-b14c-baed1a9e7c68/.

34. Scott Ostler, "Waiting for Lefty to React," *Los Angeles Times*, May 12, 1986, part III, 3.

35. Filip Bondy, "Oldham Wants a Trade," *Daily Sports News*, January 20, 1987, 41.

36. Bob Sakamoto, "In the End, Jordan's No. 1," *Chicago Tribune*, May 17, 1985, Section 4, 2.

37. David Moore, "The Rockets Rise to the Top Earlier than Expected," *Fort Worth Star-Telegram*, May 18, 1986, B5.

38. Jim Barnhart, "Not Talking," *The Pantagraph*, May 31, 1985, B1.

39. John Hillyer, "Jackson-Krause Bond Deeper Than Bulls Ties," *The Commercial Appeal*, June 12, 1991, D6.

40. Daryl Gadbow, "FVCC Loses a Team but Phil Jackson Gets to Coach," *Missoulian*, January 26, 1983, 13.

41. Michael Madden, "Cowen's Competitive Spirit Gets Major Test in Minor-League," *The Boston Globe*, December 8, 1984, 29.

42. Jackson, *Eleven Rings*, 62.

43. Lazenby, *Mindgames*, 118.

44. Johnette Howard, "Chicago Less Bullish on Coach," *Detroit Free Press*, January 17, 1986, 4D.

45. Associated Press, "Michael Jordan, Toast of the NBA," *St. Petersburg Times*, February 9, 1985, C1.

46. Pete Ryan, "Michael Jordan? He's a Gold Mine," *The Albuquerque Tribune*, January 12, 1985, TV-2.

47. Mike McGraw, "Anstey, Bulls in Olympian Dilemma," *The Daily Herald*, March 2, 2000, Section 2, 3.

48. Chuck Swirsky, "John Paxson," *Timeout Bulls with Chuck Swirsky* (podcast), Episode 10, December 27, 2016.

49. Paul Knepper, *The Knicks of the Nineties: Ewing, Oakley, Starks and the Brawlers That Almost Won It All*, Jefferson, NC: McFarland, 2020, 39.

50. Bob Sakamoto, "Bulls Shuffle, Deal," *Chicago Tribune*, June 19, 1985, Section 4, 1.

51. Charles Oakley, *The Last Enforcer: Outrageous Stories from The Life and Times of One of the NBA's Fiercest Competitors*, New York: Gallery Books, 2022, 22.

52. Donn Esmonde, "Smrek's Potential Excites NBA," *The Buffalo News*, June 19, 1985, D1.

53. Bob Sakamoto, "Bol Presents Big Problem for Bulls," *Chicago Tribune*, December 19, 1985, Section 4, 2.

54. Phil Rogers, "Who's Best Guard in SEC?" *The Shreveport Journal*, February 27, 1980, C1.

55. Jim Turner, "Suns Beam Over Macy," *The Logan Leader*, January 7, 1980, 5.

56. Associated Press, "Kyle Macy Having Day in Sun, Others for Suns," *The Messenger*, June 25, 1980, 19.

57. Bob Sakamoto, "Bulls Looking at Macy," *Chicago Tribune*, September 5, 1985, Section 3, 8.

58. Tony Moton, "Country Kid Finds New Life in the Big City," *The Courier-Journal*, January 12, 1986, C3.
59. David Moore, "Spurs Fans Hot Without 'Ice,'" *Fort Worth Star-Telegram*, November 1, 1985, 16E.
60. Lazenby, *Mindgames*, 119.
61. Thomas Bonk, "Michael Jordan to Have Foot Unwrapped Before Christmas," *Los Angeles Times*, December 3, 1985, Section III, 3.
62. Wes Lukoshus, "Always Ready, Bulls' Higgins a 'Coaching Delight,'" *The Times*, January 18, 1985, B1.
63. Bob McCarthy, "Showing Them Up," *The Fresno Bee*, July 14, 1985, D1.
64. Bob Sakamoto, "Higgins Is Fighting for Survival with the Bulls," *Chicago Tribune*, October 10, 1985, Section 4, 7.
65. UPI, "Jordan Heard Bone Crack," *Kenosha News*, November 5, 1985, 17.
66. Wire Reports, "Chicago Bulls Acquire Brewer to Replace Injured Jordan," *The Belleville News-Democrat*, November 6, 1985, D6.
67. Bob Sakamoto, "No Merry Bulls Until Christmas," *Chicago Tribune*, November 15, 1985, Section 4, 3.
68. Bob Sakamoto, "Jordan Hurting, but So Are Sonics," *Chicago Tribune*, November 2, 1985, Section 2, 3.
69. Associated Press, "Bulls' Jordan Must Remain in Cast 2 Weeks," *The Daily Register*, December 13, 1985, 4B.
70. Bob Sakamoto, "Taking Bulls by the Horns," *Chicago Tribune*, December 28, 1985, Section 2, 1.
71. Filip Bondy, "Richardson's Loss Will Be Felt by Nets," *Bangor Daily News*, January 2, 1986, 13.
72. Howard, "Chicago Less Bullish," 4D.
73. Bob Sakamoto, "Woolridge Back, Jordan on Way," *Chicago Tribune*, March 8, 1986, Section 2, 2.
74. John Crumpacker, "Loyola's Mighty Smith," *The San Francisco Examiner*, March 1, 1986, C1.
75. Bob Sakamoto, "Gervin Points Way over Knicks," *Chicago Tribune*, March 10, 1986, Section 3, 2.
76. Halberstam, *Playing for Keeps*, 168.
77. Wojnarowski, "Jerry Krause Joins Woj."

Chapter 4

1. S.L. Price, "Jordan Lifts Game to Prove Point," *The Sacramento Bee*, November 14, 1986, C3.
2. "NBA Notes," *The Titusville Herald*, March 13, 1993, B4.
3. Ed Schuyler, Jr., "NBA Draft Ends, But...," *Lansing State Journal*, April 25, 1973, C1.
4. Phil Jasner, "Collins: Talks with Bulls Weren't Interviews," *Philadelphia Daily News*, May 16, 1986, 135.
5. Phil Jasner, "Future May Be Bullish for Collins," *Philadelphia Daily News*, May 15, 1986, 127.
6. Skip Myslenski and Linda Kay, "Odds & Ins," *Chicago Tribune*, May 16, 1986, Section 4, 2.
7. Associated Press, "Stan Albeck Gets Walking Papers," *Great Falls Tribune*, March 20, 1986, 3B.
8. William Rentschler, "Sports Moguls Are Nothing but Spoiled Brats with Large Egos," *Times-Press Streator*, July 25, 1986, 4.
9. Associated Press, "NBA Playoffs/Notes," *Durham Morning Herald*, June 3, 1986, D1.
10. Jim O'Donnell, "Albeck Finds a Brave New World," *The Daily Herald*, October 22, 1986, Section 3, 5.
11. UPI, "Albeck Fired as Bulls Coach," *The Times*, May 19, 1986, 11.
12. Jim Barnhart, "The Bulls," *The Pantagraph*, January 7, 1987, B1.
13. UPI, "Collins to Coach Chicago Bulls," *The Daily Sentinel-Tribune*, May 24, 1986, 13.
14. Sam Goldaper, "Jordan Guns Like Bulls Coach Would've Liked to," *The Albuquerque Journal*, November 20, 1986, B9.
15. Bernie Lincicome, "Krause Curiously Comes Up Short," *Chicago Tribune*, June 18, 1986, Section 4, 1.
16. John Schulian, "Dallas Loses 'Big D' Title to Duke and Denny," *St. Joseph News-Press*, March 31, 1986, 9.
17. Bob Sakamoto, "Sold on Sellers," *Chicago Tribune*, June 18, 1986, Section 4, 1.
18. Halberstam, *Playing for Keeps*, 204.
19. Associated Press, "Will This Draft Be as Good to Bulls as the Last Two?" *Southern Illinoisan*, June 17, 1986, 11.

20. Halberstam, *Playing for Keeps*, 204.
21. Bob Sakamoto, "Auerbach after 2d High Pick," *Chicago Tribune*, June 15, 1986, Section 4, 6.
22. Bob Sakamoto, "Bulls Knuckling Down for Draft," *Chicago Tribune*, June 5, 1986, Section 4, 2.
23. Lincicome, "Krause Curiously," Section 4, 1.
24. Bob Sakamoto, "Bulls Give Up Green for Pistons' Cureton," *Chicago Tribune*, August 23, 1986, Section 2, 1.
25. *Ibid.*, 5.
26. Associated Press, "Veteran Sikma Requests Trade," *The Clarion-Ledger*, May 29, 1986, 3D.
27. Sakamoto, "Bulls Knuckling Down."
28. Jim Rothgeb, "Sikma Trade Grabs Spotlight at Sonics' Forum," *Kitsap Sun*, June 12, 1986, C2.
29. Halberstam, *Playing for Keeps*, 203.
30. Bob Sakamoto, "Pacers Near Deal for Macy," *Chicago Tribune*, September 17, 1986, Section 4, 6.
31. Wolff, *Big Game, Small World*, 166.
32. Bob Sakamoto, "Bulls Hope Colter Not Too Unselfish," *Chicago Tribune*, October 17, 1986, Section 4, 3.
33. Bob Sakamoto, "Bulls Spotlight Sellers, Colter," *Chicago Tribune*, June 21, 1986, Section 2, 1.
34. Jim O'Donnell, "Collins Needs to Grow Accustomed to His New Bulls," *The Daily Herald*, October 7. 1986, Section 2, 4.
35. Mitch Chortkoff, "Lakers Still Looking for More Help," *News-Pilot*, October 17, 1986, B2.
36. Randy Minkoff, "Look for Bulls to Eventually Trade Jordan," *Matton Journal Gazette*, October 15, 1986, B4.
37. UPI, "Bulls Sign Alfredick the Great," *Northwest Herald*, October 24, 1986, 15.
38. Doug Thomas, "7-Year NBA Veteran 'Confident' as Racer," *World-Herald*, January 28, 1992, 19.
39. Jim Obradovich, "Sellers Hopes to Make Believers of Bulls' Buyers," *The Rock Island Argus*, October 24, 1986, 16.
40. Smith, *The Jordan Rules*, 30.
41. Gene Seymour, "Do 1986 Bulls Have a Prayer?" *The Times*, November 1, 1986, B1.
42. Bob Verdi, "A Sweet Payoff for Bulls' Sweat," *Chicago Tribune*, November 2, 1986, Section 4, 2.
43. Johnette Howard, "General Manager Krause Picking Bulls Apart," *Detroit Free Press*, November 4, 1986, 6D.
44. Gene Seymour, "Collins Gets Coaching Honeymoon," *The Times*, November 6, 1986, C1.
45. Bill Gleason, "Jordan Makes Bulls Winners," *South Bend Tribune*, November 13, 1986, D2.
46. Bob Sakamoto, "Sellers' Father Unsold on Son's Suspension, Fine," *Chicago Tribune*, December 28, 1986, Section 3, 11.
47. Bob Sakamoto, "Krause Finds Bulls Character Pleasing," *Chicago Tribune*, November 17, 1986, Section 3, 5.
48. Phil Jasner, "Trades by Sixers Create Traffic Jam in Backcourt," *Philadelphia Daily News*, January 2, 1987, 92.
49. Pippen, *Unguarded*, 42.
50. Bob Sakamoto, "NBA Draft Lacks Superstars But...," *Chicago Tribune*, June 21, 1987, Section 3, 12.
51. Wojnarowski, "Jerry Krause Joins Woj."
52. Tyrone Bogues, *Muggsy: My Life from a Kid in the Projects to the Godfather of Smallball*, Chicago: Triumph Books, 2023, 84.
53. Knight-Ridder News Service, "Little Guy Bogues May Go Big," *Herald and Review*, June 21, 1987, B5.
54. Bob Ryan, "Bob Ryan's Mock Draft," *The Boston Sunday Globe*, June 21, 1987, 92.
55. S.L. Price, "Draft Day Arrives Amid Much Head-Scratching," *The Sacramento Bee*, June 22, 1987, D3.
56. Bob Sakamoto, "Bulls May Be Working OT to Get Pippen," *Chicago Tribune*, June 22, 1987, Section 3, 3.
57. Sakamoto, "Krause Works OT in Pulling Off Coup," Section 4, 1.
58. *Ibid.*
59. Bill Cartwright, "Horace Grant," *The Bill Cartwright Show* (podcast), Episode 8, December 29, 2020.
60. Bill Fleischman, "Draft a Reunion for Dunbar High," *The Spokesman-Review*, June 24, 1987, D4.
61. Bill Cary, "Wolf's Choice Really

No Choice at All," *The Reporter*, April 19, 1983, 6.
62. Isaacson, *Transition Game*, 62.
63. Wojnarowski, "Jerry Krause Joins Woj."
64. Lazenby, *Blood on the Horns*, 84.
65. Bob Sakamoto, "Newest Bulls Already Pals," *Chicago Tribune*, June 24, 1987, Section 4, 3.
66. Gene Seymour, "Jordan Truly Is Too Good to Be True," *The Times*, February 7, 1988, B7.

Chapter 5

1. Thomas Bonk, "The Next Time, Jordan Might Be Asking for $4 Million Per Season," *Los Angeles Times*, November 3, 1987, Part III, 7.
2. Thomas Bonk, "Michael Jordan," *The Sacramento Bee*, November 7, 1987, C6.
3. Thomas Bonk, "Jump 23," *Los Angeles Times*, November 3, 1987, part III, 7.
4. Inquirer Wire Services, "Basketball," *Philadelphia Inquirer*, November 8, 1987, 17D.
5. Gene Seymour, "Bulls Are Better, but How Much?" *The Times*, December 30, 1987, C1.
6. Bob Sakamoto, "Title-Hungry Gilmore with Celtics," *Chicago Tribune*, January 9, 1988, Section 2, 3.
7. Art Spander, "Cartwright Big in More Ways Than One," *San Francisco Examiner*, October 24, 1979, 61.
8. Mitch Chortkoff, "Bulls Aren't Just Jordan," *News-Pilot*, February 2, 1988, B3.
9. Johnette Howard, "Fame and Fear," *Detroit Free Press*, October 22, 1985, 4D.
10. Gene Seymour, "Sellers' Market Not in Chicago," *The Times*, May 5, 1988, C1.
11. Bob Sakamoto, "Bulls Deal Threatt for Vincent," *Chicago Tribune*, February 26, 1988, Section 4, 3.
12. UPI, "Is It Jordan or the Bulls Bringing in the Crowds?" *Chippewa Herald-Telegram*, February 27, 1988, B12.
13. Linda Kay and Mike Conklin, "Odds & Ins," *Chicago Tribune*, May 9, 1988, Section 3, 2.
14. Bob Sakamoto, "Reinsdorf, Krause and Collins Savor the Bulls' Special Moment," *Chicago Tribune*, May 9, 1988, Section 3, 7.
15. Associated Press, "Chicago, Malone to Talk?" *The Charlotte Observer*, May 28, 1988, 7B.
16. Bob Sakamoto, "Lakers Still Best in the West—for Now," *Chicago Tribune*, June 6, 1988, Section 3, 11.
17. Sam Smith, "Bulls' Trade Talk Is Centering on Oakley," *Chicago Tribune*, June 16, 1988, Section 4, 3.
18. Associated Press, "Knicks Get Oakley from Bulls," *Record-Journal*, June 28, 1988, 12.
19. Haize & Pat, "Sam Smith."
20. Isaacson, *Transition Game*, 22.
21. Bob Ryan, "UCSB's Shaw Fits into Celtics' Future," *Santa Maria Times*, July 3, 1988, 15.
22. Gene Seymour, "Medical Bill May Not Be Cure for Ills," *The Times*, June 29, 1988, B1.
23. Paul Sullivan, "Bulls No. 1 Pick Isn't Top Pick of Fans, as Usual," *Chicago Tribune*, June 29, 1988, Section 4, 8.
24. Lee Shappell, "Krause's Bulldozing Could Weaken Team," *The Arizona Republic*, September 18, 1988, D17.
25. Sam Smith, "Bulls Sign Perdue for 5 Years," *Chicago Tribune*, July 30, 1988, Section 2, 1.
26. David Benner, "Oakley Production Small on Return to Chicago," *The Indianapolis Star*, January 1, 1989, B-8.
27. Cartwright, "Horace Grant."
28. Paul Sullivan, "Resilient McKinney Bounces to Top," *Chicago Tribune*, July 28, 1988, Section 4, 1.
29. Jerry Sullivan, "Is This the Year NBA's Posse Rounds Up Lakers, Celtics?" *The Olympian*, October 30, 1988, 6D.
30. Roy S. Johnson, "Former NBA Player Bill Cartwright Talks About What Playing with Michael Jordan Was Really Like," AL.com, May 13, 2020, YouTube, https://www.youtube.com/watch?v=jvDeU5Tp0b4.
31. Peter May, "Scrutiny Continues for Bulls' Mr. Bill," *Hartford Courant*, December 6, 1988, C6.
32. David Aldridge, "Salary Cap, Jordan's Pay Keep Bulls on Hold," *The Miami Herald*, January 13, 1989, 4E.
33. Compiled from News Services, "Air Jordan Is the Choice of Overseas

Promoters," *St. Louis Post-Dispatch*, January 8, 1989, 9D.

34. Tom Farrey, "Stress Is Just a Way of Life for NBA Coaches," *The Arizona Republic*, March 21, 1989, C3.

35. Jim Hodges, "City of Angles," *Los Angeles Times*, June 16, 1999, D4.

36. Sam Smith, "Cavaliers Send Bulls an Ominous Message," *Chicago Tribune*, April 24, 1989, Section 3, 3.

37. Sam Smith, "Bulls May Be a Trade Away from an NBA Crown," *Chicago Tribune*, April 2, 1989, Section 3, 8.

38. Chris Juzwik, "Bulls Only Putting Off the Obvious," *Northwest Herald*, May 7, 1989, C3.

39. Bernie Lincicome, "Even with Hair, Bulls Inspired," *Chicago Tribune*, May 4, 1989, Section 4, 10.

40. Drew Sharp, "Knicks Have All the Tools—Except Maturity," *Detroit Free Press*, April 11, 1989, 5D.

41. Greg Logan, "Rice: Triangle's Third Leg," *Newsday*, April 2, 2000, C5.

42. Dispatches, "Only the Bulls Believe They're Not a One-Man Team," *The Evansville Press*, May 9, 1989, 18.

43. Dan Weaver, "NBA Hoops Do a Disservice to the Sport of Basketball," *Spokane Chronicle*, May 29, 1989, C1.

44. Barry Temkin, "A Familiar Scenario at NBA Pre-Draft Camp," *Asheville Times*, June 8, 1989, C1.

45. Jeff Snook, "McCloud Ready for NBA," *The Palm Beach Post*, June 26, 1989, 7C.

46. Bob Ryan, "Order of Tuesday's NBA Draft Remains a Mystery," *Santa Maria Times*, June 26, 1989, 13.

47. Associated Press, "Bulls Draft Talent," *The Star-Democrat*, June 29, 1989, 3B.

48. Ibid.

49. K. Shrijith, "'You Really Want Me to Do That?' A Phone Call from Michael Jordan to Olive Garden That Marked a Big Change in His 7 Ft Teammate's Career," *Essentially Sports*, October 22, 2002, https://www.essentiallysports.com/nba-basketball-news-you-really-want-me-to-do-that-a-phone-call-from-michael-jordan-to-olive-garden-that-marked-a-big-change-in-his-7-ft-teammates-career/.

50. Dick Weiss, "Collins Has Taken Bulls by the Horns," *Philadelphia Daily News*, May 26, 1989, 108.

Chapter 6

1. Edward J. Finkel, "Phil Jackson New Bulls Coach; Vows to Bring Low-Key Style," *The Arizona Republic*, July 11, 1989, C2.

2. Mike Kern, "Collins Firing Spurred by Feud," *Philadelphia Daily News*, July 7, 1989, 100.

3. Bill Conlin, "New Approach to All-Star Voting," *Philadelphia Daily News*, July 17, 1989, 85.

4. Kurt Begalka, "Some Like It Hot," *Northwest Herald*, July 14, 1989, 8.

5. Doug Hoogervorst, "Doug Collins—A Victim of Bulls' Mismanagement," *The Daily Tar Heel*, July 20, 1989, 42.

6. Pippen, *Unguarded*, 61.

7. Bob Verdi, "Collins' Unceremonious Firing Really Was His Graduation," *The Arizona Republic*, July 8, 1989, D3.

8. Sam Smith, "Reinsdorf Saw Imminent Disaster," *Chicago Tribune*, July 9, 1989, Section 3, 12.

9. Halberstam, *Playing for Keeps*, 259.

10. Gene Seymour, "Bulls' Jackson Not Afraid to Coach Jordan," *The Times*, January 21, 1990, B1.

11. Isaacson, *Transition Game*, 48.

12. Sam Smith, "Collins' Fall Told in Jackson's Rise," *Chicago Tribune*, July 11, 1989, 5.

13. John Delong, "Younger Gaines Has Taken a Circuitous Route Back to Basketball," *Winston-Salem Journal*, April 30, 1995, C6.

14. Sam Smith, "Jordan's 54 Rescue Bulls," *Chicago Tribune*, November 4, 1989, Section 2, 1.

15. Peter May, "Jackson Lightens Up Bulls," *Hartford Courant*, November 12, 1989, E7.

16. Sam Smith, "Bits & Pieces on Chicago's Teams," *Chicago Tribune*, November 23, 1989, Section 4, 15.

17. Sam Smith, "To Jordan, Trainer Pfeil Is Magical," *Chicago Tribune*, May 15, 1989, Section 3, 6.

18. Gene Seymour, "Time to See What Krause Can Produce," *The Times*, February 20, 1990, C1.

19. Bob Wojnowski, "Mature Bulls Are Ready to Test Haughty Pistons," *The Reporter Dispatch*, May 20, 1990, D9.

20. Bernie Lincicome, "No Covering Up This Bulls' Mess," *Chicago Tribune*, June 4, 1990, Section 3, 12.
21. Lee Shappell, "College Not a Place to Get Schooling," *The Arizona Republic*, June 10, 1990, D8.
22. Sam Smith, "Bulls Seek Depth Answer in Question-Mark Hopson," *Chicago Tribune*, June 27, 1990, Section 4, 1.
23. Wojnarowski, "Jerry Krause Joins Woj."
24. Al Lagatolla, "Krause Makes Big Error with Chicago Only Pick," *Journal Gazette*, June 29, 1990, B-3.
25. Kevin Ball, "Bulls Get Their Man: A Winner," *Northwest Herald*, July 22, 1993, B1.
26. Lazenby, *Mindgames*, 272.
27. Paul Sullivan, "Jordan Gets to Air Out Swings as Sox Guest Batter," *Chicago Tribune*, July 25, 1990, Section 4, 4.
28. Andrew Bagnato, "Jordan Shows Natural Talent Is No (Leftfield) Façade at Comiskey," *The Evening Sun*, July 26, 1990, B2.
29. Sam Smith, "Writers Say Team Has Been Doing Them Wrong," *Chicago Tribune*, December 7, 1990, Section 4, 7.
30. Howard Blatt, "Ex-Net Hopson Not Raging with Bulls," *Daily News*, January 9, 1991, 55.
31. Lazenby, *Blood on the Horns*, 52.
32. Associated Press, "Jordan Expresses Disappointment in Bulls' Management," *Hartford Courant*, January 26, 1991, B7.
33. Brian Biggane, "Bulls Eyeing Third Shot at NBA Finals," *The Palm Beach Post*, March 24, 1991, 7C.
34. Mitch Chortkoff, "What Can Be Better Than Being Best?" *The Daily Breeze*, March 17, 1991, C6.
35. Mark Heisler, "Team May Be Good, But Reviews Aren't," *Los Angeles Times*, March 31, 1991, C7.
36. Clifton Brown, "The Stuff of Champions: Bulls Have What It Takes," *Star-Phoenix*, March 25, 1991, B3.
37. Ibid.
38. Lee Shappell, "All Disgruntled Jackson 5 Sings Basketball Blues," *The Arizona Republic*, February 24, 1991, D6.
39. Joe Mooshil, "Jordan Is the Rock on Which Bulls Are Built," *Petaluma Argus-Courier*, May 31, 1991, 5.
40. Stan Hochman, "The Builder of the Bulls," *The Philadelphia Daily News*, June 13, 1991, 93.
41. Sam Smith, "Bulls Give Pippen New Deal," *Chicago Tribune*, June 14, 1991, Section 4, 5.
42. Ira Winderman, "A Bull Market," *South Florida Sun Sentinel*, June 14, 1991, C1.
43. Sam Smith, "Up and Away, Bull Sky High over the NBA," *Chicago Tribune*, June 17, 1991, Section 7, 1.
44. Dinces, *Bulls Markets*, 23.
45. Larry Bennett, *The Third City: Chicago and American Urbanism*, Chicago: University of Chicago Press, 2020, 92.
46. Ed Sherman, "Jackson's Aides in Background, on Solid Ground," *Chicago Tribune*, June 17, 1991, Section 7, 21.
47. Associated Press, "NBA's Salary Cap Challenging Franchises," *The Lincoln Star*, July 24, 1991, 31.

Chapter 7

1. Lee Lowenfish, *Baseball's Endangered Species: Inside the Craft of Scouting by Those Who Lived It*, Lincoln: University of Nebraska, 2023, ix.
2. Ibid., 79.
3. Mike Conlin, "Odds & Ins," *Chicago Tribune*, July 29, 1991, Section 3, 9.
4. John O'Malley, "Grant Claims Double Standard," *The Times*, October 4, 1991, E-6.
5. Sam Smith, "Jordan-Grant Truce Leads Bulls' Unity Bid," *Chicago Tribune*, October 5, 1991, Section 3, 1.
6. Michael Arace, "Bulls Settle Down to Defending Their Championship," *Hartford Courant*, November 3, 1991, C7.
7. John O'Malley, "Being Like Mike Not All It's Cracked Up to Be," *The Times*, October 11, 1991, E-1.
8. Melissa Isaacson and Paul Sullivan, "Is Krause Having Fun Yet?" *Chicago Tribune*, June 3, 1992, Section 4, 4.
9. Associated Press, "Idled Olajuwon Files a Grievance," *Corpus Christi Caller-Times*, March 26, 1992, D4.
10. Mark Heisler, "Battle Lines Drawn in Chicago War," *Los Angeles Times*, November 24, 1991, C10.
11. Mitchell Krugel, "Bulls' Krause Enjoying the Last Laugh," *The Times*, November 3, 1992, D-4.

12. Mark Heisler, "It's Been No Life of Riley for Knicks," *Los Angeles Times*, December 8, 1991, C7.
13. Sam Smith, "Jackson Coach of Year? Writer's Bullish on Idea," *The Charlotte Observer*, April 2, 1992, 4B.
14. Melissa Isaacson, "New Season for Bulls, but Don't Forget Old One," *Chicago Tribune*, April 21, 1992, Section 4, 5.
15. Robes Patton, "Few Teams Likely to Block the Run of the Bulls," *South Florida Sun Sentinel*, April 23, 1992, 9C.
16. S.L. Price, "The Silent Treatment," *The Miami Herald*, April 24, 1992, 1D.
17. Barry Stanton, "Nice Run, but There's More to Be Done," *Gannett Suburban Newspapers*, May 18, 1992, 39A.
18. Terry Pluto, "Cavs Notes," *The Akron Beacon Journal*, May 20, 1991, D3.
19. David Dupree, "Pippen Pulls Bulls' Wagon," *Great Falls Tribune*, June 1, 1992, C1.
20. Ailene Voisin, "Smits's Emergence at Center Upsets Pacers' Chemistry," *The Atlanta Constitution*, December 8, 1991, E19.
21. Paul Sullican, "Kersey: Flagrant Call 'Ridiculous,'" *Chicago Tribune*, June 15, 1992, Section 3, 16.
22. Gary Binford, "Knicks Outrace Bullets," *Daily News*, July 9, 1992, 62.
23. Steve Love, "U.S. Turns Up Intensity, Conks Croatia," *The Wichita Eagle*, July 28, 1992, 5B.
24. Associated Press, "Injuries and Croatians Fail to Stop Dream Team," *News-Journal*, July 28, 1992, 1-C.
25. Ed Sherman, "Critics, Appearance Aside, Krause a True Winner," *Chicago Tribune*, June 19, 1992, Section 9, 9.
26. Marc Hansen, "Not Bad Work If You Can Get It," *The Des Moines Register*, November 5, 1992, Section S, 1.
27. Craig Hodges, *Long Shot: The Triumphs and Struggles of an NBA Freedom Fighter*, Chicago: Haymarket Books, 2017, 171.
28. Melissa Isaacson, "Jordan Backup Job Tough to Fill," *Chicago Tribune*, October 5, 1992, Section 3, 4.
29. Brian Biggane, "Years, Time Finally Catching Up to Bulls," *The Palm Beach Post*, November 15, 1992, 14C.
30. Examiner Staff Report, "3-Way Deal Brings Rookie to Warriors," *San Francisco Examiner*, September 19, 1992, C-6.
31. Sam Smith, "Jordan's Scoring Must Fit Team Plan," *Chicago Tribune*, October 4, 1992, Section 3, 12.
32. Melissa Isaacson, "Perdue Hears Minutes Ticking Away," *Chicago Tribune*, October 11, 1992, Section 3, 14.
33. Bob Ryan, "Bulls' GM Doesn't Deserve Bad Rap," *Naples Daily News*, June 3, 1997, 3C.
34. Don Markus, "Gold Mettle Season," *The Baltimore Sun*, December 17, 1992, 8C.
35. Melissa Isaacson, "Bulls' Malaise Weighing Heavily on Jordan," *Chicago Tribune*, January 31, 1993, Section 3, 15.
36. Ira Winderman, "Will McCray See Bulls Evolve or Dissolve?" *South Florida Sun Sentinel*, February 7, 1993, 4C.
37. Isaacson, *Transition Game*, 1–3.
38. Bernie Lincicome, "Enough of Jordan Left for No. 3?" *Chicago Tribune*, February 14, 1993, Section 3, 1.
39. Barry Cooper, "Bulls Discover Point in 6-foot-10 Kukoc," *The Orlando Sentinel*, June 17, 1993, D-7.
40. David Steele, "Ewing Concedes MVP; He'd Rather Have Title," *Newsday*, May 26, 1993, 141.
41. Bernie Lincicome, "Bulls Down 2 Is Good Sign for Knicks," *Daily News*, May 26, 1993, 7.

Chapter 8

1. Tom Groeschen, "To Bulls, Blount Is Keeper," *The Cincinnati Enquirer*, July 2, 1993, D3.
2. Dan Bickley, "Cheers Don't Follow Reinsdorf Successes," *Northwest Herald*, October 4, 1993, 10.
3. Dinces, *Bulls Markets*, 81.
4. Mike Decourcy, "Bulls Pick Up Pieces to Begin Life After Jordan," *Blade-Citizen*, October 27, 1993, C-3.
5. Sam Smith, "Grant Now an All-Star," *Chicago Tribune*, February 2, 1994, Section 4, 3.
6. Gery Woelfel, "Grant Set to Hit Road," *The Journal Times*, February 12, 1994, 1D.
7. Cory Meinecke, "Red-Hot Starts Overshadow Suns' Success," *Detroit Free Press*, December 14, 1993, 3C.

8. Lazenby, *Blood on the Horns*, 75.
9. Shaun Powell, "Who Needs Mike?" *Newsday*, January 2, 1994, 13.
10. Jeff Vorva, "T-U-R-M-O-I-L Spells Doom," *Northwest Herald*, May 29, 1994, 9.
11. Melissa Isaacson, "Bulls Keep Nucleus for Title Run with an Eye on the Future," *Chicago Tribune*, February 25, 1994, Section 4, 3.
12. Stan Hochman, "Daly's the Man You Want, Harold," *Philadelphia Daily News*, May 5, 1994, 87.
13. Isaacson, *Transition Game*, 217.
14. Shaun Powell, "Bulls Remain Confident Series Will Go to a Game 7," *Kenosha News*, May 20, 1994, 21.
15. Kevin Ball, "Bulls in Odd Position—Out of Work," *Northwest Herald*, May 24, 1994, Section B, 1.
16. Sam Smith, "Hard-Working Cartwright, Paxson Represent Character of Their City," *Chicago Tribune*, May 26, 1994, Section 8, 3.
17. Sam Smith, "Spiteful Krause Strikes Again—And Bach's Gone," *Chicago Tribune*, June 1, 1994, Section 4, 3.
18. Roland Lazenby, "My Response to Sam Smith," *Medium*, May 6, 2020, https://medium.com/@lazenby/my-response-to-sam-smith-c2c23d00c02e.
19. Melissa Isaacson, "Bulls Aide Bach Shown the Door," *Chicago Tribune*, June 1, 1994, Section 4, 2.
20. Sam Smith, "Pippen's Name Surfaces among Predraft Rumors," *Evansville Press*, June 27, 1994, 19.
21. Dick Weiss, "Bulls Start to Shop Pippen's Seat," *Daily News*, June 28, 1994, 52.
22. Sam Smith, "Grant Opens Negotiations with Magic Brass," *Chicago Tribune*, July 29, 1994, Section 4, 4.
23. Melissa Isaacson, "Bulls Begin Digging Again," *Chicago Tribune*, October 8, 1994, Section 3, 2.
24. Corky Meinecke, "Bulls Should Make Deal to Get Spurs' Rodman," *Detroit Free Press*, October 29, 1994, 3B.
25. Roger B. Brown, "Another Bull Run," *Fort Worth Star-Telegram*, January 11, 1994, Section C, 1.
26. Bernie Lincicome, "Even Jordan's Jersey Doesn't Want It Over," *The Rock Island Argus*, November 2, 1994, C3.
27. Isaacson, "Why Do People Hate His Guy?" Section 3, 9.
28. Mark Heisler, "With These Resolutions, Watch Out in '95," *Los Angeles Times*, January 1, 1995, C4.
29. Mal Florence, "Morning Briefing," *Los Angeles Times*, January 20, 1995, C2.
30. Mike Nadel, "Pippen Is Feeling the Strain," *Thousand Oaks Star*, February 8, 1995, SW7.
31. Sam Smith, "No End to Pippen Trade Rumors," *Chicago Tribune*, February 9, 1995, Section 4, 3.
32. Mitch Lawrence, "Teams Dialing 911 for Basketball Help," *The Californian*, February 22, 1995, B-4.
33. Mark Heisler, "Will Writers Ever Deliver MVP Trophy to Malone?" *Los Angeles Times*, April 9, 1995, C4.
34. Tim Povtak, "Grant 'Looking for Jerry Krause,'" *The Orlando Sentinel*, May 19, 1995, M-2.

Chapter 9

1. Ronald Tillery, "Not Protecting Armstrong Makes Cents," *The Times*, June 17, 1995, D-3.
2. Sam Smith, "Toronto Picks Armstrong; May Not Trade Him," *Chicago Tribune*, June 25, 1995, Section 3, 3.
3. Bernie Lincicome, "Disaster Will Come from This Desperate Move," *Chicago Tribune*, October 3, 1995, Section 4, 2.
4. Corky Meinecke, "In Their Desperation, Bulls Turn to the Wrong Rodman," *Detroit Free Press*, October 3, 1995, 2D.
5. Bob Verdi, "The Rodman-for-Perdue Was a Real Steal for the Bulls," *Simi Valley Star*, October 8, 1995, C10.
6. Ian O'Connor, "A Cattle Drive," *Daily News*, May 3, 1996. 71.
7. Jeffrey Drenberg, "Hawks Curtail Nathan's Dream," *The Atlanta Journal*, December 15, 1995, D10.
8. Terry Armour, "Krause's Peers Name Him League's Top Exec," *Chicago Tribune*, May 9, 1996, Section 4, 6.
9. Scott Howard-Cooper, "How Much to Keep the Bulls Intact?" *Los Angeles Times*, June 11, 1996, C4.
10. Leila Rahimi, "Tim Floyd Describes His Relationship with Jerry Krause," *Bulls Talk Podcast* (podcast), April 24, 2020.
11. Randy Minkoff, "A New Line for

Jerry Krause," *Chicago Tribune*, September 22, 1996, Section 17, 1.

12. Bernard Fernandez, "The Endgame?" *Philadelphia Daily News*, April 15, 1998, 69.

13. Sam Smith, "Jackson Fortunate Contract Is Only for 1 Year," *Chicago Tribune*, June 21, 1996, Section 4, 12.

14. Knight-Ridder Newspapers, "Rodman Talks with Chicago Not Going Smoothly," *Southern Illinoisan*, July 20, 1996, B1.

15. Terry Armour, "Bulls Now Hope Rodman Doesn't Hold a Grudge," *Lancaster New Era*, August 3, 1996, B-3.

16. Jeffrey Denberg, "Big Project Ahead of Schedule," *The Atlanta Constitution*, October 20, 1996, E13.

17. Lazenby, *Mindgames*, 392–394.

18. Greg Logan, "Krause Explains Train of Thought," *Newsday*, April 22, 1998, A91.

19. Jeff Vorva, "Jordan Near Top of Bulls Hit List," *Northwest Herald*, July 24, 1997, 8.

20. Chris Baker, "Clippers' Loss Becomes Bulls' Gain," *Los Angeles Times*, April 3, 1997, C8.

21. Terry Armour, "Pippen Enters Fray Over Williams' Beef," *Chicago Tribune*, July 16, 1997, Section 4, 8.

22. Jim Litke, "Feeling Like Millions of Bucks," *Potomac News*, July 25, 1997, C1.

23. Ryan Rudnansky, "Jerry West's Relationship with Lakers' Phil Jackson Was Far from Perfect," *Bleacher Report*, October 18, 2011, https://bleacherreport.com/articles/900652-jerry-wests-relationship-with-lakers-phil-jackson-was-far-from-perfect.

24. Pippen, *Unguarded*, 226.

25. Craig DeVrieze, "Jerry Krause Deserves a Slap for His One-Last-Run-and-Done Attitude," *Quad-City Times*, July 27, 1997, 2S.

26. Skip Bayless, "If Krause Is Off the Card, This Dance Can Go On," *Chicago Tribune*, June 16, 1998, Section 4, 5.

27. Nancy Armour, "Nobody Wants to Be Remembered as the Guy Who Broke Up the Bulls," *Wilmington News-Journal*, June 20, 1998, 6.

28. Bayless, "If Krause Is Off the Card," Section 4, 5.

29. Terry Armour, "Jackson Bids Farewell: 'It's the Right Time,'" *Richmond Times-Dispatch*, June 23, 1998, E6.

Chapter 10

1. Terry Armour, "Mini-Camp Ends Business; Lockout Begins," *Chicago Tribune*, July 1, 1998, Section 4, 7.

2. K.C. Johnson, "Floyd Installed as Favorite Among Bulls' Final Four," *Waterloo-Cedar Falls Courier*, July 3, 1999, B4.

3. K.C. Johnson, "This Time He Seems to Mean It," *Chicago Tribune*, July 17, 1998, Section 4, 7.

4. Terry Armour, "Floyd Reportedly Having 2nd Thoughts about Bulls," *Chicago Tribune*, July 20, 1998, Section 4, 1.

5. David Teel, "Iowa Standout Decides to Take Another Road," *Daily Press*, August 3, 1998, D1.

6. Nancy Armour, "Bulls Officially Make Floyd Head Coach," *The Dothan Eagle*, January 16, 1999, 6-C.

7. Marc Hansen, "Floyd Impressive in Chicago Debut," *The Des Moines Register*, July 24, 1998, 4S.

8. Sam Smith, "First Job Is Bringing Fans Back," *Chicago Tribune*, January 7, 1999, Section 4, 4.

9. Terrence Armour, "Shooting the Breeze and Shooting Around," *Chicago Tribune*, January 12, 1999, Section 4, 6.

10. Steve Aschburner, "Free Agents: Who's Headed Where," *Star Tribune*, January 17, 1999, C8.

11. Sam Smith, "This Signing Just What Bulls Need," *Chicago Tribune*, January 26, 1999, Section 4, 3.

12. Sam Smith, "In the End, Pippen Proves Gracious," *Chicago Tribune*, January 23, 1999, Section 3, 1.

13. Mark Heisler, "In Chicago, Rebuilding a Bunch of Bull," *Los Angeles Times*, May 16, 1999, D11.

14. Chris McCoskey, "The NBA Rumor Mill," *The Jackson Sun*, January 18, 1999, 3C.

15. Rick Gano, "Barry Steps into Size-23 Air Jordans," *Northwest Herald*, January 26, 1999, 1.

16. Terrence Armour, "Barry's Here for a New Start," *Chicago Tribune*, January 26, 1999, Section 4, 3.

17. Doug Darroch, "'First Dance' Is Awkward," *Philadelphia Daily News*, January 25, 1999, 101.
18. Todd Zolecki, "Bulls Are Out with the Old," *Northwest Herald*, February 4, 1999, B1.
19. George Willis, "The Death of a Dynasty," *The New York Post*, February 10, 1999, https://nypost.com/1999/02/10/the-death-of-a-dynasty-egomaniac-krause-to-blame-for-bulls-fall/.
20. Steve Rosenbloom, "Hit&Run," *Chicago Tribune*, April 1, 1999, Section 4, 1.
21. Terry Armour, "10 Years Later, Back to Lottery," *Chicago Tribune*, May 19, 1999, Section 4, 3.
22. Alex Kennedy, "After the Last Dance: An Oral History of the 1998-99 Chicago Bulls," *Hoops Hype*, May 18, 2020, https://hoopshype.com/2020/05/18/nba-the-last-dance-chicago-bulls-1998-1999-michael-jordan-phil-jackson-scottie-pippen-tim-floyd-jerry-krause-toni-kukoc-new-oral-history-documentary/.
23. Howard Tsumura, "Bull Market Beats Bears," *The Province*, May 23, 1999, A76.
24. Chris Young, "Luck of Draw Lands Bull First Over-All Pick," *The Toronto Star*, May 23, 1999, C8.
25. Sam Smith, "Knicks Try to Hem Pacers with Altercations," *Chicago Tribune*, June 7, 1999, Section 3, 4.
26. Mike McGraw, "Who Will End Up in Toddlin' Town?" *The Daily Herald*, June 13, 1999, Section 2, 3.
27. Chicago Tribune, "Unknowns Striving to Improve Draft Position," *The Dispatch*, June 9, 1999, D4.
28. Mike McGraw, "NBA Draft Camp Intriguing for Floyd," *The Daily Herald*, June 10, 1999, Section 2, 5.
29. Nancy Armour, "Brand Visits Jordan's Playground," *Albuquerque Journal*, July 2, 1999, D8.
30. Associated Press, "Artest Signs for Three Years with Chicago," *Intelligencer Journal*, July 16, 1999, C-4.
31. Matt Youmans, "Bulls' Roster Soon to See Brand New," *The Times*, July 6, 1999, D-1.
32. Terry Armour, "Winter Arrives in L.A.," *Chicago Tribune*, July 17, 1999, Section 3, 1.
33. Justin Hagey, "National TV Brings Bulls Back This Season," *Northwest Herald*, July 23, 1999, 7.
34. Terry Armour, "Bulls, Floyd Short-Handed Again," *Chicago Tribune*, July 22, 1999, Section 4, 2.
35. Jeffrey Demberg, "Cash Talks, Oakley Won't," *The Atlanta Constitution*, August 8, 1999, H2.
36. Sam Smith, "Hawkins Should Be Asset for Bulls," *Southern Illinoisan*, August 15, 1999, 5C.
37. Mike Triplett, "Biding Their Time," *The Sacramento Bee*, October 19, 1999, C3.
38. Nancy Armour, "Bulls: From NBA's Champs to Chumps," *Tallahassee Democrat*, January 1, 2000, 3C.
39. Justin Hagey, "Pippen's Top Choice Is Bulls' Best Team," *The Northwest Herald*, January 4, 2000, 5.
40. Steve Wyche, "Jordan Joins Wizards' Front Office," *Washington Post*, January 20, 2000, A1.
41. Marc Fisher, "Hiring Has Impact Beyond Franchise," *Washington Post*, January 20, 2000, A1.
42. Associated Press, "Bulls Dynasty Officially Dies with Trade," *The Odessa American*, February 17, 2000, 6D.
43. Mike McGraw, "Kukoc, Sixers a Good Fit," *Daily Herald*, February 17, 2000, Section 2, 7.
44. Kent McDill, "Formerly 'Hated' Starks Given a Bulls Uniform," *The Daily Herald*, February 17, 2000, Section 2, 7.
45. Associated Press, "Starks Wants out of Chicago," *The Daily Oklahoman*, February 27, 2000, 10-B.
46. Mike McGraw, "Starks' Request to Void Contract Awaits Ruling," *The Daily Herald*, March 2, 2000, Section 2, 3.
47. Ohm Youngmisuk, "Artest: I'll Miss Starks," *Daily News*, March 23, 2000, 78.
48. Jimmie Tramel, "Heat, Knicks on Starks' Short List," *Tulsa World*, April 9, 2000, B2.

Chapter 11

1. Justin Hagey, "Blake Says Mihm Fits Bulls' Need," *The Northwest Herald*, June 8, 2000, 5.

Notes—Chapter 11

2. Peter May, "Jordan Isn't Displaying Wizardry in Front Office," *The Boston Globe*, June 11, 2000, D6.

3. Fred Mitchell, "Mihm Says He Could Fill Tall Order for Bulls," *Chicago Tribune*, June 13, 2000, Section 4, 4.

4. Jeff Gordon, "Yo, Jerry, It's 2000," *St. Louis Post-Dispatch*, July 12, 2000, D2.

5. Mike McGraw, "Top Draft Pick Fizer Says His Two Children Are 'What I Live For,'" *The Daily Herald*, June 30, 2000, Section 2, 4.

6. Wire Services, "Duncan, Hill Are Shown the Kingdom of Magic," *Democrat and Chronicle*, July 4, 2000, 3D.

7. Dan LeBatard, "Free-Agent Sweepstakes Leads Duncan, Hill into Magic's Fantasyland," *The News & Observer*, July 10, 2000, 5C.

8. Sam Smith, "Top Agent: Players Set the Agenda," *Chicago Tribune*, July 26, 2000, Section 4, 4.

9. Sam Smith, "Why Won't Anyone Play with Me?" *Chicago Tribune*, July 30, 2000, Section 3, 1.

10. Ian O'Connor, "Layden Will Be Challenged to Put Knicks Among Elite," *The Courier-News*, August 1, 2000, C-4.

11. Nancy Armour, "Mercer Relishes Task of Rebuilding Bulls," *Press Journal*, August 3, 2000, B2.

12. Ibid.

13. Brian Robb, "The Pitino Files: The Ron Mercer Trade Paid Off Down the Line for Celtics," *Boston Sports Journal*, May 21, 2020, https://www.bostonsportsjournal.com/2020/05/21/pitino-files-ron-mercer-trade-paid-off-line-celtics.

14. Michael Wilbon, "Never a Dull Moment with Iverson, Krause," *The Buffalo News*, August 6, 2000, B-8.

15. K.C. Johnson, "Brand Not Ready to Give Up," *Chicago Tribune*, January 4, 2001, Section 4, 5.

16. K.C. Johnson, "Bulls Won't Be Rushed into Turning Rookies Lose," *Chicago Tribune*, January 23, 2001, Section 4, 1.

17. Ira Winderman, "Trail of Confusion," *South Florida Sun-Sentinel*, May 13, 2001, 9C.

18. K.C. Johnson, "Record 6 Preps Part of NBA List," *Chicago Tribune*, May 19, 2001, Section 3, 7.

19. Mike McGraw, "For White, Wizards Would Be Top Choice," *The Daily Herald*, June 14, 2001, Section 2, 4.

20. Enquirer Wire Services, "Super-Sonics' New GM Says No Player Is 'Untouchable,'" *The Cincinnati Enquirer*, June 17, 2001, C6.

21. Sam Smith, "Bulls' Power Move: A Trade of Brand," *Chicago Tribune*, June 18, 2001, Section 3, 2.

22. K.C. Johnson, "Bulls High on South-Sider Curry," *South Bend Tribune*, June 18, 2001, B6.

23. SHOWTIME Basketball, "Tyson Chandler / Ep 196," *All the Smoke* (podcast), September 7, 2023.

24. Billy Witz, "Chandler Ready for NBA Draft," *The Californian*, June 23, 2001, C1.

25. Brian C. Hedger, "Surprises Galore at Bulls Headquarters," *The Times*, June 28, 2001, C1.

26. Jonathan Abrams, *Boys Among Men: How the Prep-to-Pro Generation Redefined the NBA and Sparked a Basketball Revolution*, New York: Crown Archetype, 2016, 184.

27. Nick Hut, "New Faces Make Bulls Interesting," *Northwest Herald*, July 18, 2001, B1.

28. Sam Smith, "Jordan's Best Move? Rejoin His Old Team," *Chicago Tribune*, September 7, 2001, Section 4, 1.

29. John Smallwood, "Jordan Itching to Play," *Philadelphia Daily News*, October 2, 2001, 85.

30. Mike McGraw, "Krause's Search 'Very Easy,'" *The Daily Herald*, December 29, 2001, Section 2, 3.

31. Nick Hut, "Rose Trade Looks Inevitable," *Northwest Herald*, February 19, 2002, 6.

32. Dan Gelston, "Pacers, Bulls Make Seven-Player Trade," *Signal*, February 20, 2002, B4.

33. Barbara Barker, "Mad About Yao," *Newsday*, May 2, 2002, A90.

34. Knight Ridder Newspapers, "Duke Guard Likes Idea of Being a Bull," *Herald & Review*, June 10, 2002, B1.

35. Rich Evans, "Marshall Gets Less $$$ to Sign with Chicago," *Deseret News*, August 17, 2002, https://www.deseret.com/2002/8/17/19672277/marshall-gets-less-to-sign-with-chicago.

36. Ron Higgins, "Around the League," *Commercial Appeal*, April 6, 2003, C12.

Chapter 12

1. Chortkoff, "What Can Be Better Than Being the Best?" C6.

Bibliography

Books

Abrams, Jonathan. *Boys Among Men: How the Prep-to-Pro Generation Redefined the NBA and Sparked a Basketball Revolution*. New York: Crown Archetype, 2016.

Aiello, Thomas. *Hoops: A Cultural History of Basketball in America*. Lanham, MD: Rowman & Littlefield, 2022.

Araton, Harvey. *When the Garden Was Eden*. New York: HarperCollins Publishers, 2012.

Bennett, Larry. *The Third City: Chicago and American Urbanism*. Chicago: The University of Chicago Press, 2020.

Bogues, Tyrone. *Muggsy: My Life from a Kid in the Projects to the Godfather of Smallball*. Chicago: Triumph Books, 2023.

Crandall, Russell, C. *Drugs and Thugs: The History and Future of America's War on Drugs*. New Haven, CT: Yale University Press, 2020.

Dinces, Sean. *Bulls Markets: Chicago's Basketball Business and the New Inequality*. Chicago: The University of Chicago Press, 2018.

Halberstam, David. *Playing for Keeps: Michael Jordan and the World He Made*. New York: Random House, 1999.

Hodges, Craig, with Rory Fanning. *Long Shot: The Triumphs and Struggles of an NBA Freedom Fighter*. Chicago: Haymarket Books, 2017.

Isaacson, Melissa. *Transition Game: An Inside Look at Life with the Chicago Bulls*. Champaign, IL: Sagamore-Venture Publishing, 1994.

Jackson, Phil. *Eleven Rings*. London: Virgin Books, 2014.

Klier, John D., and Slomo Labroza, eds. *Pogroms: Anti-Jewish Violence in Modern Russian History*. Cambridge: Cambridge University Press, 2004.

Knepper, Paul. *The Knicks of the Nineties: Ewing, Oakley, Starks and the Brawlers That Almost Won It All*. Jefferson, NC: McFarland, 2020.

Lazenby, Roland. *Blood on the Horns: The Long Strange Ride of Michael Jordan's Chicago Bulls*. New York: Diversion Books, 2013.

Lazenby, Roland. *Mindgames: Phil Jackson's Long Strange Journey*. Chicago: Contemporary Books, 2002.

Lewis, Robert. *Chicago's Industrial Decline: The Failure of Redevelopment, 1920–1975*. Ithaca, NC: Cornell University Press, 2020.

Lowenfish, Lee. *Baseball's Endangered Species: Inside the Craft of Scouting by Those Who Lived It*. Lincoln: University of Nebraska, 2023.

Mendelsohn, Joshua. *The Cap: How Larry Fleisher and David Stern Built the Modern NBA*. Lincoln: University of Nebraska Press, 2020.

Nicholson, James C. *1968: A Pivotal Moment in American Sport*. Knoxville: The University of Tennessee Press, 2019.

Oakley, Charles. *The Last Enforcer: Outrageous Stories from the Life and Times of One of the NBA's Fiercest Competitors*. New York: Gallery Books, 2022.

Pippen, Scottie. *Unguarded.* New York: Atria Books, 2021.
Royko, Mike. *Boss: Richard J. Daley of Chicago.* New York: E.P. Dutton, 1971.
Smith, Sam. *The Jordan Rules.* New York: Simon & Schuster, 1992.
Trutor, Clayton. *Loserville: How Professional Sports Remade Atlanta—and How Atlanta Remade Professional Sports.* Lincoln: University of Nebraska Press, 2021.
Walley, Christine J. *Exit Zero: Family and Class in Postindustrial Chicago.* Chicago: University of Chicago Press, 2013.
Wolff, Alexander. *Big Game, Small World: A Basketball Adventure.* Durham, NC: Duke University Press, 2022.

Magazines, Newspapers, Websites

The Akron Beacon Journal
AL.com
Albuquerque Journal
The Albuquerque Tribune
Arizona Republic
Arlington Heights Herald
Asheville Times
The Atlanta Constitution
The Baltimore Sun
Bangor Daily News
The Belleville News-Democrat
Blade-Citizen
Bleacher Report
The Boston Globe
Boston Sports Journal
The Buffalo News
The Californian
The Central New Jersey Home News
The Charlotte Observer
Chicago Reader
Chicago Studies
Chicago Tribune
Chippewa Herald-Telegram
The Cincinnati Enquirer
The Cincinnati Post
The Clarion-Ledger
The Commercial Appeal
The Courier-Journal
The Courier-News
The Daily Breeze
The Daily Herald
Daily Intelligencer Journal
The Daily Oklahoman
The Daily Register
The Daily Sentinel-Tribune
Daily Sports News
The Daily Tar Heel
Dayton Daily News and Journal Herald
The Des Moines Register
Deseret News
Detroit Free Press
Dialogue: A Journal of Mormon Thought
The Dothan Eagle
Durham Morning Herald
Economic Geography
Essentially Sports
Evansville Courier and Press
Evansville Press
The Evening Sun
Fort Worth Star-Telegram
The Fresno Bee
Gannett Suburban Newspapers
Great Falls Tribune
The Hartford Courant
Herald and Review
The Herald-Palladium
The Indianapolis Star
Intelligencer Journal
The Jackson Sun
Journal Gazette
The Journal of Economic History
The Journal Times
Kenosha News
Kitsap Sun
Lancaster New Era
Lansing State Journal
Las Cruces Sun-News
The Lincoln Star
The Logan Leader
Los Angeles Times
The Manhattan Mercury
Matton Journal Gazette
Medium
The Messenger
The Miami Herald
Missoulian
Naples Daily News
The New York Post
The News and Observer
News-Pilot
Newsday
Northwest Herald
The Odessa American
The Olympian

The Orlando Sentinel
The Palm Beach Post
The Pantagraph
Petaluma Argus-Courier
Philadelphia Daily News
The Philadelphia Inquirer
Potomac News
Press Journal
The Province
Record-Journal
The Reporter
The Reporter Dispatch
Richmond Times-Dispatch
The Rock Island Argus
Quad-City Times
The Sacramento Bee
St. Joseph News-Press
St. Louis-Post Dispatch
St. Petersburg Times
San Francisco Examiner
Santa Maria Times
The Shreveport Journal
The Signal
South Bend Tribune
South Florida Sun Sentinel
Southern Illinoisan

Spokane Chronicle
The Spokesman-Review
Sports Illustrated
The Star-Democrat
Star-Phoenix
Star Tribune
The Sunday Oklahoman
Tallahassee Democrat
The Terre Haute Tribune
Thousand Oaks Star
Time
The Times
The Times and Democrat
The Times Herald
Times-Press Streator
The Titusville Herald
The Toronto Star
Tulsa World
USA Today
Washington Post
Waterloo-Cedar Falls Courier
Wichita Eagle
Wilmington News-Journal
Winston-Salem Journal
World-Herald

Podcasts

All the Smoke
The Bill Cartwright Show
Bulls Talk Podcast

Locked on Bulls
Timeout Bulls with Chuck Swirsky
The Woj Pod

Index

Abdul-Jabbar, Kareem 13, 49, 50
Ackerley, Barry 142
Adams, Alvan 37, 42
Ainge, Danny 44, 79
Anderson, Nick 105, 106
Anthony, Greg 137, 187
Archibald, Nate "Tiny" 32, 33, 35, 69
Armour, Terry 157
Armstrong, B.J. 77, 106, 128, 130, 141, 145, 150, 173, 174
Arnold, Murray 59
Auerbach, Red 54, 80, 124, 193, 201
Axelson, Joe 85, 86

Babcock 96
Badger, Ed 42
Bagarić, Dalibor 181
Bailey, James 44
Banks, Gene 61, 64, 69, 85, 91
Barkley, Charles 1, 126, 134, 165
Barry, Brent 166–167, 169, 173
Barry, Rick 24, 35, 44
Barry, Sam 21
Battier, Shane 185
Bayless, Skip 161
Baylor, Elgin 84, 152
Bellamy, Walt 11
Benjamin, Corey 168
Bergfeld, John 69
Berkow, Ira 17
Berry, Bill 189
Bianchi, Al 30, 108
Blackhawks 48, 136
Bogues, Tyrone "Muggsy" 84
Bowen, Bruce 176
Bowie, Anthony 128
Bowie, Sam 50, 154
Boyz II Men 146
Bradly, Bill 52
Brandon, Terrell 175

Brisker, John 73
Brown, Clifford 117, 184
Brown, Kwame 184, 185, 186
Brown, Randy 163, 167, 183
Brown, Warren 17
Bryant, Kobe 104, 157, 172
Bryant, Mark 165, 167
Buechler, Jud 165
Burrell, Scott 166
Buse, Don 35
Buss, Jerry 49

Caffey, Jason 100, 139, 167
Calhoun, David "Corky" 35
Capicchioni, "Lucky" Luciano 127
Carr, Kenny 42, 43
Carr, M.L. 144
Carroll, Joe Barry 43, 44, 79, 80
Chamberlain, Wilt 13, 22, 26, 30, 37
Chambers, Tom 85
Chandler, Tyson 3, 5, 184, 185, 186, 187, 188, 189, 190, 191
Cleamons, Jim 110, 120, 172
Collins, Doug 72, 73, 74, 75, 76, 81, 82, 83, 85, 86, 88, 91, 92, 94, 98, 102, 103, 106, 107, 108, 109, 110, 111, 188
Collins, Jimmy 32, 33, 34
Corzine, Dave 51, 52, 77, 93, 94, 95, 98
Cowens, Dave 37, 59
Crawford, Jamal 3, 5, 180, 181, 184, 188, 190
Crown, Lester 39, 48
Cummings, Terry 50
Cureton, Earl 76, 77
Curry, Eddy 3, 5, 184, 185, 186, 187, 188, 189, 190, 191
Curry, Stephen 24

Dailey, Quintin 55, 57, 63, 66, 68, 69, 76
Daly, Chuck 65, 140, 151

215

Index

Dantley, Adrian 38, 111
Davis, Brad 43
Davis, Charles 105
Davis, Walter 116
Dawkins, Darryl 38
Dawkins, Johnny 74, 75, 76, 79, 80, 92, 117
Douglas, Leon 113
Dukan, Ivica 154, 181
Duncan, Tim 170, 172, 173, 179, 181, 187
Dunleavy, Mike 108
Dunleavy, Mike, Jr. 190
Durant, Kevin 76

Edwards, James 94, 95, 152, 157
Ehlo, Craig 75
Einhorn, Eddie 48
Ellis, Dale 116
Enright, James 17, 27
Erickson, Keith 25

Fenwick, Becky 60
Ferry, Bob 27, 34
Ficker, Robin 125
Fitzsimmons, Cotton 64
Fizer, Marcus 5, 169, 180
Floyd, Tim 58, 60, 155–58, 161, 164, 165, 168, 170, 172, 174, 177, 180, 182, 184, 187, 188, 207, 208

Gaines, Clarence 12, 22, 23, 27, 28, 61
Gaines, Clarence, Jr. 110, 136, 154, 196
Gasol, Pau 186
Gervin, George 61, 63, 64, 65, 67
Gilliam, Armen 85, 86
Gilmore, Artis 41, 55, 87, 90, 91, 92, 93, 96
Gleason, Bill 17, 82
Grant, Harvey 87, 98
Grant, Horace 1, 5, 7, 77, 85–88, 95, 97–100, 104, 105, 110, 112–14, 116–18, 120, 122, 125, 129–31, 134, 136–41, 144, 147, 149, 150, 154, 162, 172, 179–81

Halberstam, David 2, 110, 124
Haley, Jack 105, 152
Hamblen, Frank 163, 164, 172
Hamnik, Al 10
Hansen, Bob 128
Hardaway, Anfernee 150, 173
Hardaway, Tim 105, 106
Harpring, Matt 191
Hasselman, Fred 18
Hawkins, Connie 36
Hawkins, Hersey 173, 174

Helland, Erik 154
Hemond, Roland 60
Higgins, Rod 52, 64, 65, 175
Hill, Brian 169
Hill, Grant 139, 172, 181
Himes, Larry 109
Hinrich, Kirk 164
Hinson, Roy 74
Hochman, Stan 140
Hodges, Craig 101, 102, 104, 105, 112, 118, 128
Hoiberg, Fred 174, 184
Hollins, Hue 141
Holton, Michael 68
Holzman, Red 11, 12, 54, 58, 73, 92
Hopkins, Bob 42
Hopson, Dennis 86, 113, 116
Horry, Robert 148
Hornacek, Jeff 137
Houston, Byron 127, 128
Howard, Juwan 160
Hughes, Alfredick 80
Hughes, Larry 176

Isaacson, Melissa 2, 5, 98, 110, 131, 141, 142
Iverson, Alen 177

Jackson, Phil 1, 7, 10, 11, 39, 51, 52, 58, 59, 81, 88, 104, 107, 108, 110, 111, 114, 115, 119, 122–25, 129, 130, 132, 137, 140–42, 145, 147, 148, 150, 151, 154–64, 168, 172, 181, 188
Jamal, Douglas 175
Johnson, Earvin "Magic" 1, 44, 49, 54, 55, 63, 92, 94, 118, 127, 137
Johnson, Eddie 79, 80, 85
Johnson, Clint 12, 22, 23, 27
Johnson, Ken 61
Jordan, Michael 1, 5–8, 10, 11, 19, 40, 50–53, 55, 60–76, 78–83, 88–91, 93–99, 101–6, 109–23, 125–28, 130–32, 134–37, 139, 142, 144–50, 152–56, 158–62, 164, 166, 170, 173, 175, 176, 180, 185, 187, 188, 190, 193
Juzwik, Chris 103

Karbofsky, Gertrude 13, 14
Karbofsky, Paul 13, 14
Kay, Linda 73
Kerr, Johnny 5, 6, 27, 30, 98
Kerr, Steve 1, 110, 137, 138, 148, 163, 165
Ketner, Lari 170
Klein, Dick 25, 30, 31, 48
Kleine, Joe 91
Krystkowiak, Larry 78

Index

Krzyzewski, Mike 75, 170
Kukoč, Toni 5, 110, 111, 113–16, 127, 131, 133–35, 137, 139–41, 144, 148–50, 154, 157, 161, 163, 167, 169, 172, 174–77
Kunkel, Pam 154
Kupchak, Mitch 49

Lagatolla, Al 114
Laimbeer, Bill 65, 96
Lauderdale, Priest 157, 167
Lazenby, Roland 2, 22, 52, 64, 87, 114, 138, 142, 158
Lincicome, Bernie 74, 103, 146
Lloyd, Earl 12
Longley, Luc 140, 141, 154, 161, 165
Loughery, Kevin 50, 51, 57, 58, 125
Lowenfish, Lee 7, 18, 19, 20, 121, 192

MacArthur, Douglas 103
MacLeod, John 35–37, 42, 58, 108
Macy, Kyle 63, 64, 77, 78
Maggette, Corey 169, 170
Mahorn, Rick 95, 105
Majerle, Dan 97, 98, 157, 169
Malone, Karl 1, 67, 92
Maravich, Pete 33
Marshall, Donyell 191
Mason, Anthony 151
McCloskey, Jack 5, 86, 140
McDyess, Antonio 166
McGrady, Tracy 161, 169, 176, 181, 182
McHale, Kevin 76, 80, 157, 191
McKinney, Billy 67, 84, 100
McMahon, Jack 25, 37
Meinecke, Robert "Corky" 145, 151
Mercer, Ron 182, 183, 189
Meyer, Ray 41
Michałowicz, Wojciech 130, 146, 154
Mihm, Chris 179, 180
Miles, Darius 180
Miller, Andre 190
Miller, Brad 183, 189
Miller, Reggie 139
Ming, Yao 184, 190
Moncrief, Sidney 44
Monroe, Earl "The Pearl" 7, 12, 22, 27, 28, 152, 181
Motta, Dick 30–33, 38, 39, 72
Mureşan, Gheorghe 135–136
Murphy, Calvin 32
Myslenski, Skip 73
Nance, Larry 75, 85, 94

Nelson, Don 124, 128
Nixon, Norm 43, 63, 66
Nowitzki, Dirk 76

Oakley, Charles 61, 67, 68, 76, 77, 83, 85, 87, 93, 95–98, 100, 104, 132, 152, 180, 187
O'Connor, Ian 182
O'Koren, Mike 43, 44, 59
Olajuwon, Hakeem 50, 84, 92, 123, 129, 151, 165, 187
Oldham, Jawann 57, 77, 93
Ollie, Kevin 189
O'Neal, Jermaine 179
O'Neal, Shaquille 104, 149, 157, 160, 172
Owens, Billy 176

Parish, Robert 38, 39, 76, 80, 114, 157, 191
Patterson, Steve 123
Patton, George 47, 103
Patton, Landey 32
Paxson, John 61, 62, 66, 78, 82, 83, 94, 106, 118, 120, 134, 141, 192
Perdue, Will 5, 96–98, 105, 109, 110, 116, 129, 136, 138, 140, 141, 145, 151, 152, 154, 173, 174
Perkins, Sam 50, 113
Peterson, Buzz 78, 164
Petrovic, Drazen 112, 113
Pfeil 111
Pinckey, Ed 85
Pippen, Scottie 1, 4–7, 36, 76, 77, 83–86, 88, 91, 93, 95, 101, 102, 109, 112, 114, 116, 118, 120, 125–28, 130, 134, 136–39, 141–45, 147–51, 154, 156, 157, 159, 161, 162, 165, 166, 173, 175, 177, 180
Pitino, Rick 108, 161, 183
Porter, Howard 33

Rashad, Ahmad 146
Reed, Willis 37, 51, 84
Reinsdorf, Jerry 4, 5, 8, 11, 47, 48, 51–54, 57, 59, 60, 67–69, 71–74, 79, 87, 90, 96, 101, 102, 108, 109, 114, 119, 126, 130, 135, 136, 142, 144, 156–60, 162, 168, 175, 192, 193
Richmond, Mitch 142
Riley, Pat 5, 125, 190, 191, 193
Rivers, Doc 93
Roberts, Anthony 42
Robertson, Oscar 38
Robinson, David 85–86, 151, 173, 187
Robinson, Eddie 188
Robinson, Glenn 139, 142
Robinson, Will 72
Rodman, Dennis 1, 84, 115, 145, 151–54, 156, 157, 161, 165, 170
Rogers, Roy 165, 166
Rosengard, David 52–53

Index

Russell, Bill 13, 30, 35, 37, 124, 193
Ryan, Bob 17

Sabonis, Arvydas 179
Sampson, Ralph 84, 85, 92, 128, 187
Sanchez, Arturo 42
Sanders, Jeff 106, 115
Saperstein, Abe 15, 25
Schayes, Danny 96
Sellers, Brad 75–77, 79–84, 91, 92, 94, 101, 102, 104–6, 109, 180
Seymour, Gene 92, 98
Schaefer, Chip 172
Sharman, Bill 42, 43
Sikma, Jack 42, 77, 84
Silas, Paul 152, 163
Simpkins, Dickey 100, 139, 167
Skiles, Scott 69, 76, 163
Skinner, Brian 186
Sloan, Jerry 6, 7, 23, 24, 26, 35, 39, 40, 44, 51, 87, 97
Smilgoff, Jim 17, 18
Smith, Dean 64, 79, 87, 146
Smith, Keith 69
Smith, Kenny 85, 87
Smith, Sam 2, 9, 20, 51, 54, 80, 109, 114, 122, 123, 141, 142, 144, 156, 182, 185, 188
Smith, Wendell 17
Smits, Rik 96, 97
Sparrow 94, 95
Sprewell, Latrell 148
Stack, Jim 154
Stack, Karen *see* Umlauf, Karen
Stackhouse, Jerry 166
Starks, John 132, 176–78
Starr, Keith 41
Steinbrenner, George 47, 48
Stern, David 48, 49
Stockton, John 191
Szczerbiak, Wally 169, 190

Telander, Rick 5, 6, 13, 14, 16, 19, 48, 54, 57, 60, 70, 75, 115, 151, 155
Theus, Reggie 50
Thibault, Mike 59
Thomas, Isaiah 1, 5, 15, 93, 94, 182, 189
Thompson, John 57
Thomsen, Ian 17, 127, 164

Thorn, Rod 49–51, 53, 57, 73, 190
Threatt, Sedalle 83, 85, 94. 95
Tisdale, Wayman 50
Truman, Harry 47
Tucker, Trent 128
Turpin, Mel 50

Umlauf, Karen 8, 19, 20, 52, 53, 66, 73, 87, 90, 100, 135, 167, 174

Vermeil, Al 8, 20, 60, 61, 82, 94, 97, 98, 100, 101, 103, 110–12, 117, 129, 132, 139, 152, 154, 157, 159, 167, 173, 176, 186, 193
Victor 32, 38
Volkov, Alexander

Walker, Antoine 183
Walker, Darrell 77, 175
Walker, Jimmy 12
Wallace, Rasheed 160, 179
Walsh, Bill 60, 109
Walsh, Donnie 189
Washington, Harold 119
Washington, Jim 26
Webber, Chris 176
West, Doug 148
West, Jerry 5, 48, 96, 157, 158, 160, 190, 193
Westhead, Paul 69
Westphal, Paul 35, 37
Whitsitt, Bob 114
Wilkens, Lenny 77
Wilkins, Gerald 128
Williams, Brian 158, 159
Williams, Buck 103, 104
Williams, Jay 184, 190
Williams, Jayson 115
Williams, Pat 31, 32, 37, 38, 181
Williams, Reggie 86
Williams, Scott 129, 134, 136, 140, 141, 144, 191
Winter, Morice Fredrick "Tex" 21, 22, 36, 58, 59, 81, 88, 103, 107, 109, 110, 120, 172
Wojnarowski, Adrian 18, 19, 52, 109, 113
Wolf, Joe 83, 87, 115, 117
Woolridge, Orlando 51, 55, 57, 61, 68, 69, 79, 90, 96, 103, 172

www.ingramcontent.com/pod-product-compliance
Ingram Content Group UK Ltd.
Pitfield, Milton Keynes, MK11 3LW, UK
UKHW060455150426
5217IPUK00028B/2088